Voice *of*
Rebellion

HOW MOZHDAH
JAMALZADAH
BROUGHT HOPE
TO AFGHANISTAN

Voice of

Rebellion

ROBERTA STALEY

GREYSTONE BOOKS
Vancouver/Berkeley

Greystone Books Ltd.
greystonebooks.com

Cataloguing data available from Library and Archives Canada
ISBN 978-1-77164-413-6 (cloth)
ISBN 978-1-77164-414-3 (epub)

Editing by Jennifer Croll
Copy editing by Shirarose Wilensky
Proofreading by Jennifer Stewart
Jacket design by Laura Shaw Design
Text design by Nayeli Jimenez
Jacket photograph by Howard J. Davis from the set of the film *Red Snow*
Photographs courtesy of Mozhdah Jamalzadah, except for the two photos on plate 12, courtesy of Barack Obama Presidential Library
Printed and bound in Canada on ancient-forest-friendly paper by Friesens

Permission for all lyrics quoted in this book granted by Mozhdah Jamalzadah.

Some names and identifying details have been changed to protect the privacy of individuals. Conversations have been re-created based on interviews, and some events may not have occurred precisely as depicted. The author and publisher have made every effort to ensure that the information in this book is correct.

Greystone Books gratefully acknowledges the Musqueam, Squamish, and Tsleil-Waututh peoples on whose land our office is located.

Greystone Books thanks the Canada Council for the Arts, the British Columbia Arts Council, the Province of British Columbia through the Book Publishing Tax Credit, and the Government of Canada for supporting our publishing activities.

Canadä

BRITISH COLUMBIA | BRITISH COLUMBIA ARTS COUNCIL
An agency of the Province of British Columbia

Canada Council   Conseil des arts
for the Arts   du Canada

This book is dedicated to the girls and women of Afghanistan, who continue to fight for human rights and gender equality. In the midst of perennial war, they endure and they hope, drawing courage from those who have come before.

Contents

PART 4: A WOMAN'S POWER 2011-2019

Prologue

"CUT!" YELLED THE director.

Mozhdah Jamalzadah flipped the front of the burka up over her head, breathing in the fresh, sagebrush-scented breeze blowing off the parched hills of Kamloops, feeling the heavily beaded sweat along her hairline dissipate. The addition of the heavy dark wig made the burka almost unbearable in the baking heat. Mozhdah sighed. There were many hours of filming still ahead for *Red Snow*—a movie about a Canadian Armed Forces soldier who is taken prisoner by the Taliban in Kandahar while fighting for peace and security in Afghanistan.

The blue burka belonged to Mozhdah's mother, Nasrin, and as Mozhdah wore it, she couldn't help but think about the journey it had taken. Many years ago, Nasrin, along with her husband Bashir, escaped from Kabul, the capital of Afghanistan, as civil war ravaged what was left of the country following the Soviet Union's ten-year battle against fierce mujahideen warriors. At the time, Mozhdah was just five years old. The Jamalzadah family fled disguised as peasants, with

Nasrin donning the burka, transforming her from an educated urbanite into a silent and obedient Afghan wife and mother. The ruse had worked; Mozhdah and her family eventually made their way to Vancouver, Canada. This symbol of female subjugation had been a means to freedom, and Nasrin had kept it carefully wrapped in tissue paper until now, like a talisman.

But arriving in Canada had been the beginning—not the end—of Mozhdah's odyssey. Growing up, she faced racism and struggled to fit into her new country. Later, as a teen, she learned to sing, with Afghanistan as her muse. Obsessed with the thought of helping Afghanistan—and especially Afghan women—Mozhdah returned to the country of her birth to launch her own television talk show, based upon *The Oprah Winfrey Show*. But to some Afghans, Mozhdah was just another foreign invader, and she was eventually forced to flee, brutalized and defeated.

Today, surrounded by film cameras, under the shimmering heat, with the director poised to call "Action!" Mozhdah pulled the burka back down over her head. Yes, she thought, this blue burka—this is where the story truly begins.

PART 1

Seeking Asylum

1989–1991

CHAPTER 1

Betrayal

T HE KNOCK ON the door was hard and authoritative, startling Bashir Jamalzadah and causing him to draw a sharp intake of breath. The students looked up curiously. Bashir, who was at the board writing the outline for the day's lecture, put the chalk down, brushed his hands against his carefully pressed dress pants, and smiled, despite a feeling of foreboding, at his students. He walked to the door and opened it only slightly so that his students couldn't see who stood outside.

Outside, dressed in regulation pillbox cap and sand-colored uniform, stood a soldier. "Professor Jamalzadah," the man said brusquely in Farsi, Afghanistan's official language alongside Pashto.

It was a statement, not a question. Bashir took in the soldier's clear green eyes, his sun-baked face, and how the uniform hung in folds on the gaunt frame. These days, with intellectuals and opponents to Afghanistan's Soviet-backed president Mohammad Najibullah Ahmadzai's government disappearing without a trace, a soldier at your workplace meant only one thing: arrest. Yet there was something vaguely familiar and nonthreatening about this thin young man with leathery brown skin.

Bashir forced himself to remain calm, professional. "I am Professor Jamalzadah. May I help you?"

The soldier introduced himself as Hadi. "Do you remember me," he asked, lowering his voice, "from your psychology and English classes three years ago?"

Of course—those green eyes. Hadi was one of the young student teachers who had come through Bashir's classes at Kabul Pedagogical Institute. It seemed Hadi had been recruited into the Afghan National Army to fight the mujahideen opposing President Najibullah Ahmadzai's government. The battle between the national government and mujahideen—Islamic guerrilla fighters who battled the Soviet Union following its 1979 invasion—had turned Kabul into a heap of rubble from shelling and rocket bombardments. Yet students still came to Bashir's pedagogy classes, clinging to any semblance of normalcy and the desperate hope that the violence would someday end.

"I remember you," Bashir said. He looked at the young man. What could he possibly want? Bashir opened the door just wide enough to slip through. He ensured it clicked shut behind him to prevent them from being overheard. "Why are you here?" Bashir asked.

"The Afghan army is coming to arrest you. They are on their way. You must leave—immediately." Hadi looked fearful.

Bashir stuttered in alarm. "Why? When? Now?"

"I don't know the reason, but why does it matter? They are coming. I am risking my life to tell you this. You must go!"

Bashir looked at Hadi. "Yes, I will go now. But I have to speak briefly with my students first. Tell me, Hadi, why are you warning me? You're a soldier of the Afghan army."

Hadi's face softened slightly. "Because you are a good man and a good teacher. You taught me a lot. Maybe one day, *insha'Allah*—God willing—I will be a teacher once again—if the mujahideen and Soviets do not bomb this country into oblivion. Now go! Quickly!"

"Thank you," Bashir said. "You must go now too! *Khuda hafiz*—God protect you."

Bashir watched his former student walk swiftly down the hallway, straight and proud. He leaned against the door, trying to slow his breathing and his heart's thudding, wiping a trickle of sweat from his forehead with his shirtsleeve. He could plead an upset stomach to the students. He listened for approaching footsteps from the nearby stairwell or hallways but heard only the soft buzzing of busy classrooms and the droning of instructors.

Bashir opened the door and walked towards his desk. "I am so sorry," he said. "My lunch isn't agreeing with me. I am going to have to leave. Please stay here until the bell rings so you don't disturb the students in the rest of the school. Read chapters five and six at your desk, and we'll discuss at tomorrow's lecture."

Bashir gathered up his papers and textbook and placed them in his faded, worn leather satchel. He walked to the door and turned. "See you tomorrow. I am sure I will feel better by then." As he left, he could hear an outbreak of murmuring. The students sensed that something was amiss—something more than indigestion.

What if soldiers had already arrived at the university? They would have to go to the main office first, to find out his classroom number. Bashir lengthened his stride, trying not to break into a jog, the satchel bumping hard against his leg. He headed for the stairs leading to a door at the back of the building. Once outside, he could cross the university grounds and hail a taxi. His leather-soled shoes slapping the stairs, Bashir came to a back door at the university, opened it slowly and walked outside, shielding his eyes from the bright sun, peering for military vehicles or soldiers. His fear turned to anger. The director of Kabul Pedagogical Institute, Ghafoor Alipour, had obviously followed up on his threat. A member of Afghanistan's ruling Communist party, called the People's Democratic Party of Afghanistan, or PDPA, Ghafoor acted as a spy, monitoring the students and teachers for anti-government dissent. He despised Bashir for his refusal to support the PDPA, as well as Bashir's criticism of the brutal repression of President Najibullah Ahmadzai's KHAD security force. Similar to the Soviet Union's KGB, KHAD had rounded up, then tortured and killed thousands of scholars, judges, teachers, government and diplomatic officials, and members of Islamic organizations. Their arrests had filled Pul-e-Charkhi prison beyond bursting.

Ghafoor had boasted to Bashir that he could have him forcibly conscripted into the Afghan army. Bashir had thought Ghafoor's threats simple intimidation. Not only was Bashir one year shy of forty, the cutoff date for recruitment, but also his profession as a teacher made him exempt from army duty. But the army was desperate for manpower and had taken to kidnapping teenage boys off the streets of Kabul. They likely wouldn't balk at enlisting Bashir.

Out on the roadway, Bashir blended in with the few pedestrians scurrying about their business. He walked quickly and when he spotted a yellow-and-white taxi, flagged it down, yanked the door open, and slid gratefully into the dim interior. What was he to do? He didn't dare go home to his wife, Nasrin, and three children: Mozhdah, five; two-year-old Masee; and the new baby, Safee. Surely that would be the first place the Afghan army would look for him. The only place he could think to hide was at the home of his friend Haider.

"Where do you want to go?" the cabby demanded, staring in his rearview mirror at Bashir, who was lost in thought.

"Sorry," Bashir mumbled, and blurted out an address.

The driver steered his car into traffic. Bashir let his body sink low in the back seat and kept his head down. When the taxi pulled up to the destination, Bashir handed him several dirty Afghani notes for payment. It was late afternoon. His friend might not be home yet. He slipped out of the cab and, looking nervously left and right, headed into the apartment building.

NASRIN CONTINUED ROCKING Safee in her arms, even though the infant had fallen asleep twenty minutes ago. She paced the living room, watched out the window as the twilight faded into darkness. The window, opaque with dirt, was splintered into a spider web of cracks from the shock waves of bombs that mujahideen guerrillas launched into Kabul daily. Masee played quietly on the living room carpet with toy trucks and cars. Mozhdah, her long-haired five-year-old daughter, played with dolls in her bedroom. Nasrin smiled sadly: the dolls were arguing about who was going to drive to the Gardens of Babur for a picnic. Mozhdah had grown up on stories of the beauty of the gardens, created five hundred years ago by the Mughal emperor Babur. It was a place where families would go for picnics and sit on the grass to eat freshly made *bolani*—flatbread stuffed with spinach, leeks, or potatoes—mint-flavored yogurt, naan, rice, and almond cookies, called *kulche badami*, amid the scent of red, pink, and yellow roses and fruit trees. Along with the rest of Kabul, this oasis had been laid to waste.

Mozhdah's childhood, Nasrin thought bitterly, had been corrupted by nightly bombing raids and the constant threat of death and hunger. For the sake of normalcy, Bashir and Nasrin had started Mozhdah in preschool a few months ago. It was just a few blocks away, and Nasrin; her mother, Tafsira, who lived with them; or another relative would walk Mozhdah to school. Then, one day, Mozhdah's cousin Najib, who was tall for his age, was kidnapped by Afghan army soldiers after he dropped Mozhdah off. His parents went to the army base to beg for his release, showing proof that he was only fourteen—seven years younger than conscription age. But the final straw was when someone poured poison into the school's water tank. Mozhdah wasn't harmed, but Nasrin and Bashir never let her return.

This wasn't a childhood, Nasrin thought. Mozhdah should be growing up with memories of play and travel, family and feasting, school and learning. Instead, her world consisted of blasted brown earth and rubble, tremors from dropped bombs, screams of terror and agony in the night, flaming buildings, smoke, and machine-gun fire.

Nasrin's own good memories were fading, and now it was as if they had been only dreams. Before they were married and had children, Bashir and Nasrin would spend their free time exploring the city. They bought fresh naan, cooked to soft perfection in a clay tandoor oven. Packing homemade chutney, yogurt, and fried eggplant, the couple would take a bus to the Gardens of Babur to eat a picnic lunch. They made adventurous plans: Bashir would pursue a PhD at the University of the

Philippines, where he had already attained a master's degree in English, and Nasrin would go with him, leaving Afghanistan for the first time in her life.

The only thing that seemed real anymore was the omnipresent scent of kerosene that fueled the tiny stove Nasrin used to heat water to cook, bathe, and wash dishes and clothes. Life was stripped down to the essentials: find enough food to feed the family, boil water for cleaning and drinking and making tea. Boil water to sanitize Safee's diapers. Try to keep the children, who spent much of their time indoors, stimulated— and try to comfort them when they were terrorized by the bombardment of missiles, which one nightmarish day reached three hundred hits on the city. Nasrin was grateful for the support and help of one of her brothers, Hafiz, who sometimes brought them extra food. She also relied heavily upon Tafsira's calm presence and her ability to amuse the children. But the civil war was taking its toll. Bashir had developed asthma from stress, as well as from breathing the air turned gray-brown by smoke from the building fires sparked by missile hits. As the couple lay under the blankets, Nasrin would remain awake, listening to the sharp wheeze of Bashir's breathing, wondering if this night would be their last.

Surfacing from the depths of her dark musings, Nasrin realized how late Bashir was. What had happened to him? He should have arrived home long ago, perhaps with fresh naan. The children would soon be clamoring for food. Nasrin clutched Safee closer to her chest. Should she go look for Bashir at the university—let them know he was missing? But it was closed by now. And there was the impending curfew.

She went to the kitchen; luckily, there were potatoes in the cupboard.

Mozhdah wandered in. "Where is Daddy?" she demanded.

"He had to stay late at work, Mozhdah *jan*," Nasrin said, referring to her with a term of endearment meaning "beloved." "He has meetings tonight. He won't be home until later."

"What about the curfew?" Mozhdah asked.

Although Nasrin and Bashir did their best to hide the worst of the war from the children, the curfew was a part of daily conversation. In addition to carrying identity cards, everyone had to be inside between 10:00 PM and 4:00 AM. Movement in and out of Kabul was severely restricted, and even diplomats were only allowed a six-mile range of movement from the city center. Mozhdah didn't really know what a curfew was, and Nasrin suspected that she thought of it as something alive—a monster that came out at night that made people disappear.

Nasrin wondered if Bashir's ongoing conflict with his boss, Ghafoor Alipour, had anything to do with his lateness. Bashir was an easy target because of his educational background. The University of the Philippines had been founded by the Americans in the early twentieth century, and Ghafoor believed Bashir was sympathetic towards the United States. In Ghafoor's mind, Bashir's anti-government sentiments and connection to America extended back to childhood. Bashir had grown up in the northwestern Afghanistan city of Herat, a place famed for its arts and architecture. His open-minded parents had allowed him to attend secular school in addition to a religious madrassa. Bashir excelled at his studies, eventually entering Kabul University to study English pedagogy.

Following his graduate degree in the Philippines, Bashir had returned to Kabul. His arrival was unfortunately timed. Three days later, there was a coup d'etat by the Communist PDPA. During the Saur (April) Revolution, PDPA revolutionaries massacred the self-proclaimed president Mohammed Daoud Khan and his family on either April 27 or 28, 1978. Five years before that, Khan had overthrown his cousin King Zahir, the country's last twentieth-century leader who had championed democracy and liberal ideals. But despite its Communist rhetoric, the PDPA showed little inclination and even less ability to bring about a socialist revolution, becoming embroiled in fighting between two murderous wings: the Parcham and Khalq. Ghafoor was as thirsty for power as the party he belonged to. When Bashir refused to join, Ghafoor took it upon himself to punish him. Although teachers were exempt from conscription, Ghafoor insisted to his PDPA connections that Bashir was a poor role model to students.

The next morning, with Bashir still missing, Nasrin fed the children scraps from last night's dinner. The night had been quiet, and Tafsira took Mozhdah and Masee to play in the sunlight in the front yard. Nasrin glanced out the window at them and saw a man in a jacket, his upturned collar partly hiding his face, striding up the walkway. He stopped to say hello to Tafsira and the kids. As the man turned towards the house, Nasrin realized it was Nazir Khalji, Bashir's best friend. There was only one reason for him to be here: he must know something. Nasrin flung open the door before Nazir could even knock.

"Where is Bashir?" she demanded.

Nazir raised an eyebrow and said, *"Salaam."* He took off his shoes and walked into the living room, settling himself onto a floor cushion.

Nasrin flushed at her rudeness. "I've been so worried. Bashir always comes home straight after work. Have you seen him? Do you know where he is?"

"You must not," Nazir responded, "tell anyone what I am about to tell you."

"I won't say anything," Nasrin said impatiently. "Where is he?"

Nazir explained that Bashir was in hiding, after being tipped off that his arrest was imminent.

"Where?"

"I can't tell you that."

"Can I see him?"

"No."

"Is he okay?"

"Yes, he is fine. Worried about you, the children, and Tafsira."

"Is he close?"

Nazir told her it was too dangerous for her to know such information. The Afghan army could come and question her. He was surprised that soldiers hadn't come pounding on the door already. They would have no qualms about torturing her to elicit information, Nazir told her darkly.

Nasrin's breath caught in her throat. "What can we do?"

Nazir looked at Nasrin for several seconds without speaking. "I see no other option," he finally said, "but fleeing the country to Pakistan or Iran."

Nasrin glared at Nazir. "We have three small children. Safee is just a few months old. How will we get the money to get to Pakistan or Iran? It's dangerous. The routes out of Kabul are overrun by mujahideen. We will all be killed!"

"Certain death awaits you here," Nazir countered. "At least there is some hope in escape."

Nasrin felt a surge of panic. "Where will we get the money?"

Nazir responded calmly. "Bashir mentioned you have savings, enough, possibly, to escape Kabul." He got up, walked towards the door, and opened it. "Don't worry," he said gently, looking at Nasrin. "We'll figure everything out."

The kindly tone caused Nasrin's eyes to smart with tears. How could she not worry? "Tell Bashir I love him. Tell him that the children and I are okay," she said.

Later, awake in the night, Nasrin considered Nazir's words. He was right—there was no future here. Their life was a ghoulish game of waiting for a missile to drop on their house, to be hit by a stray bullet, or to be thrown into prison and tortured. She got up in the dark, feeling her way in bare feet, tiptoeing along the cold tile floor, a blanket wrapped around her thin, shivering frame. She could hear the thud of bombs in the distance. *Please*, she prayed, *stay away from my children tonight*.

Nasrin walked down the short hallway to her mother's room and knocked on the door. *"Gul,"* Nasrin whispered, using an affectionate nickname meaning "flower." "Are you awake?"

"Of course," Tafsira replied. "Come in. I never sleep anymore. Here in Kabul, to sleep is to be dead," she said, laughing softly at the bitter joke. "Nasrin *jan*, what did Nazir say to you today? It is causing you distress. I see it in your eyes."

"You can't tell anyone what I am about to tell you," Nasrin said.

"What is it?"

Nasrin reached out in the dark for her mother's hand. "Bashir wants us to flee to Iran or Pakistan. I think that this is the right thing to do. There is no future here—for me, or your grandchildren. You will come with us, of course."

The silence was as heavy as the darkness.

"No," Tafsira said. "I am too old to run away. I would not survive such a journey. I was born in Afghanistan, and I will die in Afghanistan." She paused. "I don't want you to go, Nasrin *jan*. The war will be over soon and we can rebuild our lives."

Nasrin said nothing, tears in her eyes. "But, *Gul*, how can you say that? It will not be over. Your Afghanistan—my Afghanistan—is gone. I can't stay here and doom Mozhdah, Masee, and Safee to a life of war. Bashir is in danger. We are all in terrible danger, every second of our lives. I can't live like this anymore. I just can't."

She began to weep. Tafsira took Nasrin into her arms, and both of them cried deep into the night.

THE NEXT DAY, Nasrin busied herself with sweeping the rugs and rubbing heavy dust off the surfaces with a cloth, hoping Nazir would show up again. As night began to settle, she heard a soft knock on the door.

It was Nazir. "Any news?" Nasrin asked, almost before she opened the door.

"*Salaam*, Nasrin," Nazir said. "I would love some tea."

"*Salaam*," Nasrin responded. "Tafsira!" she called out to her mother, who was in the kitchen. "Can you bring tea for Nazir and me?"

"Bashir sends his love," Nazir said. "I hope you have told no one of plans to leave for Iran or Pakistan."

"I told Tafsira," Nasrin confessed. "I want her to come too. But she is stubborn and refuses to leave. She thinks peace will come."

Nazir sighed. "This country," he said, "will never know peace again. Bashir agrees that the only solution is to escape to

Pakistan. Financing is a problem, but he has a solution. Nasrin, do you think you can organize a group of people who want to leave Kabul? You could pool resources to rent a vehicle to take you to Pakistan through the Paktia mountains."

Nasrin thought about how little money she and Bashir had saved, a few thousand Afghanis. "We have hardly any savings," Nasrin admitted, looking at Nazir, her voice low and fearful.

Nazir nodded. "Nasrin, you will have to sell everything: jewelry, clothes, furniture, pots and pans, even the children's toys and clothes. And secretly, to family only," Nazir warned.

"Yes, I think I can do that," Nasrin said in a small voice. Everything, she thought, her entire life—gone, as if it had never been. Then, a desperate escape south out of Kabul, encountering Afghan army checkpoints along the way. If they survived that, they would face mujahideen-held territory. Where would she find the courage?

CHAPTER 2

Escape from Kabul

NASRIN SAT IN the living room, holding herself stiffly to hide her trembling. Hafiz leaned back against one of the red cushions, sipping chai. Hafiz was Nasrin's favorite sibling—a half brother and the eldest of five sons from her father's first marriage. All the siblings looked up to him, often went to him for advice, even though they were now adults.

Nasrin's tea had gone cold. "A missile hit an apartment just a block away the other night," she said, her voice shaking. There was no need to describe the high-pitched whine and vibrating air, like a meteor falling from the sky, followed by a boom that felt like a volcanic eruption—Hafiz knew the sound all too well. Worse was the terrified weeping of the children: Mozhdah, Safee, and Masee. The only thing Nasrin could do was take them in her arms and crouch down in a corner of a room farthest from the windows, whispering to them to keep their heads down, telling them it would be okay. After the shock of impact, Nasrin could hear the shouts of neighborhood men running to the flaming, smoking rubble to search for survivors.

"It is only a matter of time..." Nasrin's voice trailed off.

"So let's make a plan," Hafiz said firmly.

"Bashir has let me know through a, uh, contact, that we should go to Pakistan with a group to help pay for a truck to take us through the mountains. We have no passports," Nasrin said anxiously.

The Afghan government refused to give passports to people like Bashir and Nasrin who weren't supporters of the Communist government. A clandestine escape was the only way out. The quickest route to Pakistan would be via the main road south from Kabul to the province of Logar. From there, a road ran east to Paktia, the mountainous frontier region bordering Pakistan. The roads were peppered with checkpoints, manned by Afghan army soldiers, whose job it was to stop the exodus of fleeing citizens, as well as search for mujahideen weapons going in to or out of Kabul.

As Nasrin and Hafiz talked, a plan crystallized. Hafiz knew two other families also desperate to leave Kabul. One was his brother-in-law Rahmat Hasanzi and his family. There was also the family of Haji Abdul Shakoor Yousef. Hafiz made a quick calculation; in all, seventeen people would be escaping to Pakistan: nine children and eight adults.

Haji Yousef would be vital to a successful escape, Hafiz said. He was a cousin of a mujahideen leader in Logar, whose name was Commander Rawani. The commander would help facilitate their flight into Pakistan, connecting them with local drivers who had vehicles sturdy enough to navigate the steep, rugged mountain passes into Pakistan.

Travel to Logar would be highly dangerous. Shortly after the 1979 Soviet invasion, Logar became the heart of mujahideen activity, largely because of its proximity to Pakistan, which provided training centers and funneled money and weapons supplied by America, Iran, and China to the guerrilla fighters. Many mujahideen groups maintained their headquarters in the border city of Peshawar in Pakistan. Logar had also been where mujahideen leaders planned guerrilla attacks on Soviet targets. The Soviets had retaliated with a vengeance, leveling entire villages and killing all the inhabitants to try to intimidate Afghans and deprive the fighters of shelter and food. News blackouts didn't stop reports of Soviet atrocities from reaching Kabul. In the rural areas, where mujahideen built pockets of resistance, the Soviets undertook bombing raids with Mikoyan-Gurevich MiG-21 fighter-bomber jets and Mil Mi-24 helicopter gunships, often referred to as flying tanks. Soldiers would carry out systematic searches of the villages and, if a single bullet was found, shoot male family members. The Soviets destroyed crops and irrigation systems, killed animals, and at times, slaughtered entire villages, from women to babies.

To make it past the army checkpoints along the main road into Logar, Nasrin, her family, and the other escapees would have to disguise themselves as rural villagers, pretending they had come to Kabul to sell harvest vegetables like melons and eggplants. The women would wear burkas over long, loose-fitting kurta shirts, the men would be unshaven and don *shalwar kameez* with shawls and flat-topped, brimless woolen *pakol* hats. Nasrin would get her mother to scour the marketplace for used roughhewn outfits and the thick, heavy scarves, called chadors, that peasant children wore. They could take

nothing with them—no books, toys, or Western clothing—
nothing to identify them as urbanites.

Nasrin had already started selling the children's books and
clothes, as well as her jewelry, including gold bangles and a
favorite gold and pearl necklace. She thought longingly of her
collection of elegant high-heeled shoes. She had bought them
before the Soviet invasion, when Kabul was referred to as the
Paris of Asia, and young, educated women like Nasrin looked
to Europe for fashion inspiration, wearing short skirts, the
latest hairstyles, and heels. She would get a pittance for them,
but every cent was needed not only for transportation, food,
and water but also for bribe money, called baksheesh, that
would—God willing—get them through checkpoints.

The most frightening part was how to get all four families to the bus stop where they would catch a bus to Logar
province. They could not gather at one family's home, then
travel en masse—that would draw attention. Nasrin suspected
that some of her neighbors were spies for the PDPA government and had been keeping watch for officials in case Bashir
returned home. If he showed up, they would alert the army,
which would send soldiers swooping in for an arrest. They
could not leave the house in peasant clothes during daylight;
that too would arouse suspicion. Only one bus for Logar left
Kabul each day, and that was in the early morning. The curfew
lifted at 4:00 AM. How would they get to the bus stop in time?

Nasrin's eyes suddenly widened. She looked at Hafiz, grinning. "Atiq! Of course! Why didn't I think of him before?"

Atiq was Nasrin's cousin and a recruit of the Afghan
National Army. His main job was driving the military generals to official functions, which meant he had access to a jeep
at all hours of the day and night.

"A jeep is too small for all four families," Hafiz pointed out.

"Atiq could make several trips," Nasrin countered.

"Can he be trusted?" Hafiz asked.

"Of course. He is family," Nasrin replied.

It was decided. Nasrin would contact Atiq and propose a plan to drive all four families in an army jeep to the Logar bus stop. It sounded insane, Nasrin thought. It sounded desperate. But then, they were desperate.

NASRIN HAD GOTTEN a message to Atiq to meet her close to her house at a small park that was now a dismal landscape of brown flower beds, dead trees, and missile craters. Skeletal dogs with dirty, short tan coats skulked about, noses close to the ground in search of food. To the casual passerby, it looked as if Atiq had stopped Nasrin: an authoritative soldier questioning a civilian. She explained to him how Ghafoor Alipour had tried to have Bashir conscripted into the Afghan army. She then outlined the escape plan to Pakistan through Logar and the need for the four families to pool resources to pay for a driver and truck to navigate the mountain passes into Pakistan. But first, they needed someone to pick up all the families from their homes and drive them to the bus stop.

"It's crazy," Atiq said, his face grim. "What if I'm stopped? Why would I have peasants in my jeep? And seventeen people? That's at least two, probably three trips to the bus station. And I'll have to pick up Bashir, wherever he's hiding."

"But you'll do it?" Nasrin asked.

Atiq looked at Nasrin and his face softened. She was much thinner than the last time he had seen her, with a pale face and dark bags under her eyes from lack of sleep. The plan would put him in grave danger. If caught, he would be tortured and killed, leaving his own wife and children destitute. But, Nasrin was his cousin. "There is a dinner for the generals at the Hotel Inter-Continental this Thursday. It will be a night off for me, so I'll be free to take all of you to the bus."

Nasrin slipped Atiq a piece of paper on which she had written everyone's address. "We will get word to everyone to be ready to go Thursday night," she said.

The families, Atiq emphasized, had to keep watch and be ready to slip as unobtrusively and silently as possible into the jeep as soon as it stopped outside their home. They must carry very little: water and a bit of food. "I will not wait for them," said Atiq. "Tell them that."

"We will be ready," Nasrin said, nodding. "*Khuda hafiz*— peace be upon you. Thank you—a million times thank you."

NASRIN DREW THE thick dark curtains shut. It was only late afternoon, but Mozhdah and Masee needed to get some sleep before the late-night rendezvous. She closed the bedroom door, heard them whispering and giggling. They were already dressed in traveling clothes. She prayed they would fall asleep.

A brown burlap sack holding Safee's clean diapers was already waiting by the front door. In between the folds of cloth she had hidden Bashir's master's degree, as well as his undergraduate degree and teacher education certificate. Nasrin couldn't find her own teacher's certificate, but told herself it was of little consequence. When would she have the opportunity to teach again, she thought, pouring boiled water for Safee's formula into a green-striped half-gallon thermos. She eyed with consternation the simple brown Afghan vest waiting on the kitchen counter.

Before Kabul became a moonscape of broken buildings, Bashir and Nasrin had loved to go to the Old City and walk among the kiosks selling kites and spices like turmeric and saffron, as well as rose petals for making rose oil for perfume. They would hunt for coins once used as currency along the Silk Road, the ancient trade network connecting East and West, from China to the Mediterranean Sea. Bashir and Nasrin would find rough-edged coins of silver, gold, or brass covered with delicate Persian writing—some of the coins dated back a thousand years. Nasrin could not bring herself to sell the collection of two hundred coins and had spent several evenings creating tiny pockets on the outside of the vest for secreting each one. She tried the vest on, dismayed at its heaviness, knowing she would be carrying Safee as well.

"Bulletproof," she said aloud, smiling grimly.

Nasrin peered out the window that looked out onto the road in front of the house, keeping watch for headlights. Her silky blue burka lay folded on the burlap sack holding the diapers, naan, a container of water, the thermos with boiled water and infant formula. Tafsira waited with Nasrin, but they didn't speak. In the past few weeks, they had said everything that they could possible say and vented every emotion: recrimination, regret, grief, and then, simply, resignation and love. Off in the distance, Nasrin spied a dim suggestion of headlights.

"He's here, *Gul*," Nasrin whispered to Tafsira. "Let's get the children up. Quickly." Nasrin took the heavy vest and pulled it over her narrow shoulders, draped the burka over her arm, and then picked up the sleeping Safee. Tafsira went into the bedroom to shake Mozhdah awake and pushed her to the door, carrying Masee.

Mozhdah was on the point of tears. "Why do we have to get up now? I'm tired."

"Shhh, Mozhdah *jan*," said Nasrin. "We are going on a bus. It'll be fun."

"I don't want to go on a bus ride," Mozhdah pouted, slipping her feet into shoes.

A military jeep pulled to a stop opposite the apartment. The driver killed the engine. Nasrin waited. What if it wasn't Atiq? What if their escape plot had been discovered, and this was a soldier come to arrest them? She heard the sound of a vehicle door opening—the noise magnified in the dark and the silence. Nasrin heard quick, soft footsteps against the cement walkway. She waited. There was a knock on the door.

Nasrin quietly opened it. It was Nazir.

"Let's go. No talking," he whispered.

"Are you ready, *Gul*?" Nasrin whispered, turning to look at Tafsira, her hand on the doorknob.

"Yes, Nasrin *jan*," Tafsira murmured. "Go!"

They trod lightly down the stairs, Tafsira holding the hands of Mozhdah and Masee, who had woken up, too numb with sleep to complain. They quickly crossed the road and Nazir opened the back door of the jeep.

"Nasrin, let me take Safee," he said. "Jump in."

"Atiq—you came! Thank you!" Nasrin exclaimed softly as she clambered onto the hard, cracked leather seats.

Atiq craned his neck and grinned. "I said I would, didn't I?"

Nasrin threw the burlap bundle onto the floor and jumped, gasping in alarm, as she sensed another person in the back.

"It's me—Bashir."

"Oh, Bashir," she cried, throwing her arms around him, noting the bony frame and scratchy, untrimmed beard.

"Hand me Safee," Bashir said. Nazir handed the baby to Nasrin, who passed the bundle to Bashir, who gently kissed his son, still asleep. As Nazir hoisted Mozhdah into the jeep's back seat, she yelped with joy, "Daddy?" Masee, plunked next to Nasrin, climbed over his mother to reach his father for a hug.

Nasrin slipped out of the jeep.

"Where are you going?" Bashir said anxiously.

"Give me a second," she said, walking towards Tafsira, who waited a few feet away. She stood in front of her mother and gripped her shoulders. "Please, come with us!"

"No, I will only be a burden," Tafsira said. "I will not come."

"Then promise me we'll see each other again," said Nasrin, tears rolling down her cheeks.

"God willing," said Tafsira, and after one desperate, hard hug, she turned away from her daughter, the outline of her body dissolving into the night, as if she no longer existed. They would never see each other again.

Nasrin climbed back in the vehicle and pulled the door shut, flinching at the loud metallic clang. She quickly pulled the burka over her head, grateful for its privacy, hiding the tears she didn't want her children or Bashir to see. The jeep pulled away from the curb, bouncing over bumps, rocks, and potholes—taking them from fear and hopelessness into dread.

About twenty minutes later, the headlights of the jeep illuminated the outline of rows of buses and low-slung, small buildings off in the distance. Atiq stopped the jeep and turned off the ignition.

"You have to get out here," he said, turning around. "The area is patrolled by Afghan soldiers, and I don't want to be stopped and questioned. Your friends are here already. I dropped them off earlier."

"Oh, Atiq," exclaimed Nasrin, grabbing his arm and squeezing it. "I can't thank you enough."

"Nasrin *jan*, no need to thank me. Just get to Pakistan safely."

Nasrin looked through the mesh of her burka at Nazir, who sat in the front passenger seat. "Thank you for helping us get here, for helping keep my husband safe, for supporting me when I was crazy with worry."

Nazir smiled. "Now it is your turn to keep Bashir safe—and he you. Remember, Nasrin, you are a peasant woman—do not respond to any man's questions. Leave everything to Bashir."

Nasrin took Safee from Bashir, who opened the jeep door and put out his hands to Mozhdah and Masee. One at a time, he lifted them onto the cold, dusty ground. He then grabbed the burlap sack. Atiq turned on the ignition and shoved the stick shift into first gear, pulling a U-turn to return to the city. There was no going back now.

It was cold and too early for the dawn light to help them navigate the rocky, uneven ground. A conservative Afghan woman walks several steps behind her husband, so Nasrin followed Bashir at a respectable distance, her frightened breathing magnified in the oppressive blue sheath. She placed her feet carefully on the ground in front of her, feeling her way in the blackness, blinded by both the dark and the burka.

They stopped when they came close to a row of parked buses, dented, dirty, and rusting, with thinning tires. About thirty feet away from the buses, their friends sat huddled together on the ground, the children leaning against their parents, eyes wide with fear. The men, in linen *shalwar kameez* and long heavy vests, sat on folded layers of burlap sacks—the kind used to carry produce to the city from farms outside Kabul. Bashir walked up to them, murmured *"Salaam,"* and looked cautiously around, noting the bus stop was being patrolled by several pairs of soldiers, dressed in heavy brown camouflage uniforms and black leather boots, cradling AK-47s. One pair of soldiers stared at them and began walking over.

Nasrin quickly pulled Mozhdah's chador down over her head to hide her eyes. It would not do for the soldiers to see her daughter's soft, smooth cheeks and clean, shiny hair, so different from the pinched, sunburned face of a peasant girl who had spent her young life picking vegetables and fruit, hauling water, washing clothes, and gathering and spinning wool. Nasrin chided herself; Mozhdah's chador and traditional tunic and baggy pants were too clean. She should have made more of an effort to make them ragged and shabby.

The soldiers turned on a square flashlight and shone it directly into the faces of the men, sweeping the beam slowly across the huddled blue forms of the women, who clutched their children. The flashlight lingered on Mozhdah, who turned her face towards the light.

The taller soldier barked in Farsi: *"Az koujastin?"* (Where are you from?)

"Logar," Bashir said, shielding his eyes with a hand.

"Kouja mirein?" (Where are you going?)

"Logar," Bashir repeated.

The soldier stared at Bashir in the harsh light as the group held their breath. Then he snapped the light off, turned away, and walked off with his fellow soldier.

Gray sky emerged in the east, hinting at the approaching dawn. About fifteen minutes later, thin rays of sun grazed the frost on the ground, turning it to crystals. A naan seller slowly walked by, a stack of bread in a cloth bag, and Bashir bought several warm, fragrant discs, enough to last them the day.

The bus drivers arrived, unlocked their vehicles, and turned on their ignitions, warming up the engines, choking the air with black exhaust. Bashir, along with Hafiz, walked over to one of the drivers, whose jacket was stained with motor oil and grease. They were the only people getting on the bus to Logar. A wad of worn, grubby Afghani bills exchanged hands. Bashir beckoned and all seventeen piled aboard. Nasrin stared out the windows as the dawn morphed into day. She cradled Safee tightly, trying to stay calm.

An hour later, with the sun still in the eastern sky, the bus slowed and braked to a stop with a grinding screech of metal that set Nasrin's teeth on edge. Hearing harsh voices, she peered through the dirty window. They had arrived at an army checkpoint, consisting of a small mud-brick shack snug against a pile of sandbags on top of a horseshoe-shaped hard dirt wall. Two soldiers came over to the bus, and the driver pulled the door crank, allowing them to stomp on board.

"Don't say *anything!*" Nasrin whispered to Mozhdah and Masee, seated beside her.

The soldiers walked slowly, looking carefully at each person, picking up the burlap bags and shaking them. One stopped beside Nasrin and stared at her hands—smooth and pale, with neat nails—as she cradled Safee.

"*Az koujastin?*" he barked.

Nasrin stayed silent and Bashir responded, "Logar."

"You're lying." The soldier laughed scornfully. "You're from Kabul!" The soldier turned, yelling at the bus driver, "These people are from Kabul! Don't lie to me!"

Nasrin stopped breathing. The bus driver said nothing, got up, and beckoned the soldier to follow him. Jumping stiffly onto the hard ground, the driver walked casually over to join a group of soldiers standing near the sandbagged mud wall. Pulling a cigarette out of a pack in his pocket, he offered cigarettes to the soldiers, then lit his own smoke with a match, inhaled deeply, and began chatting. The soldier from the bus joined them.

Nasrin was terrified. She kept her head down, murmuring to Safee, who grabbed at the unfamiliar mesh hiding his mother's face. Then their driver walked back to the bus, took a final, heavy drag from his cigarette, and flicked the butt to the ground. He jumped on board, slipped into the driver's seat, turned on the ignition, and put the bus into first gear. Nasrin glanced at the soldiers, who stood outside smirking. Why hadn't they been arrested?

Bashir, seated ahead of Nasrin, turned his head slightly and said gently, "Are you okay?"

"Yes," Nasrin lied.

"It is a good thing," Bashir chuckled, "that Afghan soldiers are so corrupt."

The bus passed through two more checkpoints. Each time, there was an intimidating search by soldiers and a payment of baksheesh. By the time their stop came, at a collection of mud-walled homes that could barely be called a village, Nasrin estimated it was about 2:00 PM. They piled off the bus, stiff and hungry, and thanked the driver profusely, telling him how much they admired his cool-headed negotiation skills.

Haji, whose cousin was the famous mujahideen commander, led the way past the single-story, light brown homes with their uneven flat roofs and large plastic water jugs outside.

Logar seemed deserted. They walked for about five minutes until they came to a larger home surrounded by a high wall made of mud bricks enclosing a large courtyard. Nasrin could just see the top of the roof over the wall, which was pockmarked with bullet holes. Part of the wall had collapsed—possibly from a Soviet rocket—and been inexpertly rebuilt. Off in the distance, a herd of sheep, tan and dirty white, grazed on the brown grass.

"We're here," Nasrin said to Masee and Mozhdah.

"You mean Pakistan?" Mozhdah asked, puzzled.

"No, Mozhdah *jan.*" Nasrin laughed. "This is our friend's home. We're here for a short visit."

They came to the closed front gate and Haji called out a greeting. A man in *shalwar kameez*, with a *pakol* hat and worn leather sandals, AK-47 slung across his chest, opened the gates. They were expected, as Haji had managed to get a message to Commander Rawani that they would be coming. The families shuffled in. Through the burka face mesh, Nasrin spied hens with dusty feathers scratching in the dirt and a gray-brown donkey standing near a wizened tree, its eyes nearly closed and head bowed, swishing its tail, enjoying the tepid sun warming its back. She ached to take off the heavy vest and burka.

There was no glass left in the windows and plastic had been nailed over some of the openings. They followed their escort to the house and, after taking off their shoes, entered. They were then led into what Nasrin assumed was the living room. There were no homey comforts, no rich, thick Afghan carpets as there would normally be in a house of this size, just thin cotton floor mats and some faded pillows, or *boleshts*, propped up against the wall for people to lean against when sitting on the floor.

The group settled themselves against the *boleshts*, and soon an elderly man came into the room carrying glass cups on a tray. He left the room and returned with two large pots of chai. He seemed incurious about the group, and Nasrin wondered how many hungry, thirsty, and frightened stragglers bound for Pakistan had stopped at the compound.

As they sipped their tea, a man walked into the living room. His face was deep brown, with rivulets of wrinkles around his eyes and mouth and an aquiline hooked nose. He wore dusty pale khaki pants with side pockets, a tan shirt, and a long dark vest. A traditional white-and-black checkered *shemagh* scarf hung loosely around his neck and a woolly *pakol* rested on his head. He had a black moustache, wiry beard, and penetrating, intelligent eyes. He placed his hand on his chest: "*Salaam.* I am Commander Rawani."

Nasrin and the others murmured a greeting and thanked the commander for his hospitality.

Haji got up to greet Rawani. "Cousin!" he said, embracing the commander.

"I heard that you were stopped at three checkpoints, but the soldiers were easily bribed," Rawani said, a grin widening across his face. "They are greedy for baksheesh and easily manipulated. We will drive them out of power yet."

Nasrin looked at Bashir and raised her eyebrows. This was the famous Rawani, a commander of Mahaz-e Milli-ye Islami-ye Afghanistan, the National Islamic Front of Afghanistan, considered one of the most moderate of the mujahideen groups that fought to drive out the Soviets before 1989 and was now trying to overthrow the Communist PDPA government. Mahaz-e Milli was one of the famous Peshawar Seven, a loose alliance of seven factions created in the early 1980s to oppose the Soviet-backed PDPA. Unlike other more fundamentalist mujahideen groups, members of Mahaz-e Milli were royalists who advocated for the return from exile of King Zahir, as well as democracy and a free press.

"We are honored to be guests in your home," Bashir said, as Rawani settled himself on the floor, reached for a cup, and poured himself some tea.

The elderly man who had followed Rawani into the room took the empty pots of tea away and returned with them replenished. Commander Rawani, a Pashtun who was fluent in Farsi as well as his native Pashto, began telling the group about the struggle he was leading, how his mujahideen fighters had to move to new locations almost every night to avoid being bombed, and how terribly the people of Logar had suffered, under first the cruel Russian soldiers and now the Afghan National Army, which had inherited the Soviets' savagery.

"I will tell you a story," said Rawani, "about one especially terrible day in Logar."

Rawani began telling them about a village called Padkhwab-e Shana. The village had a remarkable gift: an underground river the villagers used for drinking and irrigation. In the fields, where farmers pastured their sheep and cattle, a complex irrigation system called a karez had been created over many years, allowing animals and crops to be watered easily from wells dug down into the flowing water source. In addition to surface channels that allowed easy irrigation, deep underground tunnels were built as well that preserved water during times of drought. They also provided shelter for villagers escaping bombardment.

Padkhwab-e Shana was built near a point where the river rises quite close to the earth's surface and irrigates a vast and flourishing vineyard. Near the middle of the village, the stream naturally descends. Long ago, stairs were cut into the earth and a tunnel created. People would walk down these steps into a cool, dim cave and fill buckets of water for drinking, washing, and cooking.

About half a mile away, the Soviets had set up an encampment with seven thousand soldiers. Several years ago, Commander Rawani continued, early one morning, as dawn broke, warning came to the villagers that Soviet soldiers from the nearby garrison were en route to Padkhwab-e Shana to press-gang the village men and boys into military service. There was no time to escape into the countryside, so more than a hundred boys and men fled down the stairs into the tunnel leading to the underground river. When the Soviets arrived, all the males had vanished, except for the elders, who stood outside the village store, drinking tea.

The soldiers searched the homes, finding them empty. The Soviet commander assumed that the men and boys had hidden underground and angrily demanded that two of the elders go into the tunnel to tell everyone to come out of hiding. The elders descended the stairs and then returned, reporting that there was no one down there. Unfortunately, one of the men in hiding, named Sayyid Hassan, panicked, and came running up the stairs into the sunlight. The Soviet commander roared at the two elders, accusing them of lying.

Sayyid shook his head. Only one other villager was down there, he told him unconvincingly.

The Soviet commander ordered Sayyid to retrieve the man and bring him to the surface. Sayyid scurried down the carved clay stairs into the darkness but didn't return.

The commander didn't wait long. He turned to two soldiers and barked orders. They leaped into a military jeep and roared off in the direction of the Soviet garrison.

The return of the soldiers was first marked by a bright flash of sun on metal and dust churned by big tires. It wasn't soldiers in jeeps who were coming but two large tankers. The commander talked to the drivers, who drove off and parked next to two well shafts. They got out and unleashed hoses from the huge vehicles. One began pumping gasoline into a well shaft. The other driver pumped kerosene into another well. The choking smell of petroleum drifted over the village like poison.

Several other Soviet soldiers, wearing protective gear and gas masks, and carrying bags of a dry white chemical, trotted down the tunnel stairs and emptied the bags into the gasoline-and-kerosene-infused waters. While this was going on, other soldiers rounded up the remaining villagers and pushed them together into a group to watch. Two more soldiers moved to the entrance of the tunnel leading down to the underground river and began firing into the hole. Explosions rocked the ground, shaking it like an earthquake, and the agonized shrieks of the dying rose from the tunnel.

They were burned alive—105 people. Twelve children were among the dead. It took a week for the villagers to winch out all the bodies.

Nasrin sat on the floor, stunned, blinking away tears. She had heard stories about the cruelty of the Soviets but nothing close to this. Commander Rawani apologized for telling such a tragic tale. But such sadism and cruelty were what the mujahideen had been fighting all these years, he said.

"When you arrive in Pakistan," he added, "inform others what Afghans are enduring. Do not forget us." He then smiled and said, "Tonight we will celebrate the new life that awaits you all!"

Later, in the dark, the women were cordoned off from the men in an area of the living room farthest from the open windows. There was no plastic covering these windows, and the freezing wind blew into every corner. Mozhdah and Masee snuggled next to Nasrin, curled up like kittens to keep warm. Nasrin kept Safee close to her chest, with the burka spread over top of her and the three children. She could hear the faint sound of men's voices coming from rooms in the far end of the house and the constant trudge of footsteps. She couldn't sleep, kept awake by the story of the cruel massacre, by the coins digging into her flesh, and by the cold wind that never ceased to blow.

BREAKFAST WAS EARLY—before the sun came up—consisting of tea and fresh naan that was baked outside by two men, former Afghan National Army soldiers who had been captured by Commander Rawani's soldiers and turned into house servants. Nasrin had spoken briefly to them while she was boiling water in the kitchen. This fate, they said, was better than life in the Afghan army.

A truck and driver had been hired the previous day with the help of Commander Rawani.

"How much?" Nasrin whispered to Bashir.

"Eighty thousand Afghanis, split four ways," Bashir replied.

"Will we have any money left after this?" Nasrin asked worriedly.

"A little," he responded.

The truck was a six-wheeler, badly dented, with paint faded by dust, wind, and time. The truck bed had thick wooden slats topped by metal slats, and a latch door at the back. It would provide shelter from the wind while hiding them from prying eyes. Nasrin went to the back and looked inside, catching a whiff of manure. Obviously, the truck had been used for transporting livestock, but at least it had been swept out and doused with water.

Nasrin had refilled the thermos with boiled water and washed Safee's baby bottles. Commander Rawani and the driver, a man in his fifties with a loosely tied green turban, skin as brown as cardamom pods, and hands blackened with motor oil, stood talking quietly, enjoying a cigarette. Another man, young—too young to grow a beard—tall, slender, and light of skin, cradling a heavy submachine gun with a huge drum magazine for bullets, stood with them.

The driver turned to the tired group. "We must go right away," he said, "there are reports of army movement in the area."

Bashir helped Nasrin into the back of the truck, then handed her Safee and the burlap sack, some fresh naan inside. When it came time to put Mozhdah and Masee into the back of the truck, Bashir grabbed them and swung them high in the air, making it a game, causing them to shriek with laughter.

Everyone clambered aboard. Commander Rawani came to the back of the truck as everyone settled into a spot on the uncomfortable metal floor. "There are places along the roadways," he said, "where you can stop for food, water, and shelter. You will meet many mujahideen who are not part of Mahaz-e Milli. They might rob you." He was sending one of his men, Mahboob, to accompany them to Pakistan and keep them from harm. "*Khuda hafiz*—may God protect you," the commander said, putting his right hand over his heart. He moved aside to let Mahboob leap lightly into the back of the truck. The young man stood tall, cradling his weapon.

"This man," Haji announced to the group, "is my nephew."

The group smiled and greeted Mahboob warmly.

"*Tashakur*—thank you! *Khuda hafiz!* *Tashakur! Khuda hafiz,*" the families yelled to their host as the truck roared to life, spewing diesel fumes that made them choke.

As the vehicle lurched forward, the fumes lessened and Nasrin breathed easier. But the noise of the engine grew louder, making her wonder if their journey might be over before it even started. No—it wasn't the truck engine, Nasrin realized, looking up into the sky. It was a low-flying jet, the morning light bouncing off its steel exterior, streaking towards Commander Rawani's headquarters. The families all stood up in the truck, clinging to the top metal bars for balance, to watch. Even from a couple of miles away the boom of the bombs hitting the earth felt like a blow to the chest. Black smoke swirled into the air and Nasrin felt sick, realizing how narrowly they had escaped. Had Commander Rawani been killed? Mozhdah and Masee, who couldn't see over the sides of the truck, looked stricken.

Nasrin sat down hard on the metal floor, holding Safee close, and put her face into his blanket, letting it absorb her silent tears.

CHAPTER 3

The Road to Terai Mangal

THE ENGINE GROWLED as the truck climbed the rock-strewn, dusty dirt mountain roadway. The families sat silent, shaken by their narrow escape from the air assault. When she thought back to the urgency in Commander Rawani's voice as he saw them off, Nasrin had a sense that he knew an attack was imminent. Quite possibly he had evaded it. But she wondered if the elderly housekeeper who served them their tea, as well as the two men who baked the naan, had also eluded the bombing.

Nasrin turned to Bashir. "What route are we taking to Pakistan?"

"The road to Terai Mangal, a pass almost directly on the Durand Line dividing Afghanistan and Pakistan," Bashir responded. "Mujahideen bring supplies into Afghanistan through there—food, weapons, money, medicines. Afghans also bring illegally cut lumber over Terai Mangal into Pakistan."

"It doesn't sound very safe," Nasrin said quietly so that the others in the truck wouldn't hear her.

"No, it's not," Bashir said. "Groups of mujahideen hide along the path, and they can be as dangerous as the Soviets, especially if they suspect you are a spy for the PDPA. But we have no choice—it is the only way for us to get through the mountains with children."

Nasrin bit her lip. Surely the mujahideen would let women and children pass safely; they posed no threat. As the day wore on, Nasrin felt boredom mix with trepidation as she listened for the sound of approaching planes. Everyone complained about their aching backs from the constant slam of body against metal as the truck plunged in and out of potholes, over rocks, and around hairpin turns, belching black diesel into the air with each gear shift. But there was beauty too. When Nasrin handed Safee to Bashir to hold so that she could stand and stretch, she stared in awe at the craggy, precipitous gray and brown rock faces of the mountains, patchy with ice, their peaks partly hidden by hoary, brooding clouds. Far in the distance she could see blue mountain peaks enveloped in an opaque mist that made them appear two-dimensional. Putting her face into the wind, Nasrin inhaled pure air—the breath of ancient rock—as clean and fresh as new snow.

It was late afternoon when the autumn sun disappeared behind a mountain peak and the air became frigid. Nasrin shivered and her hands quickly stiffened in the cold. Within minutes, they were plunged into darkness, and Nasrin wondered if they shouldn't halt their journey for today—but where? It wouldn't be safe, she thought, to keep traveling along the narrow road with its steep drop-offs and unexpected turns. Then the vehicle stopped and the ignition was turned off. The engine sighed, like an animal relieved of a heavy burden. She heard male voices, speaking in Pashto.

"Can we get out now?" Nasrin asked Bashir.

"Let me check," said Bashir, groaning as he used the slats to pull himself upright. Their guard, Mahboob, had already leaped onto the ground.

"Mommy, I want to get out too," said Mozhdah.

"Me too!" said Masee, and before Nasrin could respond, the pair jumped out of the truck after their father.

Nasrin looked at Safee and nuzzled his cheek. "Let's get out of this horrible thing," she said, handing Safee off to one of the other women so that she could stretch, muscles and tendons creaking and popping, then slip on her burka.

Nasrin gingerly climbed down out of the truck and took Safee back. Several yards away a group of about a dozen mujahideen sheltered in a lee of rock. A campfire was burning, its smoke fragrant. Over the low orange flames hung a black iron pot on a wooden spit, and cast-iron teapots sat on the edge of the fire near the hot embers. Mozhdah and Masee came to stand close to Nasrin, watching as Mahboob and the men joined the intimidating group of guerrilla soldiers, who were dressed in long shabby vests, *shalwar kameez*, and sandals. Several lit cigarettes, and the smell of burning tobacco mingled with the scent of campfire.

Most mujahideen were culturally and religiously conservative, so they considered it inappropriate for women they didn't know to come anywhere near them. Mahboob had told the group, should they encounter mujahideen during their journey, that all they had to say was *"Kada da,"* meaning, "There are women and children—it is a family moving." The presence of women meant the mujahideen would neither approach the group nor even look inside the truck. Bashir and Mahboob strode back to the women and said that the soldiers had received communications via radio that the families would be arriving.

"They have food ready for us," Bashir said.

"I'm starving," Nasrin confessed.

Just as it was inappropriate for the women to stand near the mujahideen, it wasn't tolerable that they should come close to or eat at their campfire. So Mahboob and the men got a small blaze going a little way away from the soldiers, using embers and cached twigs and branches, to keep them warm while they ate. Bashir, Hafiz, and Haji went over to the mujahideen and came back carrying large plates, called *ghorie*, piled high with *palaw*, a traditional rice dish. Seated on the ground, the four families dug in, using the fingers of their right hands to ravenously scoop food into their mouths.

"Mommy," exclaimed Mozhdah. "This is delicious!"

"I know!" Nasrin said, giving Safee rice grains on the tip of her finger. "Eat all you want—there's lots."

After the meal, Mahboob told the families that the mujahideen had heard what happened to Commander Rawani's headquarters. All the mujahideen had escaped the air attack, but the two naan makers had been killed, the house and compound obliterated. Nasrin's stomach heaved, and she thought she might throw up. She glanced at her fellow travelers—their faces stricken, eating slowed.

Nasrin forced herself to finish her *palaw* and glanced surreptitiously at the guerrilla soldiers' campground. At the edge of the light thrown by the campfire, she could see about a dozen machine guns lying on a piece of canvas. They would be safe with this group of fighters but might well freeze to death in the mountain air without shelter.

"Where are we going to sleep tonight?" she asked Bashir.

Bashir shrugged and directed Nasrin's question to Mahboob. "Is there a shelter for the women and children to sleep in?"

"There is a *chaikhana*—a teahouse—a half mile or so away," Mahboob said. "The road is fairly straight, so we can drive there safely in the dark."

"Then we should get going," Bashir said, and the families murmured their assent, having cleaned the *ghorie* of any last bits of rice.

They stood up, brushed the dirt off their clothes, hoisted the children into the back of the truck and climbed aboard. Mahboob and the men walked over to the group of mujahideen to thank them and wish them well.

The journey to the overnight shelter took about twenty minutes. The abandoned *chaikhana* was a hut with a flat corrugated iron roof that looked too small for ten people to lie down in, let alone seventeen. Mahboob walked slowly around the area, his hands ready on his weapon, then popped inside and came out a few seconds later. The building, Nasrin realized, must have been used by thousands of refugees who had escaped to Pakistan over this pass since the Soviets invaded ten years ago.

"It is safe," Mahboob announced. "The women can start a fire in the stove. There is wood on the other side of the building. There is also water in a storage tank," he said. "We'll sleep here and rise before dawn. It is very close quarters, but you will manage. I will stand guard outside."

Nasrin ducked inside the black interior with the other women. Surely there were candles or oil lamps? They felt around inside, bumping into one another, stepping on toes, which made them giggle.

Bashir ducked his head inside. "What's going on?" he said cheerfully. "Some matches would help," he said, handing Nasrin a box.

"I found a kettle!" Nasrin said, groping around a clay cookstove. "Go get water, Bashir, so we can make tea."

An hour later, with a small fire warming every inch of the room, except the dirt floor, which remained ice cold, everyone arranged themselves for sleeping, somewhat like a marketplace display of eggplants, Nasrin thought, smiling at the image. Nasrin let her thoughts drift to her past excursions with Bashir, hunting for another exotic coin to add to the collection. These bloody coins, she thought, as they poked into her body through the vest. Why hadn't they collected something soft?

Safee's hungry gurgles nudged Nasrin out of her doze. The fire in the stove had gone out, and the air in the *chaikhana* was musty with the odor of dirty bodies. She needed fresh air. Trying not to wake those still sleeping, Nasrin grabbed the burlap sack with the baby bottles and thermos and tiptoed over the bodies, opening the door just wide enough to slip through, softly murmuring, "Shhh" to the hungry infant. Bright stars hung in the graying darkness. Nasrin jumped at the silhouette of Mahboob, crouched on the ground, alert, his machine gun across his lap.

"*Salaam*, Mahboob. *Sobh bakhair*—good morning," whispered Nasrin.

"*Sobh bakhair*," Mahboob responded.

About fifteen feet from the *chaikhana*, Nasrin spied a round boulder where she could sit to feed Safee. She wrapped him tightly in his blankets and her burka to keep him warm, shaking a bottle filled with now-tepid water until the infant formula powder dissolved. That Safee didn't protest about the lukewarm milk showed how hungry he was. By the time she returned to the hut, everyone in the *chaikhana* had woken and was stretching outside in the growing dawn. All wanted tea. Everyone groaned how hungry they were and dug into sacks and bags for leftover naan.

Yawning, Bashir walked over to Nasrin and kissed Safee on the forehead. "If all goes well, we'll be at Terai Mangal on the Pakistan border tomorrow," he said.

Warmth. Food. Safety. Freedom. But, until then, many unforeseen dangers, worried Nasrin.

THE MORNING SUN, gold and pale, hung in the eastern sky, warming Nasrin's face. She grimaced as the truck hit a pothole, causing her to bite her tongue. The driver slowed the vehicle and stopped, then turned the engine off and jumped out. Had the huge pothole snapped part of the undercarriage or given them a flat tire? She could hear the driver and Mahboob talking, then detected a strange voice. Bashir and the rest of the men jumped out of the truck. Nasrin strained to listen but couldn't make out what was being said. She handed Safee to Mozhdah and, pulling her burka down over her head, jumped out. Bashir and the rest of the men were standing near an empty truck that had its hood up, the engine emitting an acrid smell.

"What's going on?" Nasrin asked Bashir.

"This truck has broken down. Our driver is from the same village as this man. We're going to have to help him get the truck going again," Bashir responded.

"How long could that take?" Nasrin said worriedly.

"Until it's fixed." Bashir sighed.

"But we don't have food," said Nasrin.

"None?"

"We ate all the *palaw* from the other night. We have a bit of naan left. Safee still has powdered milk. But I have to boil more water."

Bashir shook his head with worry. "I'm sure we'll get the engine going again soon."

"Let's hope," Nasrin responded.

The sun crept west across the sky, and still the two truck drivers tinkered and hammered with their tools, occasionally jumping into the cab to try the ignition. The engine refused to turn over.

The children dug holes in the hard ground with sticks and made houses out of piled stones in the bright sun. Gradually, the light began to change, throwing deep, cold shadows onto the rough track. Nasrin felt a growing fury. They had paid their driver a fortune to take them to Pakistan. She walked over to the men, whose heads were deep in the engine, while sockets, wrenches, and screwdrivers lay on a dirty, oily cloth on the ground.

"*Salaam*," Nasrin said politely.

The drivers ignored her.

"Nasrin!" Bashir called out in warning.

Nasrin didn't look at Bashir. "We have been here for hours," she told the drivers. "The children are hungry. They are thirsty. We must get going."

No response.

"Night will fall soon and we have only traveled a few hours today. We won't arrive in Pakistan tomorrow. It is too dangerous, staying here," Nasrin's voice rose in frustration.

Bashir hurried over and grasped Nasrin's arm, pulling her firmly away and down the path. "You must understand, Nasrin," Bashir said urgently. "They are from the same village—the same family. Our driver would as soon join the Afghan army as leave a relative stranded. We have no choice. We must stay until the truck is fixed."

"But they're not going to get it going. They've been at it most of the day," Nasrin protested. "Maybe the driver should come with us and look for a mechanic—or engine parts—in Terai Mangal," she said.

Bashir suddenly snapped his head around and began scanning the rocky terrain. "Where are those voices coming from?" Shouting could be heard from far away.

"I don't know," Nasrin responded nervously.

"Listen," Bashir said softly.

They turned at the sound of shouting from Mahboob, who had cupped an ear with his right hand, the better to hear the faraway voices. He grinned broadly, waving at a craggy hilltop several hundred yards away.

"Yes! We would love some food!" he yelled. "Thank you!"

Bashir and Nasrin looked at each other, puzzled, and walked towards Mahboob.

"Who are you talking to?" Bashir asked.

"Some mujahideen have been watching us from their lookout and noticed that we have children and no food," said Mahboob. "They are going to send a large plate of *palaw* and potatoes to feed us."

"The mujahideen lookouts don't miss much," Bashir remarked.

"No, they don't," Mahboob agreed.

A mujahideen soldier, carefully navigating the treacherous boulders and scree, arrived about twenty minutes later carrying a *ghorie* heaped with *palaw*. The drivers took a break to eat as well, scooping the rice and potatoes into their mouths with hands dirty with grease. Nasrin was pleased that the potatoes were soft enough to feed to Safee. It was as if the food were a restorative for the moribund engine too, as it roared to life only fifteen minutes after the drivers returned to their tinkering, causing everyone to choke on the cloud of black, oily diesel exhaust filling the air. They cheered through their coughing. Five minutes later, the two trucks resumed their respective journeys, one uphill and east towards Pakistan, the other downhill and west towards Logar.

It was twilight now, and Nasrin looked up at a sliver of a new moon in the sky between mountain peaks. She thought of the people she loved who were left behind in Kabul and wondered if they were looking up at the same beautiful, pale light.

"We're still alive, *Gul*," she whispered. "We're still alive."

Trying to make up for lost time, the driver drove well into the night, but at a crawl over the rocky, twisting road. Nasrin's nose and ears felt like ice. Safee, at least, was warm and asleep, cradled tightly against her chest in a nest she had created with the diaper-stuffed burlap sack. Eventually, the truck bumped to a stop. The driver opened his door and jumped to the ground, calling out: "We have arrived at the *chaikhana*. Everyone can get out."

Relieved chatter: "What time do you think it is? How close are we to the border?"

The *chaikhana* was a utilitarian square building with a flat roof and a stainless steel chimney from which tendrils of smoke wafted. Desperate for warmth, the families walked stiffly to the door and slipped off their shoes before entering. Small oil lamps in shallow recesses along the walls flickered as cold air blew into the room. The travelers entered the main area, which was covered wall to wall with a thin, worn Afghan carpet. A middle-aged man in a turban, his face deeply furrowed, came out of an arched doorway, murmured *"Salaam,"* and laid out an enormous pink, flowered plastic cover on the rug. The children and adults returned the greeting and plopped down on the hard *toshaks*, or floor cushions. *He looks old*, thought Nasrin, *as well as sad*. Mozhdah snuggled against Nasrin with tears in her eyes and held up her hands. Nasrin clasped her daughter's icy hands in hers and blew warm air onto them until the tears disappeared.

While their host prepared a meal for them in the kitchen, Nasrin looked around, noticing a faded framed photograph of the charismatic commander Ahmad Shah Massoud, the "Lion of Panjshir," a revered hero of the mujahideen resistance against the Soviets.

"Look! Tea!" Nasrin exclaimed to Mozhdah and Masee, who had been tugging at her sleeve. Their host carried a tray with two pots of tea and cups, placing it carefully on the pink plastic covering. Nasrin poured Masee and Mozhdah each a mug loaded with sugar. "Cup the mug like this," she told them. "It will warm your hands. But let it cool a bit before drinking."

About twenty minutes later, their host brought in a tray laden with numerous serving bowls and a large stewpot of *shorwa*. Instead of the traditional Afghan dish typically brimming with summer vegetables, chunks of meat on the bone, and tomatoes and spices, this was a watery brown facsimile, with a few potatoes and thin slivers of lamb meat. Each person grabbed a chipped porcelain bowl from the stack, and Nasrin ladled out helpings to Mozhdah and Masee, giving them fresh naan for dipping. It was delicious, and Nasrin gave tiny pieces of *shorwa*-soaked naan to Safee, who clapped his hands for more, eyes wide with pleasure.

When the dishes were removed and the last remnant of sweet tea drunk, the children curled up on the *toshaks*, falling asleep immediately. Nasrin went into the kitchen with her thermos and bottles to ask the man if she could boil water for Safee's formula.

"*Tashakur.* Thank you for the meal. It was delicious." She paused, not knowing how comfortable the man would be talking to her. "What is your name?" she asked.

"Ali," he responded.

"How long have you had this *chaikhana?*"

"Four years now." Ali sighed deeply and began talking. The Soviets had killed his two children and wife in their village in Mazar-i-Sharif. There had been a nearby garrison of Soviet soldiers, and one night four of them got drunk and stupidly wandered into the village to buy apples and grapes. The mujahideen captured and killed them. In retaliation, the Soviet soldiers attacked the village in the middle of the night—bulldozed their homes, shot at them, butchered as many people as they could. The bullets somehow missed Ali, who fled, returning later to find the bodies of his wife and children. He buried them, then escaped to Pakistan with a few other survivors. When they were coming through these mountains it snowed, leaving them stranded and near death. Afterwards, Ali said, he thought that by opening a *chaikhana* at this point of the journey, he could help other Afghans.

"I'm so sorry for your terrible loss," Nasrin said in a stricken voice.

"You are blessed to have children. Keep them safe," Ali said.

"I will," Nasrin responded, her voice cracking.

After a night of restless sleep, the families were up by 5:00 AM and downed a simple breakfast of naan and tea. Today, they hoped, would be the last stage of the journey to Pakistan. They paid for the food and accommodations and climbed reluctantly into the back of the truck. Mahboob, as usual, stood up, scanning the landscape, machine gun cradled in his arms, alert and relaxed despite keeping guard all night long. Bashir held Safee, and Mozhdah and Masee snuggled against their mom, listening as Nasrin softly hummed Afghan songs from childhood.

The sun warming her face, Nasrin realized that she had dozed off. She licked the dust off her dry lips. It seemed warmer, and she was beginning to sweat underneath her heavy vest. The truck slowed to a stop. Another *chaikhana*? Authoritative voices—hard and commanding—the voices of army or police officers, sent a chill down her spine.

"Stay here," Bashir said. "Don't anyone make a sound," he whispered to the women and children. He unlatched the door at the back of the truck and jumped out.

"Where are we? Why did we stop?" Mozhdah asked nervously.

"Shhh," Nasrin responded.

In the stillness, Nasrin detected changes: the scent of vegetation, the trilling of birds—so different from the barren, cold mountain roads.

Bashir came back and beckoned to Nasrin. "Come out," he said, a wide grin on his face. "We have made it to Terai Mangal. Wear your burka," he added.

Nasrin pulled the blue cloth over her head and stumbled stiffly to the ground. She looked about. It was another world. Sparse grasses covered boulder-strewn hills while copses of stunted trees grew out of the rocky earth. Three nearby mountains rose into the air, their steep slopes covered in green.

A small group of armed men approached the group. Mahboob walked towards them, and they greeted each other warmly. Returning to the families, who stood uneasily about ten feet away, Mahboob explained he would continue on with the group into Pakistan, though he had to leave his firearm in Afghanistan, picking it up on his return. "This is the Terai Mangal pass—we have arrived in Pakistan!" he said, smiling as everyone cheered.

Mahboob handed one of the men in the group his machine gun and walked back to the truck. "Let's go!" he said.

As they drove through the gate, the road sloped downhill and the engine's growl eased slightly. Nadia, Nasrin's fourteen-year-old niece, couldn't contain her excitement and stood, holding tight to the top metal slats. Her chador blew off and her long black hair whipped around her face. "We made it!" Nadia screamed into the wind. "Yaaaay, we made it!"

Everyone laughed. It was, thought Nasrin, like being on a ship, sailing away from land onto a great big endless ocean, roiled by waves of hope.

CHAPTER 4

A Waiting Game

THE PLAN WAS to travel to Islamabad, a day's drive. But first, the families would stop in the city of Mīrāmshāh in the Pashtun tribal area of North Waziristan. Mīrāmshāh was only an hour from Terai Mangal. There was a hotel in the city that, their driver told them, was the first overnight stop for many Afghan refugees, mainly because it was cheap. An hour later, dusty, thirsty, and bruised from days of rough roads, Nasrin and the others gratefully disembarked outside the hotel. Never again, Nasrin thought grimly, would she travel in the back of a truck. The families said goodbye to their driver, who nodded curtly in response to their profuse thanks and wheeled the truck around, which belched more black diesel exhaust into the air as it lumbered down the road, returning to Afghanistan.

The four families stayed in one large room in the hotel. It had a flush toilet, a luxury after the days spent in the back of the truck. This was countered by the stench of an open sewer just outside the window. The next day, they rented a van big enough to fit all seventeen people and drove for two hours to their next destination, Peshawar, where they stopped for breakfast at a roadside kiosk that sold naan. In Peshawar, they rented two smaller vans for the 120-mile leg to Islamabad, where they would arrive at their final destination: the home of Rokai, brother-in-law of Hafiz. Rokai and his family rented part of an enormous house that otherwise stood empty. The landlord had agreed, at Rokai's request, to rent out the rest of the home to the families. Nasrin felt blessed; most Afghans ended up in tents in one of Pakistan's many refugee camps.

Pakistan grew warmer and more humid the farther they drove, the craggy mountains softening into rounded green hills. The motorways became congested with motorcycles, cars, and ornately decorated jingle trucks, so named because of the clinking metal trinkets they were adorned with. The vehicles roared only yards away from unflinching men and women clad in shalwar kameez, walking along the roadside.

It was near dusk when they reached Islamabad, Pakistan's capital, which, at the time, was a small city of just over 300,000 people. The air was filled with a cacophony of beeping horns, engine exhaust, and the enticing scent of street food: spicy rice, meat, and vegetable dishes. It took nearly an hour to find Rokai's house, and it was dusk by the time the vans parked in front of the home. Hafiz got out, walked up to the high iron gates, and called out a greeting. Within a minute, the gates swung open. Rokai joyously threw his arms around Hafiz and beckoned everyone inside.

A yard light illuminated the broad and shiny leaves of a laburnum tree, and pink bougainvillea bushes framed the wooden

front door of the three-story house. An older man, Hafiz's
father-in-law, Mohammad Ali Hasanzai, stood on the porch.

"Welcome to Pakistan!" Mohammad said. "You must be
exhausted—and hungry! I will show you to your rooms and
then take you to the kitchen for food. We've given each family
their own bedroom and bathroom. Come quickly, before all
the insects of Pakistan fly in."

Stiff, hungry, and thirsty yet excited, the families spilled
out of the vans, dragging their worldly possessions in the dirty
burlap sacks.

As she walked through the home, Nasrin stared in awe at
the cavernous hallway with its gray marbled floor and high
ceilings. Mohammad pointed out the bathroom for Nasrin and
Bashir, then escorted them to a bedroom containing *toshak*
cushions for sleeping on and some blankets.

"Here," Nasrin said to Bashir, handing him Safee. "I'm going
to have a bath."

Bashir was about to protest, then laughed and said, "Take
your time. We'll eat in the kitchen."

The bathroom was just down the hall. Nasrin opened the
wooden door. It felt like she had stepped into heaven. There
was a rusty claw-foot soaker tub and a pile of towels lying on
an elegantly carved round rosewood table. She smelled sandal-
wood soap. As warm water gurgled into the tub out of the taps,
Nasrin peeled off the layers of travel clothing: the now-hated
vest with its two hundred heavy coins, her tunic and *shalwar*
trousers, hardened with dust and sweat. When had they left
Kabul? Was it only five days ago? It felt like five years, she
thought, slipping into the clean bath water.

"We made it, *Gul*," Nasrin spoke aloud, as if her mother
were in the room. "No one was hurt. You should have come

with us. Why didn't you come?" she said, tears slowly hitting the bathwater.

SIX MONTHS LATER, the laburnum tree was a sunburst of bright yellow flowers that filled the air with sweetness. Mozhdah played in the front yard with her cousins: Farzana, Mina, Vida, and Nadia. Bored, the girls decided to slip through the narrow gap between the hedge and the cement column of the front gate to see if their friends were home from school. Walking to an adjacent house, they saw sisters Asma and Bushra, and siblings Qudsia and Faisal, still in their school uniforms of light blue *shalwar* pants and tunics. They were sitting on the front step of their home.

Mozhdah waved them over. "We're going to buy some *pakora* fritters and chutney. Come with us," Mozhdah said in Urdu, which she was picking up from the neighborhood kids.

The group walked several blocks until they reached a busy thoroughfare where the street vendors congregated, selling everything from popsicles to freshly crushed sugarcane juice, walnuts, and sweets. The children sought out the *pakora* vendor, who served the treat with bright green chutney in a paper container for two rupees. Sharp and tangy, the chutney went perfectly with the spicy, crunchy snack. Mozhdah received a small allowance from her dad, most of which she spent on *pakora*. She spied two women in blue burkas hurrying down the street, and wondered if they might be from Afghanistan. She wanted to speak to them in Farsi—ask them if they were from Kabul. Maybe they knew her grandmother, her aunties, uncles, and cousins. But she was too shy, and the women scurried quickly past, with too much purpose.

Bashir had found a job in Peshawar, an ancient city founded in the sixth century BCE by nomadic Kushans. Just six months previous, he and the other escaped families had stopped here for a breakfast of naan on their journey into Islamabad. Only forty miles east of the Afghanistan-Pakistan border, Peshawar had been inundated with thousands of Afghan refugees during the Soviet occupation. It also bustled with foreigners who worked for international non-governmental organizations (NGOs) and aid agencies. About ten miles from the city was the famous Nasir Bagh refugee camp, one of the biggest of about 150 safe havens for Afghans that had sprung up. Bashir worked as a translator there with the International Medical Corps (IMC), teaching English-speaking expats such as nurses and physicians basic Farsi. He made 6,000 rupees a month—about USD$300—enough to support his family. The IMC provided Bashir with accommodations at its compound during the week. At the end of each workweek, Bashir jumped on a bus for the 120-mile journey back to Islamabad to spend the weekend with Nasrin and the kids.

Despite their relative security, the Jamalzadah family was in limbo. Pakistan didn't grant citizenship to Afghan refugees. Bashir and Nasrin knew they could never return to Afghanistan, so as soon as Bashir arrived in Pakistan he applied for an identification card—the all-important Shanakhti Pass. It was a simple piece of paper, written in Urdu, the lingua franca of Pakistan, with a photo, one's name, and the names of family members. None of the foreign embassies would accept a refugee claim without it. As soon as he received a Shanakhti Pass, Bashir applied to the American, Australian, and Canadian embassies as a refugee. At the Canadian office in Islamabad, he was given a short form to fill out that included space for the names of family members. He made photocopies of his post-secondary degrees and teaching certificates and submitted them as a package.

One weekend, after returning home from his IMC job in Peshawar, Bashir received a letter from the Canadian office. It was another form, a much longer one this time, asking for details about his refugee claim, including any threats or actual harm he had suffered while in Afghanistan, and the possibility of mistreatment by an individual or group should he return to his home country. One question asked whether Bashir required an English translator if selected for an interview with embassy staff. Bashir jotted down "No"—grateful for his fluency in English. Once again, he returned the form to the embassy, along with photocopies of his degrees and diplomas.

Now it was a waiting game. As Bashir sat on the bus to Peshawar, he stared unseeing, lost in thought, at the passing landscape: flat farmland with neatly ploughed fields, turgid rivers, and the outline of blue mountains like a mirage on the horizon. What would Canada be like? Would the people be friendly? He couldn't think about Canada too much, for fear of getting his hopes up. What might make his refugee application stand out among the thousands that the embassy was deluged with? How were people picked?

The months crept by, and Nasrin began homeschooling Mozhdah, who had turned six. Nasrin taught her math, reading and writing, and geography. Mozhdah stared in awe at a map of Canada and tried to imagine what it was like to live in such an enormous country, which could fit more than a dozen Afghanistans into its expanse. On weekends, Bashir would tutor Mozhdah and Masee in English: "Hello. My name is Mozhdah. I am from Afghanistan. Thank you." Making her repeat the words over and over—like a mantra of hope.

It was a late afternoon one steaming summer day. Bashir had just returned from Peshawar. He was hot and tired, his dress shirt sticky with sweat from the walk home from the bus stop. Opening the gate into the yard, he watched the children, including Masee and Mozhdah, as well as some neighborhood kids, seated on the grass in the shade of the laburnum tree. They were enthusiastically rubbing the heels of their bare feet.

Laughing, he said, "What are you up to?"

"Daddy!" exclaimed Mozhdah, leaping up to hug him. "We're trying to make it rain. They say that if you rub your heels and pray, then the rains come. We need rain, right?"

"Yes, Mozhdah, we need rain. It has been very hot. That is an excellent idea: rubbing your heels to make it rain. I am sure you will be successful," he said, still laughing.

"Oh," Mozhdah said. "Mommy has a letter for you. I think she said it was from Canada."

Bashir stopped in his tracks, momentarily forgetting his fatigue. "Thank you, Mozhdah. I shall go find Mom."

Bashir kicked off his shoes at the door and walked into the cool hallway, calling out: "Nasrin, are you here? Do we have a letter from the Canadian embassy?"

He strode to their bedroom and opened the door. Nasrin was hanging clothes in the closet. She turned to Bashir. "Shhhh. Nap time," she whispered, nodding towards Safee, who lay on his back on a *toshak*, eyes closed, arms and legs splayed out.

"Letter?" Bashir whispered back.

Nasrin nodded again, towards a small table where a white envelope lay. Bashir picked it up, staring at the return address: High Commission of Canada.

He sat on the bed, slipped a fingernail underneath the envelope's flap, and opened it slowly. The paper was thick, with Government of Canada letterhead. "Dear Mr. Bashir Jamalzadah..." Bashir closed his eyes, unable to read any further. What if it was a rejection letter? He couldn't bear to think about the possibility.

Fearing the worst, Nasrin went over to him and placed a comforting arm around his shoulders. "Oh no, Bashir," she said softly.

"I actually haven't read it yet," said Bashir, opening his eyes and smiling ruefully at Nasrin, who rolled her eyes.

Bashir scanned the letter twice to make sure he understood it. And then he broke into a huge smile and hugged Nasrin and kissed her on the cheek. "We have an interview. All of us. At the embassy office."

"Really?" said Nasrin, her voice rising in excitement. "All of us get to go?"

Safee opened his eyes and blinked sleepily, looking at his parents curiously.

"Yes, they want us at the embassy office at ten o'clock next Wednesday. They are going to interview me, you, and the kids."

"Finally!" Nasrin exclaimed.

"What do you mean, 'finally'?" Bashir asked.

Nasrin moved over to the closet. "I can finally wear my beautiful shoes that I brought all the way from Afghanistan— hidden in the diaper bag!"

Bashir opened his eyes wide and shook his head, chuckling at Nasrin's optimistic daring. Safee had woken up and rolled onto his bottom, putting his hands out, thrilled to see his dad after the five-day absence.

"Yes, you're coming too, Safee," said Bashir, grabbing his younger son and holding him aloft. "We're off to the Canadian embassy!"

SEVERAL HOURS BEFORE their appointment at the High Commission of Canada on Embassy Road, Bashir called a taxi to pick them up at the house, rather than take a bus or minivan. It was better to be early than late, and a taxi would be more dependable in Islamabad's infamously chaotic traffic.

Nasrin fretted about what to wear. She finally opted for a cream-colored dopatta scarf, a symbol of modesty for Pakistani women, light brown *shalwar* pants, and a satin tunic dress in lapis blue with blue flowers and satin cuffs that complemented the fashionable black high heels smuggled out of Afghanistan.

Mozhdah wore a traditional *shalwar kameez* outfit that Nasrin had sewn; the *shalwar* pants were red, topped by an aquamarine tunic. Her long hair was kept out of her face with a flowered headband. She couldn't stop admiring herself in the bathroom mirror, making Nasrin and Bashir laugh. The boys wore new shorts, shirts, and runners. Bashir wore his only suit: gray, with a blue tie and white shirt. He polished his brown leather shoes to a high shine and carefully trimmed his beard.

The letter explained that each member of the family would be interviewed separately—even the children would have an interview without their parents present. Nasrin and Bashir briefed Masee and Mozhdah on what to say.

"Be truthful," Bashir emphasized. "Say that living in Kabul was scary because of the missiles. The bombing often woke you up at night, so the family traveled to Pakistan to be safe. You can tell the interviewer that your parents were scared too," Bashir said to Masee and Mozhdah, who nodded in understanding.

The taxi ride was uneventful, so the family was early. Nasrin (trying to keep a squirming Safee under control), Bashir, Mozhdah, and Masee disembarked carefully from the taxicab so as not to brush up against the dusty vehicle. A guard stood watch at the gate to the embassy compound, surrounded by a tall concrete wall. Bashir stated his name to the guard, who turned to another watchman seated in a tiny office just inside the fence. Their names were on the log of the day's visitors, and the guards beckoned the family inside. The compound was lush, with artfully arranged flowerbeds, and bushes and trees in bloom. A flagstone walkway led to the front door.

"Smell the jasmine and roses," Nasrin said to the children, inhaling deeply.

Inside, they were greeted by the rhythmic whump of a large slow fan that did little more than circulate the humid air. A marble floor led to a waiting area with several neat rows of chairs. A secretary sat behind a wooden desk that held some cardboard files, a container of pens and pencils, and a telephone. Other couples with children also sat waiting.

Bashir approached the secretary, who was Pakistani. "Good morning," he said nervously in English. "My name is Bashir Jamalzadah, and my family and I are here to be interviewed." He slipped his hand into his inside jacket pocket and pulled out the letter he had received from the Canadian embassy. "Here," he said, unfolding and placing it carefully on the desk.

The young woman glanced at it briefly and looked at a typed list of names on the desk. "Your appointment is at eleven o'clock," she said. "You're a bit early. If you like, you and your family can take a walk in the gardens outside."

"Thank you," said Bashir. "But we are fine waiting here."

Nasrin rolled her eyes at Bashir as he sat down in the chair beside her. "The children will squirm out of their skins if we wait here for very long," she said. "I'm taking them into the gardens."

"Don't let them get dirty," Bashir said anxiously. "And don't be longer than fifteen minutes, in case they call our names early."

Nasrin wandered the gardens for about twenty minutes, smelling the flowers while admonishing the kids not to pick them. When she returned, the children were still relatively clean, though Safee had grabbed a handful of dirt from a flower-bed and flung it at his brother. Nasrin brushed away the remnants of dirt from Masee's clothing.

The hands on the large round wall clock crawled by so slowly Bashir was convinced it was broken.

"Mr. Bashir Jamalzadah," the secretary finally announced. "Please go up the stairs and take a seat in the chairs provided. There is an interpreter there, in case you need one," she said.

The family walked up the curving stairway, feeling the smoothness of the heavy, polished, dark wood banister. A row of chairs lined the wall of the hallway, and everyone took a seat. A secretary came out of a room and beckoned Bashir to follow her up another staircase, then down a long hallway. First, he looked back at Nasrin and nodded reassuringly. After all, they had been forewarned that they would be interviewed separately.

A slender middle-aged man in dress pants and a white shirt unbuttoned at the neck came out of an office. "Mr.

Jamalzadah?" he said. "I'm an immigration official for the Government of Canada. Please come in," he said, gesturing to a chair.

An interpreter, clearly Afghan, was waiting in the office, and Bashir and the man greeted each other in Farsi. The immigration official picked up a document that Bashir recognized as the long-form questionnaire he had sent in months ago. "It indicates here that you don't need an interpreter," the official said.

"No, I don't," Bashir replied.

"Good," the man said, then directed his comment to the Afghan interpreter. "You can leave. Thank you for your time."

The official moved around the corner of his enormous wooden desk and sat down. "So... tell me your story," he said, looking keenly at Bashir. "What made you leave Afghanistan, and why do you want to emigrate to Canada?"

Bashir began his tale. He explained how he was a teacher at Kabul Pedagogical Institute and that his boss, Ghafoor Alipour, a PDPA Communist party supporter, tried to sign Bashir up for conscription to get rid of him. He talked about going into hiding and the desperate plan to flee to Pakistan through Logar province disguised as peasant farmers. He described how he and three other families bribed Afghan soldiers at checkpoints, how Commander Rawani housed and fed them, and how they narrowly escaped an aerial bomb attack at the commander's headquarters. Bashir described the cold, cramped, bone-shaking journey in the back of the truck through the Paktia mountains, and how surviving the trip felt like a miracle. And although he was grateful to Pakistan for letting him and his family stay, he explained, the government would never grant them citizenship. He wanted a home for his three children, a place for them to grow up safely and get an education.

The official looked intently at Bashir as he spoke, never moving, never looking down at his papers. "Why did you apply to Canada?" he asked. "What do you know about the country?"

Bashir smiled nervously. He knew that the country's capital was Ottawa. He also knew a bit about Montreal—how everyone spoke French. He also knew that Canada had universal health care and welcomed new immigrants. "It is a young country," Bashir said. "It is peaceful. It welcomes refugees."

The official smiled, got up from his chair, and came around the desk. "Well, I've heard enough," he said, sticking his hand out to shake Bashir's hand. "I won't need to interview your family. Let me see you out."

Relieved, but wondering if he'd said the right things, Bashir stood up and surreptitiously wiped his sweaty palms on his pants, following the official back down to the second floor.

The man shook his hand once again. "I will file my report. It's up to the adjudicators whether to accept you into Canada— or not," he said.

"Do you know when we will hear?" Bashir asked.

"I don't know. We have a backlog of refugee applications. I wish you the best of luck," the official said, turning away to trot back up the stairs.

"Let's go," said Bashir, turning to Nasrin and the kids. "You don't need to be interviewed."

"Oh," Nasrin responded in a whisper, as they walked down the staircase into the main lobby of the embassy. "Is that good or bad?"

"I honestly don't know," said Bashir. "It's a waiting game—a long one from the sounds of it. The man said there is a backlog of claims."

Weeks later, the family had still heard nothing, aside from a request asking Bashir and the family to travel to Rawalpindi, a half-hour drive away, for a medical checkup.

After that, life resumed its normal rhythm. The summer monsoons came, turning roadways into streams. Bashir stopped wondering if a letter would arrive and began to think that the family had been rejected on medical grounds. He continued work as a translator and Farsi instructor at IMC. As fall approached, the weather cooled, and with it Bashir's hopes.

Then, one October day, as he was working at his desk in the IMC building, he heard a soft knock at his office door. "Come in!" Bashir called, without looking up.

It was Nasrin's seventeen-year-old nephew Najib from Islamabad. "What are you doing here?" Bashir gasped. "Is everything okay at home?"

"You have a letter, uncle!" Najib exclaimed. "It's from the embassy. We decided to open it in case it was important. And it is! Very, very important!"

Bashir put his hand out to take the letter. He began reading: "Dear Mr. Jamalzadah." His eyes went blurry and he had to reread the opening paragraph three times. His hands shook. He, Nasrin, and the kids were going to Canada. They would pick up their tickets at the airport this Friday.

Stunned, he put the letter on the desk. He had to take it to Todd Peterson, his boss at IMC. "Come with me, Najib," said Bashir. "Thank you so much for opening the letter. I wouldn't have been home until Friday and we would have missed the plane! But," he added, "you could have called me!"

"We thought you should see the letter yourself," Najib said, laughing.

Bashir strode down the hallway towards Todd's office. His boss looked quizzically at Bashir, who was breathless with excitement. "Todd, this is Najib. He came here all the way from Islamabad today to deliver a letter."

"It must be important," Todd remarked.

"Here!" Bashir said, handing him the letter. "Read it!"

Todd read it slowly. "Congratulations!" he exclaimed, and got up out of his seat, moving around the desk to hug Bashir.

"I'll take this as your resignation," Todd said with a grin. "But before you jump on the bus, let's get everyone together so they can say goodbye." He strode into the hallway and began knocking on people's office doors, telling them that Bashir was off to Canada and they were giving him an impromptu going-away bash.

Someone ran out to buy street food, and they all went into the lunchroom to sip soft drinks and eat fresh kebabs, chapati, and plump *kachori* dumplings.

Todd took Bashir aside. "Here," he said, placing a stack of rupees in an envelope into Bashir's hand. "The rest of this month's salary plus one month extra. You won't get out of Islamabad International Airport without paying bribes."

Bashir laughed. "Thanks for letting me know."

Todd chuckled. "As soon as this little party is over, I'll take you and Najib to the bus station. Make sure that you write me when you get to Canada and let me know where you live, and tell me all about your new home. It's pretty cold there, you know."

"So I've read," said Bashir. "We'll survive. It gets cold in Kabul in the winter too, you know."

"Not like Canada," Todd said.

A short while later, with dusk falling, Todd dropped Bashir and Najib off at the busy bus station. After final handshakes, the pair climbed aboard the crowded bus, pushing past passengers with shopping bags and packages. Bashir kept his hand on the letter throughout the three-hour drive, opening it to reread it, feeling light-headed and giddy. He wanted to stand up in the bus and shout out to all the passengers that he— Bashir of Afghanistan—was taking his family to a new home called Canada.

PART 2

The Melting Pot

1991–2009

CHAPTER 5

Schoolyard Lessons

"It's too cold. I'm not getting up," Mozhdah said, sliding deeper into the cocoon of blankets on the double bed in their motel room.

"Get up," Nasrin said firmly.

"No."

Nasrin tugged the blankets off Mozhdah, who whimpered as the cold air hit her skin. She grabbed at the covers and pulled them over her head.

After a long journey from Pakistan, stopping for a connecting flight at Schiphol Airport in Amsterdam, the Jamalzadah family had landed in Toronto. An official with the Department of Employment and Immigration, who introduced himself as Mr. Campeau, met them at Pearson International Airport. After handing out parkas to the family—it was a chilly October evening—Mr. Campeau bundled the family into a van and drove forty-five minutes to Oshawa, a small, blue-collar, auto-manufacturing city east of Toronto. By the time they reached their destination—the unpretentious brown two-story Kingsway Motel—Safee and Masee had nodded off.

Bashir and Mr. Campeau dragged the luggage out of the van and placed it on the pavement. Nasrin carried Safee, still asleep, while Masee and Mozhdah stood shivering miserably in the parking lot beside their mother, waiting for Bashir and the immigration official to return from reception with a key to their ground-floor room. Little more than a day ago, they were in eighty-five-degree weather, surrounded by greenery. Here in Oshawa, the temperature was near freezing, the trees barren of leaves. Bashir unlocked the motel room door and they walked inside, looking at their new, two-room home, which included double beds with wooden headboards and nylon bedspreads; a television, desk, and chair; and a small half-fridge tucked into a corner of the room. After the intense colors, heat, noises, and scents of Pakistan, it was unbearably banal.

Mr. Campeau showed Bashir how to turn the television on and change channels. He promised to drop by in the morning to show the family around the neighborhood and take them shopping for groceries and more winter wear. He also pointed out the coffee maker and gave them a bag of sandwiches and fruit.

After Mr. Campeau left, Mozhdah plunked herself down on a bed. "I want to go back to Pakistan," she said. "I hate it here."

That had been a week ago, and Mozhdah had not warmed up to her new country, despite a shopping trip for clothes and a trip to the local museum. Nasrin tugged again at the covers pulled up over Mozhdah's head. Today was Mozhdah's first day at Clara Hughes Public School, where she would attend the grade three English as a second language (ESL) class. Bashir would walk her to school, just a few blocks away.

After Mozhdah was finally out of bed and dressed, and had eaten a bit of fruit for breakfast, Bashir bent over to help her into her snow boots and parka.

"Here's your lunch," Nasrin said, handing her a brown bag. "It's yogurt and a sandwich, like the one Mr. Campeau brought us our first night here," she said, hugging Mozhdah and kissing her on the forehead. "Have fun today. I'm sure you'll make lots of new friends."

Mozhdah felt sick. She knew little English. She didn't want to go outside in the cold. Her homesickness was growing, rather than diminishing. There was no golden sunlight here, no sweet frangipani flowers to tuck behind her ears, no *pakora* fritters with chutney, no large bold birds with bright plumage, no beautiful ladies in saris, no friendly store clerks who smiled when you waved. In Oshawa, only a few people were outside on the sidewalks, parka hoods pulled over their heads, hurrying for refuge from the cold.

She wanted to cry.

Bashir opened the motel door. "Let's go," he said brightly. "Time for school!"

Mozhdah grabbed his proffered hand, and they walked quickly to keep warm. Her other hand felt icy cold, despite the new woolen gloves.

They arrived at the schoolyard to see a few hardy kids in boots, bulky parkas, and thick mittens playing on the swings and slide. They went inside and Bashir pointed out a sign directing visitors to the office. Boots squeaking on the polished linoleum floor, they walked to the office, and Mozhdah reluctantly let go of her father's hand.

"Can I help you?" asked a woman behind a high wooden counter.

"Good morning," Bashir responded. "My name is Bashir Jamalzadah, and this is my daughter Mozhdah. We are the family from Afghanistan. Mozhdah will be starting in the grade three English as a second language class today."

"Are you excited about your first day of school in Canada?" said the woman, peeking over the counter to look at Mozhdah.

Mozhdah stared blankly at the woman.

Bashir cleared his throat. "Say hello, Mozhdah."

Mozhdah looked up at her dad. "Hello," she said in a faint voice, then peered down at the worn linoleum floor, blinking back hot tears. She knew she was about to be abandoned by Bashir in this cold, inhospitable place, and there was nothing she could do to stop it.

Bashir said, "Thank you" to the woman and took Mozhdah's hand again. They walked to the end of the hallway and turned left. "See that?" Bashir asked, pointing to a sign on a door. "That's the bathroom. If you have to go during class, don't be afraid to ask your teacher."

Mozhdah nodded numbly, her lower lip trembling.

They entered the classroom, where a young woman sat writing at a sturdy wooden desk at the front. She looked up. "Oh, hello!" she said. "This must be Mozhdah. Welcome!"

Mozhdah looked at the toes of her new snow boots.

"Mozhdah," said Bashir. "I'm going to leave you now. But I'll be outside the front doors when school is over at three PM."

Mozhdah clung to Bashir's hand. "Don't leave, Daddy," she begged, as he firmly pulled away from her tight grip. "You'll be fine," he assured her.

The teacher, beautiful, blonde, and slender, with kind eyes, came over to Mozhdah and bent down. "I see you brought your lunch," she said, speaking slowly and pointing to the brown bag. "Let's put your parka in the coatroom. Follow me." The teacher helped Mozhdah remove her coat, then led her to a wooden desk at the front of the class. She pointed to the seat, indicating that she should sit down and slip her brown bag lunch into the desk opening.

Mozhdah peered around the classroom, with its straight lines of desks, big windows, and huge blackboard at the front. Pinned to a wall was a huge blue map of the world with brightly colored continents, as well as paintings done by the students. Above the chalkboard were pictures of animals, creatures she had never seen before or even imagined, with huge brown bodies and enormous horns sprouting from their heads. Others had giant hairy jaws. These terrifying animals, Mozhdah realized, must live in Canada.

The school bell clanged, followed by the sound of stampeding boots. Red-cheeked from the cold, a group of children entered the classroom and rushed to the coatroom. They glanced curiously at their new schoolmate as they took their seats.

"Good morning, students," said the teacher.

"Good morning," they responded unevenly.

"I am happy to tell you that we have a new student today. Her name is Mozhdah Jamalzadah," said the teacher, turning to the blackboard to write Mozhdah's first and last name.

There were murmurs of surprise at the long name and strange spelling.

"Mozhdah is from Afghanistan."

Blank stares.

A boy's arm shot up. "Where is ... Af ..." he said, his voice trailing off.

"Afghanistan?" the teacher said, smiling, "is in Asia." She went to the world map and, with a long wooden pointer, placed the tip on Europe. "This is where most of you are from—Europe. What country is this?" She pointed to a place in the middle of the continent.

"Czechoslovakia!" a boy chimed.

"And what's this country?" the teacher asked, moving the pointer.

"Polska!" a young girl exclaimed.

"Yes. Poland. And what is this country?"

"Italia!" chimed another boy.

"Italy, yes."

"Now, Afghanistan is," the teacher let the pointer trail south past Greece, Turkey, Syria, and Iraq, through Iran until it hit the potato-shaped country of Afghanistan, "all the way down, down, down—here!"

The children sat entranced, their eyes open wide.

"There is a war in Afghanistan, which is why Mozhdah and her family came here. They are refugees," the teacher said.

The children murmured with excitement and awe. Mozhdah flushed with embarrassment, knowing the teacher was talking about her but unsure what she was saying.

The teacher started the other students off with a refresher lesson on the alphabet to help initiate Mozhdah into the class. She then gave Mozhdah practice sheets containing capital and small letters from A to Z. She showed her the proper way to hold the pencil and had her trace each letter to get a feel for writing English.

When the bell clanged for recess, Mozhdah stayed at her desk while her classmates charged to the coatroom to grab their coats and then ran down the hallway to play outside.

"Come," said the teacher, beckoning to Mozhdah. She helped her into her coat, then slipped into her own dark blue, quilted parka. They walked slowly outside, hand in hand.

Flakes of snow floated gently down and the frigid air hit Mozhdah like a slap. Seeing Mozhdah tremble, the teacher sighed, turned, and walked back to the classroom.

"You can practice your letters, or draw with the crayons," she said, helping Mozhdah out of her coat.

Not sure what the teacher was saying but happy to be out of the cold, Mozhdah smiled gratefully.

As winter approached, Mozhdah became confident enough to walk to school on her own. But the worsening chill only made her hate Canada even more. The walks to and from school were hell, Mozhdah thought. As the biting winds penetrated her bulky parka and snow pants, threatening to blow her tiny frame over, Mozhdah held intense conversations with God: *What did I do to deserve this? Are you mad at me?* she thought miserably, grabbing hold of a nearby fence, tree, or signpost whenever a particularly ferocious gust of winter wind threatened to bowl her over. *I'm sorry. Please forgive me for whatever I did. Please, please send me back to Pakistan!*

A motel is not a place to set down roots, and the Department of Employment and Immigration eventually moved the family to a new home on Wentworth Street in Oshawa, which meant that Mozhdah and Masee, who was in grade one at Clara Hughes, would have to change schools. By then, Mozhdah's English had improved dramatically. She had fallen in love with the intricacy of the language, enthralled that words like "to," "too," and "two" sounded the same but meant something entirely different. Speaking English was a bit like learning a secret code, she thought; you had to rely upon a word's relationship to other words in a sentence to divine the meaning.

Mozhdah wasn't happy about moving to their new apartment at 280 Wentworth Street, or having to attend a new school. She would be leaving her new best friend, Jenny Kastner, who had come up to Mozhdah during the first lunch period at Clara Hughes elementary and beckoned her to sit beside her. They became inseparable, with Mozhdah having sleepovers at the Kastner household. Even the girls' parents became friends.

On moving day, there was little more to pack than their suitcases. Their new home, a seven-story building on Wentworth Street, was imposing and unwelcoming, its brick edifice tattooed with graffiti, the hallways dingy. They had little furniture, and although Nasrin scrubbed the kitchen's thin cheap cupboard doors and small white stove, as well as the bathroom grouting, for hours, it never truly felt clean or homey. Mozhdah cringed when neighbors launched into fights, the thin walls providing little insulation against the yelling. At bedtime, Mozhdah couldn't sleep until her parents retired for the night, waiting in silence in the dark at the top of the landing, arms wrapped around her knees to keep warm, until she heard their ascending footsteps. Only then did she tiptoe into her own bedroom and slip under the covers.

Mozhdah hoped the students and her new teacher at nearby Glen Street Public School would be as nice as those in her ESL class at Clara Hughes. But when Bashir escorted her and Masee on the first day of school, she recoiled at the unfriendly stares of the other students as they walked through the yard. Mozhdah felt Jenny's absence sharply. It didn't help that Mozhdah's nearsightedness had recently been discovered, meaning she now wore a pair of oversized prescription glasses that covered half her face and tended to slip down her nose. She hated them—promised herself that someday she would purposely lose them.

After finding her new classroom, Mozhdah slipped her bagged lunch into the desk cubbyhole, laying a pencil, eraser, and a new lined notebook on the top. She looked shyly at the teacher, who was short and squat, with chopped brown hair.

"We have a new student today. Her name is … " the teacher stumbled over Mozhdah's name. "She has been in Canada for six months. Mozhdah is from Afghanistan, which is a country in the Middle East." Mozhdah cringed. Afghanistan was in Central Asia. How could the teacher not know this? The teacher pointed out Afghanistan on the classroom map. "It is located here, next to Pakistan and Iran."

Mozhdah was startled to hear a low hiss from the boy behind her: "Paki!"

"Paki?" Mozhdah queried, spinning around. "Are you talking to me?" she said, looking at the boy with tousled blond hair, his face distorted with contempt.

"Yeah, I'm talking to you, Paki!" the boy sneered.

"Mozhdah, please face the front," the teacher said firmly.

Mozhdah turned around, her face hot with anger and embarrassment. It wasn't her fault she had turned around! The horrible boy was obviously trying to insult her, accusing her of being from Pakistan. But she was from Afghanistan; hadn't he heard the teacher correctly? And besides, what was wrong with being from Pakistan, the land of *pakora* and chutney?

"Today, class, we are going to continue looking at colonial Canada and how the first European settlers met with the

Algonquian and Iroquoian Indians who were living in what is now our province of Ontario."

Indians? Had people from India come to Ontario years ago? Mozhdah was intrigued and focused on the social studies class. As it turned out, it was Indigenous nations—not people from India—who clashed with explorers and settlers from Europe as Canada was increasingly colonized. It was fascinating, and Mozhdah was disappointed when the recess bell rang. She slipped her notebook and pencil into her desk and looked around as the other students sprang up and ran into the coatroom. Mozhdah reluctantly followed at a distance—dreading standing out in the schoolyard alone.

Outside, she looked for Masee but couldn't see him in the throng of children. She walked towards the swing set and slides, her hand shielding her eyes from the bright spring sun. Suddenly, she felt a huge shove from behind and instinctively threw her hands in front of her as she collided face first with the hard ground. She lay there for a few seconds before sitting up, spitting out dirt, and grabbing her right wrist, which was throbbing with pain. She looked up to see who her attacker was. It was the boy from class, laughing.

"Hey, Paki! Go home!" he yelled, before running off, while students nearby snickered.

Mozhdah looked around to see if teachers had seen what happened but spied no adults. She got up, brushed off her coat and pants, and returned to class, where she hung up her coat and sat down at her desk, rubbing her wrist, fighting back tears of unhappiness.

THE SUMMER BREAK brought not only relief from the cold but liberation from the misery of the Wentworth Street apartment and Mozhdah's school bully. Once again, immigration officials moved the family, this time into a far nicer Oshawa apartment. In September, Mozhdah would attend nearby Mary Street Community School, which had only a few hundred students, from kindergarten to grade eight.

Mozhdah didn't know what to expect. Would the students be friendly, like those at Clara Hughes, or nasty and racist like the Glen Street kids? During Mozhdah's first recess, she was heartened when several girls came up to her and introduced themselves, asking about her family and how long she had been in Canada, and inviting her to sit with them at lunch. The next day, however, as she was walking towards class, a boy, pretending to be in a hurry, slammed into her in the hall-way, loudly hissing, "Paki!" The doppelgänger of Mozhdah's Glen Street bully tormented her at the slightest opportunity, so long as there wasn't a teacher within sight. But the attacks weren't as distressing as they were when she had attended Glen Street school. Her new friends stood in solidarity against her tormentor, glaring at him and yelling, "Shut up!" when he spat his racist epithets. It made her feel less alone—less vulnerable.

Mozhdah began to love school, especially English, check-ing out as many books from the library as was allowed, spending her spare time reading and doing homework. She earned straight As in school. She became more confident, bolder. One morning, as the students shuffled into the class, she overheard her tormentor make a grammar error: "I brang my lunch to school today," he told his friends.

"You mean you *brought* your lunch to school," Mozhdah said haughtily.

"You'll pay for that," the boy snapped.

Mozhdah laughed at the threat, masking a flutter of apprehension.

Mozhdah loved her studies, while tolerating physical education, or phys ed. Although she was good at basketball, games like baseball proved more of a challenge. She was left-handed, and the school's two lefty gloves were too big for her small hands, which meant she was better at batting than catching.

One sunny day, during a baseball game out on the school grounds, it was Mozhdah's turn to hit the ball. She grabbed a light aluminum bat from the pile beside the metal mesh backstop, stepped up to the plate, leaned forward, and gave a few determined practice swings. The pitcher lobbed an underhand pitch, aiming for the vicinity of home plate. Mozhdah swung.

"Strike one!" called the gym teacher.

"Great swing!" Mozhdah's teammates shouted encouragingly.

"Blind Paki," came a sneer from third base, where her nemesis stood, punching his fist into his glove.

Unnerved, Mozhdah tried to focus on the next pitch. She punched the ground with the bat and pushed her large glasses firmly back onto the bridge of her nose. She was determined to connect with the ball. The pitcher tossed the ball.

Mozhdah swung. "Strike two!"

"That was *so* close!" "Great swing!" "Keep it up!" her teammates shouted.

"Stupid Paki," came the response from third base. "Your parents are stupid Pakis too."

Hot fury suddenly engulfed Mozhdah. She straightened and gripped her bat hard, sprinting for third base, fueled by rage. The boy stood there, mouth agape. He guffawed brashly, then realized his danger as Mozhdah bore down upon him, bat held high like a sword. He turned to flee—too late—and Mozhdah swung the bat, knocking his legs out from underneath him. He crashed head first into the hard ground and curled into a tight fetal position. Mozhdah flung her bat away then, with a wrath born of months of torment, kicked him and rained blow after blow upon his body with her arms.

Mozhdah became vaguely aware of yelling, and someone yanked her off the screeching boy.

"Mozhdah! That's enough!" the teacher bellowed. "Go straight to the principal's office. *Now!*"

Mozhdah stomped towards the school building. She was in so much trouble but didn't care.

The principal, seated behind his desk, looked at Mozhdah perched on the edge of a chair in front of him. It wasn't like Mozhdah to get into trouble. She hung out with the other quiet, studious girls.

Mozhdah's gym teacher came striding up to the principal's office, knocking politely as he swung the door open. The principal looked at the teacher, who began to tell the story about Mozhdah's assault on her schoolmate, which had been sparked by his crass racist taunts. As she listened, Mozhdah's eyes darted defiantly back and forth between the two men, her breathing shallow and quick. Kids who got into physical altercations were suspended, and she awaited her sentencing, wondering how Bashir and Nasrin would react. She gritted her teeth to keep the tears from falling. She wouldn't cry. No way.

"Mozhdah," said the principal in a firm but not unkind voice. "Do you have anything to say for yourself?"

"He deserved it," Mozhdah said.

The principal waited. "That's all you have to say?"

"Yes," she responded. "He's a bully and he deserved what he got."

"What he did wasn't right." The principal nodded in agreement.

She looked up at him, a tiny smile of gratitude on her face.

Mozhdah was given two days' detention. Most kids would have been expelled, but she suspected that her squeaky-clean behavior until then, and the boy's offensive manners, accounted for the light sentence. She would have to stay after school for half an hour and do homework, which, for Mozhdah, wasn't punishment. The phys ed teacher told Mozhdah that he understood why she attacked the boy but to never again use violence when confronting bullies.

The next day, as Mozhdah was walking down the hallway with her friends, she saw the boy approaching. She glared at him as hard as she could as he passed. Dropping his head, he scurried past. Triumphantly, she thought that sometimes violence was the only way of dealing with certain people.

IT WAS ONE of those beautiful September early evenings, more reminiscent of summer than approaching autumn. The family was at the dinner table, eating Nasrin's aromatic Afghan dishes: steamed rice and lamb *ghorma* with potatoes and kidney beans and a side dish of eggplant. The sun, beginning its descent towards the western horizon, gleamed through the spotless windows.

"I have some news," said Bashir.

Mozhdah and her brothers barely glanced up from their dinner.

"We're moving to the province of British Columbia, to a place called Vancouver," he announced.

Mozhdah's head snapped up and she dropped her fork, which clattered loudly on her plate. "Why?" she demanded. Her heart sank. She couldn't leave Jenny Kastner, who had remained her best friend despite attending a different school. They had spent a languorous summer together, reading and swimming in Jenny's family pool. Mozhdah had just started grade six and was finally starting to feel like she was fitting into Canadian society.

"Well," Bashir said, catching Nasrin's eye, "the doctor recommended that we move someplace without all this Ontario ragweed, which is making my asthma worse. Plus, Vancouver is warmer—there's no snow in winter."

It was difficult to protest when the reason for leaving was health related, but Mozhdah would try. "Can't you try new medication?"

"No, it doesn't work like that," Bashir said. "Your mother and I have already decided to move, and a friend in Vancouver has even found us a place to live."

"So you've been planning this for a while," Mozhdah said accusingly.

"Yes, Mozhdah *jan*," Nasrin said gently. "We didn't want to ruin your summer with Jenny until we knew for certain that we had a place to stay."

"I don't want to go. I can't go. I can't leave Jenny," said Mozhdah. "And I just started school. I don't want to start over at another school after classes have started. I can't believe how mean you are!"

"We'll talk about it later," Nasrin said, her eyes narrowing.

"You'll talk, and I'll have to listen, like that will make any difference!" Mozhdah said, getting up from the table. "I'm going to Jenny's!"

Mozhdah ran all the way to Jenny's house, tears stinging her eyes. She rapped sharply on the door, heard light-footed skipping along the hallway to the foyer.

Jenny's eyes lit up when she saw Mozhdah, then darkened as her best friend's face crumpled.

"I have to move, Jenny!" Mozhdah sobbed. "Soon! To someplace far away!"

"No!" Jenny grabbed Mozhdah in a hug. She also burst into tears—two girls crying, diminished by grief, while the western sky glowed sunset orange and pink.

CHAPTER 6

Taliban Nightmares

"THIS," MOZHDAH PAUSED, "is our new home?" She looked around in dismay at the three-bedroom house, located just off Fraser Street in East Vancouver. "We left Oshawa for *this*?"

Mozhdah walked down the hallway towards the bathroom, sniffing loudly. A strange musty odor wafted from the bathroom. "Gross," she muttered.

Bashir and Nasrin's friend in Vancouver, Jacob Kosik, had found them a home that fit the family budget: the first floor of a house that had long been a rental property. They had taken a taxi from Vancouver International Airport to their new abode, looking under the plant pot on the cracked concrete front steps for the keys Jacob had hidden.

Nasrin sighed and looked around at the dirty walls, thin, stained carpet, window blinds caked with dirt, and dirtier windows. Mozhdah came back into the living room, a disgusted look on her face.

Nasrin didn't look happy either. "It's like we're Kuchi nomads." Nasrin sighed. "Forever on the move."

The family had sold whatever they could in Oshawa, packing their suitcases with the bare essentials: some bed linens, basic kitchenware, and clothes. Each of the kids had been allowed to fill a small backpack with their favorite possessions. Mozhdah had filled hers with books and a stuffed cat. Masee, who had packed his bag unsupervised by his parents, had inexplicably filled his with numerous random keys, *Archie* comic books, teaspoons, and empty juice bottles. Safee had a math game, a teddy bear, and some Disney books.

Mozhdah continued her slow meander down the short hallway. "Two bedrooms?" she exclaimed. "Am I supposed to sleep with Masee and Safee? No way!"

"I don't want to share with Mozhdah!" Safee yelled.

"Me neither!" Masee said, echoing his sibling.

"Oh, is this a third bedroom?" Mozhdah shouted from down the hallway. "It's more like a closet. Especially because... it has no window!" She returned to the living room, looking accusingly at her parents.

Bashir smiled thinly at his daughter. "You're tired, Mozhdah, we all are. Things will look better in the morning."

"You think so?" she snapped, then immediately felt guilty for being mean.

"It's the beginning of better things," Bashir said.

But you don't have a clue what that is, thought Mozhdah, deciding it was better, at this juncture, to stop railing at her parents. Right now, she was just too disappointed.

BASHIR AND NASRIN wanted to get Mozhdah and Masee, already complaining of boredom the next morning, into school as quickly as possible. On their first day, Bashir accompanied them on the half-mile walk to Sexsmith Elementary School, a three-story building with tawny brown bricks and double front doors.

Mozhdah wore her favorite outfit: red jeans, a T-shirt, and a long, colorful vest knitted by Nasrin that went down to her knees. Her long hair was loose, and she had a backpack slung over her shoulder. She walked down the broad hallways, peering through her round glasses at the names of the teachers above the classroom doors. Her grade six class had just started, and the teacher was talking in front of the blackboard. Mozhdah knocked tentatively and walked in.

"Hi, I'm Mozhdah Jamalzadah," she said shyly to the teacher.

The teacher smiled warmly at Mozhdah and directed her to take a seat at an empty desk by the window. She then turned to the students and explained that Mozhdah had moved to Vancouver from Ontario. "Please make her feel welcome," she added.

Mozhdah froze as she looked at the students, shocked. After enduring racial taunts at her all-white schools in Oshawa, she now faced a sea of brown faces, black hair, and even turbans. Waves of homesickness for Pakistan suddenly overwhelmed her, as memories came flooding back of playing with her friends in the Islamabad streets, with their kiosks, flowers, birds, and *pakora*. She could almost smell the hot salty aroma. She walked towards her desk, trying to appear nonchalant yet delighted, feeling like, in a small way, she had come home. She couldn't wait to talk to these students about where they came from and their own difficulties fitting into Canadian society.

Then, a girl sneered, "*What* is she wearing?"

Face blazing, Mozhdah sat down and distracted herself by taking a binder and a pen and pencils out of her backpack. She looked up at the teacher, trying to ignore the interrogative stares.

The teacher briefly outlined the grade six curriculum and timetable to Mozhdah, handing her a sheet detailing the days and times for each subject. The first class of the day, Mozhdah noted happily, was language arts.

At the end of class, the bell rang for recess. Mozhdah intended to lag behind, perhaps ask the teacher a few questions. But the instructor quickly gathered her papers and followed the students out the door. Mozhdah hung back, waiting to make sure she was the last person out of the room. As she walked into the hallway, a mixed group of her new class-mates, dressed uniformly in dark blue jeans and dark tops, loitered. They stopped chatting as Mozhdah walked close to their huddle.

"Hey!" one called out. "What's your name again?"

"Mozhdah."

"Why'd your parents name you after a car?" They all laughed.

"What do you mean?" Mozhdah said indignantly.

"Uh, *Mazda*?" a boy said churlishly.

"I have a question for you, *Mazda*," said another girl. "Why are you dressed like a douche?"

"Is that what all the white preppy girls in Ontario are wearing?" another chimed in.

Really? In Oshawa Mozhdah was brown, but here she was white? She couldn't win. She walked off casually, her head held high, shoulders straight—belying how utterly lonely and friendless she felt.

The lunch break came too quickly, and Mozhdah dreaded what she would do and where she would sit. All these kids had obviously known each other since grade one and teased each other like siblings, laughing and yelling boisterously in the hallway. Mozhdah might as well have been an alien. Unless somebody like Jenny—who had come up to her that first day at Clara Hughes Public School in Oshawa—invited Mozhdah to join them, she would be like space junk in perpetual orbit. She couldn't bear the thought of people staring while she wandered the lunchroom, looking for a place to sit. So, just as she had done at Glen Street Public School, Mozhdah ducked into a deserted classroom to eat her brown bag lunch. She felt sick, almost too sick to eat. Was this what the entire year would be like?

Mozhdah found respite in the sanctuary of books: she would devour two or three novels a week, in addition to her homework, in the library, where she could surreptitiously munch her lunch.

Then, one day after Mozhdah came home from school, Nasrin broke the tragic news. Mozhdah's grandmother, Nasrin's mom, Tafsira, had died of a massive heart attack in Peshawar. Nasrin was struck down by the terrible irony as well as grief. Her efforts to get Tafsira to go with them to Pakistan when the family first fled in October 1989 had been futile. But when Afghanistan spiraled into even more ferocious civil war just a few years later, it forced Tafsira, along with some other of Nasrin's relatives, to flee to Pakistan. With long-distance telephone calls to Peshawar costing $2.50 a minute, phone calls from the family in Canada were brief. Nasrin would call at night to catch Tafsira during the day in Pakistan, and Mozhdah and her brothers, wearing their pajamas, could say little more than, "Hello, how are you, Bibi?"

Mozhdah felt helpless as Nasrin wept. For Nasrin, a thread linking her to her past in Afghanistan had unraveled.

Mozhdah took comfort not only from books but also from her new kitten, Mittens. Nasrin got him from a pet store next door to the hair salon where she worked. As soon as Mittens came home, the little feline with the white paws and chest adopted Mozhdah, sleeping in her bed and following her around. And when Mozhdah had a miserable day at school, Mittens would curl up against her, his deep purr a salve for the hurt, anger, or disappointment.

Mozhdah's study habits shot her to the top of her class, which inspired constant taunts of "nerd." Some of the students, many of whom were immigrants, retained the accents of their home nations and mocked Mozhdah's perfect English pronunciation. Mozhdah feigned nonchalance. Eventually, "nerd" simply became one of Mozhdah's nicknames, in addition to "Maz," short for "Mazda," rarely uttered maliciously. One student, Darcy, constantly teased Mozhdah, a lighthearted, friendly two-way banter.

One day, "Hey, Maz," he said.

"What's up, Dar?" Mozhdah responded coolly.

"You know that English paper we're supposed to write on *Lord of the Flies*?"

"What about it?"

"Well," said Darcy hesitantly. "You know how we're supposed to write some analysis of the, um, complex . . . symbols . . . that, um . . ."

"Complex symbols that affect the novel's tone and meaning?" Mozhdah said sweetly.

"Yeah, that," Darcy said. "Have you started it?"

"Finished," Mozhdah said.

"It's not due 'til Wednesday," Darcy said, surprised.

"Why would I wait until the night before it's due to write it, like the rest of you?" Mozhdah asked.

"Well, I was wondering if you might help me write it."

"No," Mozhdah said. "I'm not your teacher."

"But you're so good at this English stuff."

Mozhdah looked at him keenly. "Tell you what: I had a bunch of examples of symbols that I had to cut, as my paper was getting too long. I'll give you those and you can use them to write your paper."

"Cool!" Darcy responded.

"For a price," said Mozhdah.

"What do you mean?"

"Five dollars. Take it or leave it. And I want the money up front."

Darcy paused, assessing Mozhdah, who looked at him with her arms crossed and eyes narrowed. Clearly, there was no negotiating.

It became a tidy racket for Mozhdah. She edited or wrote classmates' English papers and, when questions about novels were assigned for homework, gave people the answers. It meant she had money, when her family had none, and she spent every penny buying books. Moving to Vancouver had used up much of the family's savings, and in the beginning, they could barely cover rent, relying upon income assistance from the government for several months before Bashir found a job at a pizza parlor. Mozhdah's sideline not only put money in her pocket but also elevated her status among those students who had parental expectations to meet but viewed the work needed to achieve good grades as a blight on their socializing. For those students who didn't care about their grades—or what their parents thought about school marks—Mozhdah was still a target, but less so, because of her elevated new social standing.

When the last day of school finally came, Mozhdah was thrilled; she would have a full two months off to read and spend hours in conversation with Jenny on the phone. She walked slowly across the schoolyard, reading her report card, pleased to see the anticipated list of straight As. With her head down, engrossed, she didn't see her classmate Timothy approach. He grabbed the report card, glanced down at the marks, and began running around the schoolyard yelling at the top of his lungs while waving it. "Mazda's a nerd! Mazda's a nerd!" He wouldn't stop, and other students cackled as Timothy lapped the schoolyard. Mozhdah stood, blinking back tears of humiliation, until Timothy, tired of the prank, handed the report card back.

She snatched it, fuming. *I'll show all of you next year*, she thought. *Just you wait.*

IN SEPTEMBER, MOZHDAH took revenge—by sabotaging her grades. She stopped paying attention in class or doing homework, getting Cs on her first grade seven report card.

"Did you get your homework done?" Mozhdah casually asked a classmate one day as they meandered down the hallway into class.

"Nope" was the reply.

"Me neither." Mozhdah sighed. "Couldn't be bothered. Algebra—what a bore ..."

"Nerd" was incompatible with "C student," and Mozhdah discovered low grades to be her entrée into grade seven high society. The glue that held the popular kids together was gossip: about other students, celebrities, parents, clothing, music—anything but academics. She was even welcomed into the inner circle of girls who had anointed her "Mazda" on her first day, becoming best friends with one of her early tormentors, Jasleen, as well as a Polish girl named Joanna. Jasleen and Mozhdah found hilarity in other people's looks and dress, and the imagined dullness of their lives. Mozhdah was careful, however, never to humiliate anyone to their face. She knew all too well what that felt like. The girls would giggle together in class until they became so disruptive the teacher would send them out to the hallway to calm down.

For the first time since coming to Canada, Mozhdah began to pay attention to music, one of the main topics of conversation among her classmates. Her friends' tastes leaned towards heavy metal like Metallica and Aerosmith, as well as alternative rock like Nirvana. Lunchtime conversations, when the other girls weren't discussing their latest crush—a topic Mozhdah was too shy to join—often focused on the newest music on the radio.

At home, Mozhdah would listen to the pop and rock stations her friends enjoyed. She would jot down the names of the bands and their latest songs, treating it like homework, so that she could participate in her friends' conversations. Trying to appear cool by memorizing the latest pop songs was hard, far more difficult than studying English, math, or science, Mozhdah thought.

Mozhdah started to become a little less concerned about being one of the cool kids the closer to high school she got.

When the time came, Mozhdah enrolled at John Oliver Secondary School six blocks from their house. Bashir was still serving pizza by the slice nearby, while Nasrin, who had taken out a student loan to attend hairdressing school in Oshawa, was expanding her clientele at Raymond Salons.

The first year of secondary school, with its throngs of intimidating, tall, sophisticated-looking students and its serious-looking teachers who specialized in specific subjects, refocused Mozhdah's study habits. It was also a year that marked an enormous change for the Jamalzadah family, with Bashir opening up his own business, Super Wedge Pizza, on bustling Commercial Drive, a neighborhood filled with an eclectic and energetic mix of artists, professionals, lefties, and immigrants.

The family had no credit, didn't own a home, and had no collateral—they didn't even have a checking account. The only way for Bashir to open a pizza parlor was to go to a loan shark for start-up cash. A moneylender gave him and his business partner $11,500 cash, taking $1,500 right off the top for the first repayment fee. That left $10,000 to buy the pizza-making equipment and things like a phone and cash register. The landlord who leased them the space was willing to take cash for the first month's payment. The gamble paid off. The November 16 grand opening netted $600 for the day, with people lining up out the door and onto the sidewalk to buy pizza from Commercial Drive's first-ever by-the-slice pizzeria. By the end of the year, Bashir and his partner had paid the loan shark $23,000 to cover the debt.

Between Nasrin's income as a hair stylist and the money from Super Wedge Pizza, the family fortunes changed. Nasrin enrolled all three of the kids in after-school sports and academic programs. Safee and Masee, both math whizzes, attended enriched mathematics classes and took piano lessons. During the winter, the boys joined a hockey league. Nasrin tried to get Mozhdah into figure skating and ballroom dancing. "Too girly," Mozhdah sniffed.

Mozhdah rebelled against anything conventionally feminine. After Nasrin bought the kids a Sega Genesis video game console—to her eventual regret—Mozhdah became a *Mortal Kombat* fanatic. The game was a gory homage to the fantasy-horror genre, with warriors engaged in never-ending battles with the barbarous inhabitants of Outworld and Netherrealm. Mozhdah was enamored by *Mortal Kombat*'s first female combatant and special forces general Sonya Blade, who vanquished rivals like Kano, leader of the international crime cartel Black Dragon, with her Tae Kwon Do skills.

"I want to do Tae Kwon Do," Mozhdah told Nasrin.

"What's that?" Nasrin said.

"A martial art."

"Oh," Nasrin responded, a note of disappointment in her voice. She was trying to steer Mozhdah towards more feminine pursuits.

"I really want to try this," Mozhdah said.

"Okay," Nasrin said resignedly. "Let's go watch a class first."

Watching the other teens in their crisp white V-necked uniforms, called a *dobuk*, and the various colored cloth belts, and seeing the discipline and athleticism required, was thrilling. Mozhdah convinced Nasrin to allow her to join classes at the Langara Family YMCA in South Vancouver. She loved learning and refining the techniques of combat: open and closed hand strikes, the high front and side kicks, the roundhouse and flying kicks—all so difficult to master. There was only one other girl in the class, so Mozhdah often sparred with the boys. Light and quick, Mozhdah could send opponents nearly twice her size reeling backwards or watch with satisfaction as they dropped to the mat with a hard thud following a deftly delivered kick. She became good enough to think about competing.

By this point, Bashir and Nasrin began talking about opening up a hair salon. They could do it, Nasrin suggested, if Bashir sold Super Wedge Pizza. The thought was appealing. Bashir wanted to get back into teaching and the hours at the pizzeria were grueling. Why not take on another new challenge?

ALTHOUGH THE JAMALZADAH family was more financially secure, Mozhdah felt a creeping sense of dread. The Soviet Union's official withdrawal from Afghanistan on February 15, 1989—eight months before the Jamalzadah family fled the country—marked a descent into chaos. The mujahideen holy warriors who had fought the Soviet invaders focused their weapons and wrath on the national Communist government. When the government collapsed in 1992, internecine savagery ensued among the mujahideen. Homes and villages were plundered, while citizens were raped, robbed, and tortured as warlordism gripped the country.

Media reports, whether on TV or in the newspapers, were brief and often confusing, leaving Mozhdah distraught and worried for her cousins, aunts, and uncles still left in Afghanistan. She watched, fascinated, short reports about a particular mujahideen faction that went by the name "Taliban," meaning "students" in Pashto. Led by the charismatic mullah Mohammed Omar, a hollow-cheeked man with a blind right eye that he had lost in a guerrilla attack against the Soviets, the Taliban pledged security to the war-shattered populace. The group fought to crush the warlords and restore safety by imposing a harsh version of shari`a, or Islamic law. They took control of Kandahar, Mullah Omar's home province in southwestern Afghanistan, and within two years, he and his followers, mainly Pashtun tribesmen educated in madrassas in Pakistan, had gained strategic control over much of the country.

Mozhdah scoured the newspapers and waited impatiently for the international news segments on television for updates on the Taliban's expansion in Afghanistan, as the group edged ever closer to Kabul. Then, in September 1996, the Taliban captured the city of Jalalabad in Nangarhar province, only ninety-five miles from Kabul. Their next target would be the capital.

On September 27, 1996, the Taliban roared into Kabul, their symbolic white flag waving from tanks, cars, and pickup trucks, and declared the creation of a new nation: the Islamic Emirate of Afghanistan. Mozhdah's sense of dread deepened.

In the days and weeks that followed, news trickled out about the Taliban's harsh rule. Mozhdah was outraged at the injustices against women. They were ordered to leave their office jobs, though some female workers were allowed to continue working in hospitals. Women had to cover up in head-to-foot black or blue burkas and could only leave the house if accompanied by a man. Television and music— symbols of Western decadence—were also banned. One day, Bashir, after reading yet another chilling newspaper article, looked at Mozhdah. "If we were still there," he said, "you would be one of those girls the Taliban is forcing to stay at home and wear a burka."

The fact that Mozhdah had escaped such a fate filled her with a jumble of emotions ranging from relief to guilt. She knew that people she had grown up with, girls she had played with in Kabul, those unable to flee, were now under the yoke of the extremists. Mozhdah felt the heavy burden of luck: luck that her parents had the courage and opportunity to escape to Pakistan through the Paktia mountains, luck that they hadn't frozen to death or driven over a cliff on the journey. It seemed like luck, too, that the people at the Canadian embassy in Islamabad had chosen them—and not someone else—to come to Canada. Why? Others were just as deserving.

Many families had probably been far more desperate. Her family's luck, Mozhdah thought, must have come at the expense of others. What hardships had others endured because a quota had been filled when her family was granted refugee status? It was like Afghanistan was a sinking ship, and there were only a few lifeboats big enough for the thousands and thousands on board. The rest were left to drown, without any help. Where was the justice? Where was the mercy? What right did Mozhdah have to be so lucky, when others had no luck at all? She felt undeserving of her circumstances—like a thief running her fingers through a stolen hoard of jewels. Freedom at the expense of others was a bitter, bitter pill.

Mozhdah lay awake at night, the lack of sleep and her grief becoming a physical pain that never went away. In class, words would blur and she had to read passages in textbooks three or four times for them to make sense. When she did sleep, she would wake up, heart racing, from unsettling dreams. Childhood memories materialized out of her subconscious and filled her with fury and impotence. In them, Mozhdah was small, and a teacher—probably at the preschool in Kabul—was lecturing the class on how to be a good Muslim. They must uphold, without question, an unwavering belief in God and Muhammad, the teacher said. This, she continued, was *faith*, and a person had to always be conscious of and nurture it. Without faith, you couldn't be a good Muslim.

Mozhdah put up her hand and blurted: "But didn't God give us brains for asking questions?"

The other children looked at Mozhdah, some mortified, others gloating at her stupidity.

"You must never question the word of God!" the teacher admonished, glaring at Mozhdah.

Mozhdah could only drop her eyes shamefully to the ground. "I will question whatever I want," she mumbled. That was the day she rebelled against religion—if being a good Muslim meant she couldn't question things, then she could never be a good Muslim, she thought.

As she sat on the living room couch, after watching a too-brief update about Afghanistan on CNN, Mozhdah thought that there was nothing to stop her from speaking up now. But what would she say? How would she say it? Most importantly, how could she make herself heard amid the tumult of hatred and violence ravaging her country?

CHAPTER 7

Inspired by Oprah

OZHDAH WAS SEATED at the breakfast table, pushing scrambled eggs around on her plate. She had taken a few mouthfuls and washed them down with orange juice. She knew she'd be starving by second period but couldn't bring herself to eat more. It didn't matter; Nasrin always sent Mozhdah to school with snacks that she ate surreptitiously at her desk during morning classes.

Mozhdah had lain awake much of the night, images from the day's news racing through her mind. It was the only way to try to understand what might be happening to all the uncles, aunts, and cousins on Nasrin's side, as well as her mother's two sisters-in-law, nieces, and nephews, who were still in Kabul. Bashir's extended family, who lived in Herat in the northwest of the country close to Iran, were also in danger under the new regime. There was no way to communicate with them, no telephones, computers, internet, or letters. They could only piece together what the families might be suffering from a patchwork of updates from television and newspapers. Mozhdah was tormented by the thought of them being arrested. Did they have food to eat? How were the women and girls enduring the Taliban's edict on women, which amounted to virtual house arrest? Were they even alive? Mozhdah listened in fascination to CNN's Peter Arnett's interview with Osama bin Laden, the notorious terrorist and one of the world's most wanted men, who was lying low in an isolated Afghanistan mountain hideout with the Taliban's blessing. In the interview, bin Laden called for jihad—a holy war—against the United States, declaring the American government tyrannical and unjust. Mozhdah marveled at Arnett's courage, thought he'd been fortunate that bin Laden hadn't held him hostage.

Mozhdah began filling her sleepless nights by writing poems in school notebooks that she kept on a small table by her bed. She wrote about the girls who were no longer able to go to school, and the women who were beaten by the Taliban after venturing out to the market to buy naan for the children. So many mothers had desperately hungry children to feed. They were alone, without the help of husbands, sons, or brothers, who had been killed in the protracted conflicts that began with the Soviet invasion and continued through the mujahideen civil conflict to the current brutal Taliban oppression.

"Mom," Mozhdah said, getting up from the table to put her breakfast plate and glass in the kitchen sink. "I've been writing a lot of poetry lately."

"Yes?" Nasrin responded curiously.

"I was wondering if there was someone who might be able to sing some of my poetry, you know, make it into a song."

"Why don't you sing your poems yourself?"

Mozhdah laughed. "I can't sing."

"Well, you don't know that, do you? You haven't really tried," Nasrin responded.

"I don't need to try," Mozhdah said impatiently. "I already know I can't sing."

Nasrin chuckled. "You might be surprised. You've been in Tae Kwon Do for, what is it, three years now? Why not do something different? Take up guitar lessons. That way, at least you could put your poems to music."

"Hmmm," Mozhdah said. "Let me think about it."

Nasrin was friends with a local Afghan-Canadian musician, Wahid Omid, and contacted him about giving Mozhdah music lessons. Like many people in the Afghan diaspora scattered about the globe, Wahid had fled when the Soviet Union military machine rumbled into Kabul. After settling in Vancouver, Wahid became a composer, creating bright, bubbly love songs that were an amalgam of pop and traditional Afghan rhythms. He embraced music videos in the 1980s, when he was in his early twenties, and as soon as YouTube was created posted videos that introduced the diaspora to his revolutionary, modern Afghan music. Handsome, but geekily so, with enormous, trademark, round, wire-frame glasses and skin-tight black leather pants, Wahid became an Afghan heartthrob, his caramel-smooth voice crooning passionate lyrics of love and yearning in both Farsi and English. He became known among the diaspora as the Michael Jackson of the East.

"She's very motivated to learn guitar," Nasrin said to Wahid over the phone. "She has been writing poetry and wants to put it to music. But she wants someone else to sing these songs she's planning to create."

"Yes, I can help her, but she will need to practice guitar chords every day," Wahid said.

"No, no," Nasrin said firmly. "I don't want her to learn guitar. I want you to teach her to sing."

"I'm confused," Wahid said. "So you want her to come to me for guitar lessons, but I'm not supposed to teach her guitar but give her singing lessons?"

"Exactly," said Nasrin.

"Why the deception?" Wahid asked.

"Because Mozhdah thinks she can't sing. But I've heard her; she actually has a nice voice. She just lacks confidence."

Wahid paused. "She's going to hate me if I force singing lessons on her, especially if she thinks she's coming here for guitar."

"She'll get over it," Nasrin said nonchalantly. "Just be persistent—and push her," she said. "So, when can she start?"

BASHIR AND NASRIN had decided to make their dream of opening a hair salon a reality and began to look for a location close to their new home near Main Street in East Vancouver. Bashir had sold Super Wedge Pizza, making a considerable profit. There was enough money to open another, smaller pizza parlor on Hastings Street, though its profits were modest in comparison to Super Wedge. They used the rest of the money to lease a space on Main Street for an elegant salon.

Nasrin had cultivated a large clientele encompassing the Filipino, Afghan, and Punjabi communities. As soon as Nasrin's Hair Design opened in November 1998, Nasrin found herself working twelve-hour days, Monday to Saturday, doing not only cuts and color but makeup and hairstyling for bridal parties.

Mozhdah's Tae Kwon Do and homework were enough to keep her busy, but Nasrin didn't like that her daughter would be largely unsupervised until late each evening. Her solution was to have Mozhdah come straight to the salon after school, something she suspected her daughter might resist. But, she told herself, she would be teaching Mozhdah practical skills: how to cut and color hair, how to apply the dramatic makeup and create the elaborate hairstyles that Indian and other South Asian brides and bridesmaids wore to their extravagant wedding celebrations. It was also the opportunity to teach Mozhdah small-business management. Nasrin hoped it would also help her overcome the shyness that had developed during the years of being an outsider, which caused her to take refuge in solitary pursuits like reading. It would be, Nasrin thought optimistically, a wonderful mother-daughter bonding experience.

In truth, Nasrin was most worried about the possibility of Mozhdah getting into trouble after school, which was located in one of Vancouver's higher-crime neighborhoods. And despite her daughter's love of studying, Nasrin nonetheless felt that an unsupervised teenage girl was trouble waiting to happen. There was also a cultural driver—protecting the honor of daughters was deeply embedded within the psyche of Afghan parents, no matter how liberated they were.

Over dinner, Nasrin broke the news to Mozhdah that she wanted her help in the salon every day after school.

Mozhdah glared at her mother. "Why are you making me do this?" she snapped.

"Because I barely see you kids and I miss you. This is the chance for us to spend more time together and work as a family."

"You just want free labor," Mozhdah retorted. "Safee and Masee don't have to come to the salon."

"There isn't enough work for all three of you," Nasrin said.

"Well, let one of them come, then," Mozhdah countered.

Nasrin sighed. "Just think how much money you will make, helping me at the salon."

"I'm not interested in hair stuff. You went to hairdressing school. I'm going to be a lawyer. I'm going to university. I need to study."

Nasrin rolled her eyes. "Life isn't just about studying. I'll teach you to do makeup and hairstyling for Indian bridal parties."

Mozhdah glared even harder at Nasrin. "Weddings are on weekends. So that means I'll have to help you then too?" Her voice rose. "I need to do homework. And Tae Kwon Do. I have competitions coming up."

Nasrin had used up her rationalizations. "Just make sure you come to the salon after school. Or else."

The next day, Nasrin was impressed when Mozhdah showed up at the salon only ten minutes late. She smiled at her. "Mozhdah *jan*! How was your day?" Nasrin said brightly, walking towards her daughter.

"Fine," Mozhdah snapped.

"Let me show you what I want you to do," Nasrin said, pointing to the appointment book that lay open at the front desk.

Mozhdah mumbled something, let her heavy backpack thud loudly on the floor, and threw herself into the swivel seat.

"Call these clients up and remind them that they have their appointments in two days and confirm the date and time. If they aren't home, then leave a message."

Mozhdah was silent. Nasrin's eyes narrowed as she looked at her daughter's sullen, angry face. "And be polite. Be very, very polite," she warned.

As her mother returned to her client, Mozhdah muttered, "Hitler" under her breath. She could tell that her mother heard by the slight pause in her stride. Mozhdah didn't care. Rather than phone Nasrin's clients, Mozhdah slumped in the chair and laid her head on her arms. She wasn't going to call up total strangers. Let her mom do that.

Over time, Mozhdah's resentment decreased. After she had swept the salon floors, cleaned the sinks and counters, dusted the shelves with their bottles of hair products, and called clients to remind them of their pending hair appointments, Nasrin would allow her to read and do homework. As she worked, Mozhdah absentmindedly hummed the songs that she was creating with Wahid Omid, drawing admiring glances from Nasrin, who never heard Mozhdah singing at home. Self-conscious about her voice, Mozhdah tended only to practice when everyone else was busy outside the house.

"SING," WAHID TOLD Mozhdah, seated in a room in his house that had been turned into a studio. "Sing the words of the poem you wrote. I will play some chords that I think will fit the lyrics."

"I can't sing," Mozhdah said petulantly. "I don't want to sing."

"Yes, you can sing. Just try to keep in tune with the chords I play," Wahid said, careful to keep the frustration out of his voice.

"Don't blame me if your ears bleed," Mozhdah said, clearing her throat several times.

Accompanied by Wahid strumming a combination of chords, Mozhdah started humming and spoke a few words of a poem. "It's not working, Wahid," she protested.

"Yes, it's working, just sing along with the chords. Listen, this is what I'm playing," Wahid said, strumming some basic pop chords.

"You just heard what came out of my mouth, right?" Mozhdah said. "It was horrible."

"No, it wasn't," Wahid said. "I wouldn't waste your time, your mother's time, or more importantly, your mother's money if I thought you couldn't sing."

"This is all my mom's fault," Mozhdah said, glaring at Wahid.

"Well, yes. But your mother has good instincts. Try again, Mozhdah."

Reluctantly, Mozhdah continued with the singing lessons, eventually gaining confidence, marveling at the power that music brought to her poetry. To her surprise, she began to love singing. Inspired by Wahid, who knew so well the Afghan diaspora's tastes, Mozhdah began experimenting with his technique of amalgamating modern pop rhythms and instruments with ancient melodies. For the first time since moving to Canada, Mozhdah felt like she was reconnecting with her native country rather than growing ever more distant from it. Instead of simply watching her country's pain and suffering in print and television news reports, singing was a way to honor Afghanistan's rich culture. It gave Mozhdah hope that her homeland had a future beyond violence and bloodshed.

One day, while driving the family car, a new lavender-colored Toyota Corolla, Mozhdah was blasting an Afghan song, singing along to the lyrics. People she knew in Afghanistan could be listening to this very song, she thought. Sworn enemies probably listened to this song. Music made people forget their differences, made them realize that there were things to fight for—community, tradition, food, family, music—rather than fight over. Maybe, just maybe, Mozhdah thought, music was the way to bring change in Afghanistan. Currently, the United States government under President Bill Clinton was trying to negotiate with the Taliban, urging the group to expel international terrorist financier Osama bin Laden from Afghanistan, but unsuccessfully. Perhaps pursuing a law degree and going to Afghanistan as a legal expert or a member of the United Nations—besides taking years of study—would end up being an act of futility. Maybe Mozhdah could take her poems and her music and turn them into songs that she could sing to the people of Afghanistan. Could they be made to see that change was possible? Nearly everyone loved music. Was this the common denominator that would bring Afghans together? Was music what she was meant to do? Probably she was being delusional. But perhaps the time had come, Mozhdah thought, to start taking music a bit more seriously.

Mozhdah began to take her work at the beauty salon more seriously too, proud of the new skills she was developing and, even more appealing, delighted by the money she was making. Nasrin watched with satisfaction as Mozhdah began to converse with clients, rather than speaking in monosyllables. She was catching on to the basics of haircutting, highlights, and color, paying attention and asking questions when Nasrin would say, "Watch me, watch what I'm doing." Eventually, Nasrin was able to double-book clients, with Mozhdah helping color, wash, condition, and blow-dry hair. She still became slightly tongue-tied when left alone with a client, but they noted her shyness and were gracious and kind.

Mozhdah especially loved doing makeup, the more dramatic the better. On Saturdays, she and Nasrin would arrive at 4:00 AM at the home of a young woman, often from Vancouver's large Sikh community, to undertake the elaborate makeup and hair for the bride and her wedding party. For a high school student, it was a huge amount of cash—hundreds of dollars to style the bridal party's hair and makeup, ensuring it complemented the silk saris, elaborate gold jewelry, and detailed *mehndi*, or henna tattoos, on the feet and hands of the bride, symbolizing love between the betrothed. After ensuring the young women were wedding perfect, Nasrin would take Mozhdah—both of them ravenous—for breakfast at McDonald's.

The added income meant Mozhdah was able to start paying for her own music lessons. By now, she had started singing lessons at the British Columbia Conservatory of Music in Burnaby under the tutelage of mezzo-soprano performer and music teacher Melanie Adams, one of Nasrin's longtime clients. Wahid had helped Mozhdah learn how to sing and write pop songs, but Melanie taught Mozhdah how to turn her voice into a musical instrument.

"My voice won't do this. It's impossible!" Mozhdah said, as Melanie led her in vocal exercises.

"Just hang in there," Melanie said. "In five months, all of these techniques will become second nature."

Mozhdah did trust Melanie, and practiced her singing daily around the house out of earshot of the rest of the family, strengthening her voice and diaphragm and developing proper vocal technique. She learned to read music, could look at the notes and hear the song in her head. After a year, Mozhdah was able to hit a high C in the sixth octave. It completely changed how she sang pop music; it was effortless, unconstrained—powerful.

The hair salon began to feel like home to Mozhdah, and she looked forward to arriving there after school. By the time she was in grade eleven, she could do color and highlights on her own. And, if she was particularly nice to her mother, Nasrin might experiment on Mozhdah's long hair, trying different highlights, curling or straightening.

"I think I'll go goth," Mozhdah said one day.

"What does that mean?" Nasrin said with apprehension.

"You know: black makeup, black nail polish, black hair, black lipstick—that kind of thing." Goth style was popular among those students asserting independence from the mainstream fashion of the time.

"Why?" Nasrin asked.

"It's how I feel inside," Mozhdah said.

"Why?" Nasrin repeated.

"Because of Afghanistan, I guess." Mozhdah shrugged.

"You'll scare away my clients," Nasrin complained.

"They'll still love me," Mozhdah said.

For Mozhdah, relief from the desolation she increasingly felt, expressed by her monochrome appearance, came from watching *The Oprah Winfrey Show*. Nasrin's twenty-eight-inch tube TV with antennas, too heavy to lift, sat in a corner of the salon, positioned so that all the customers could see it reflected in the mirror at each cutting station. Nasrin refused to get cable, so her customers were unable to argue about changing the channel at 4:00 PM when *Oprah* came on, since it was the only show that came through clearly.

Nasrin, Mozhdah, and the clients would watch while Oprah welcomed the beautiful and famous, the experts, the downtrodden, victims of crime, authors, artists, and oddballs to her stage, providing a glimpse into the human condition—not to mention celebrity gossip.

Mozhdah was fascinated by the insights into her own behavior that Oprah's interviews gave her. Oprah seemed to define and legitimize the deep, dark feelings that Mozhdah often felt overwhelmed by. By watching how Oprah conducted interviews, Mozhdah also came to understand empathy, as well as the importance of conversing with people who held ideas different from your own—even ideas you were fundamentally opposed to.

It was remarkable, thought Mozhdah, how Oprah was able to draw out her guests' most painful or poignant experiences. It was as if these two people—the interviewee and Oprah—existed within their own bubble of intimacy. Mozhdah tried to imagine herself on that stage, conducting interviews with people from all walks of life. Was it possible to develop such poised and insightful interviewing skills? She studied Oprah's mannerisms, the way she spoke to people, how she framed and delivered discomfiting questions, how quickly she gained the trust of guests. "Listen to your instincts," Oprah said. And Mozhdah took that to heart, interpreting it to mean that she should trust her feelings, no matter what other people said.

When Oprah said, "We are all beacons of light for each other," Mozhdah thought of Afghanistan. How could light shine through the violence and oppression that lay upon her country? When Oprah undertook a special show about the effect of absent fathers—a phenomenon that was ravaging the African-American community in the United States—Mozhdah thought of Afghanistan again. Fatherless sons, said one Oprah guest, had a hole in their soul the size of the father. Mozhdah thought of Bashir, about how much he had endured, fought, and sacrificed to help his family climb out of penury when they arrived in Vancouver—going into debt to a loan shark in order to open a pizza parlor where he then worked seven days a week, twelve hours a day. Where would she, Nasrin, Masee, and Safee be without Bashir? And where would Bashir be without Nasrin? Where would any of them be without each other? There wouldn't be money for a home, martial arts classes or music lessons, hockey or tutoring for the boys. Nasrin's indomitable work ethic and strength were multiplied exponentially by Bashir's support and love. Together, they had performed a miracle of survival and the equally great achievement of successful integration into Canada. Mozhdah thought about Bashir's wise guidance, how he always spoke of human rights, especially women's rights, while she was growing up—how he made sure his children were brought up as equals. Without Bashir and without Nasrin, she too would have a hole in her soul. How would it be filled?

For Afghans, was there a way to help them fill this void? There had to be, thought Mozhdah. But she felt small, young, inexperienced, and alone. Yet listening to her instincts, as Oprah urged, Mozhdah felt that there was something she was meant to do in Afghanistan. She didn't know what that might be. But something awaited her—something just around the corner.

CHAPTER 8

The Power of Song

"YOU HAVE TO go to university. You can't just hang out at home once you graduate from high school and play video games and sleep in," said Nasrin, standing in the middle of her hair salon.

Mozhdah was sweeping strands of black hair, scattered under one of the salon chairs, into a dustpan. It was a late Tuesday afternoon and the salon was quiet, with only one client, head encased in a hair dryer, nose deep in a gossip magazine.

"I intend to go to university. But maybe not right after grade twelve." Mozhdah looked at Nasrin, who stood with her arms crossed. "I'd like to do songwriting and singing. And read." She paused. "I could help out here, save some money."

Nasrin shook her head. "I don't think you should take time off after high school. Too much time on your hands to get into trouble. It seems like a waste to me."

"You want to hear how other people are wasting their lives? You know what my friends talk about? Marriage! How many kids they're going to have. Now that's wasting your life," Mozhdah said.

"Wanting to get married and having kids isn't necessarily wasting your life—for some people," Nasrin responded. She sighed and looked sympathetically at her daughter, broom in hand, eyes bright and defiant. Her long hair had returned to its normal brown, the menacing goth phase having lasted about a year. The return to her natural color also signaled an improvement in Mozhdah's mood.

"Another thing," said Mozhdah. "I'm not opposed to university, but I need to figure out what classes I want to take and where's the best place to go. I'd like to do something that will allow me to help out Afghanistan."

Nasrin suddenly recalled a visit long ago in Kabul by one of Bashir's good friends, Sayed Aaqa, a medical doctor, when Mozhdah was only seven months old. Mozhdah, who had weighed a burly nine pounds at birth, had been lying on a blanket on the floor, chubby legs bicycling the air. Even then there was something captivating about her, a calm, perceptive, almost ethereal demeanor.

"Your daughter will move this whole country," Sayed told Nasrin.

"What do you mean—move?" Nasrin asked, pleased but puzzled.

"She will change the whole country," Sayed said.

Nasrin had never forgotten Sayed's peculiar divination. At the time, it had made her laugh, but it had stayed in the back of her mind as Mozhdah grew up. It made her push Mozhdah and challenge her, help her unlock her talents—like singing.

The path Mozhdah was going down seemed, Nasrin sensed, to be circling back to Afghanistan, making Sayed's comments seem even more prophetic. Nasrin didn't feel this with Safee or Masee, both of whom had integrated seamlessly into school, embracing Canadian culture and sports like hockey, making friends easily, weathering the vagaries of life with greater ease.

"How would you help out Afghanistan?" Nasrin asked.

"There are millions of refugees who need help, and orphans. I just need to figure things out," Mozhdah said, sweeping the last of the hair into the dustpan and tipping it into the garbage.

As the new millennium neared, there was no indication things would improve for Afghans, only more cruel repression and misery under Taliban rule. Just a few months previous, in October, reports had trickled out about mass arrests and executions by the Taliban of thousands of Shi`a Muslims, including the ethnic Hazaras, in the city of Mazar-i-Sharif in central Afghanistan. The Taliban had also allowed the country to become a breeding ground for terrorism, providing sanctuary to Osama bin Laden, believed to have masterminded the 1998 bombings of two American embassies in Africa. Around the same time, Mozhdah had watched footage on TV of a woman named Zarmeena, the mother of seven children, publicly executed with bullets to the head from a Kalashnikov in Kabul stadium. The footage had been smuggled out of Afghanistan by a women's group called the Revolutionary Association of the Women of Afghanistan.

The Associated Press was also reporting a new tactic of control and punishment by the Taliban, called wall toppling. Using a tank, they would knock over a brick wall on people as a form of public execution. Other horrors the Taliban used to enforce their harsh interpretation of Islamic law included amputating the feet and hands of accused thieves. Mozhdah read in the *New York Times* that a man named Mohammed Yaqub, who was accused of stealing $200 worth of carpets, was sentenced to have his left foot cut off. Caught once before for stealing, Yaqub's right hand had been lobbed off as punishment. Before the severing of his left foot, Yaqub was forced to undertake a ghoulish walk around Kabul stadium, displaying the shortened arm to spectators.

Mozhdah could not distance herself from these horrors, and her fury at the atrocities grew stronger. Relief only came when she was doing homework, writing music, or practicing martial arts in the gym.

"Tell you what," said Nasrin, grimacing as Mozhdah banged the dustpan harder than necessary against the bin, causing the customer under the hair dryer to glance up. "I'll buy you a car—a new one—if you go to university right after high school."

Mozhdah looked at her mom, surprised. That was hard to pass up. She peered sharply at her mom, wondering if she was serious.

Nasrin took Mozhdah's silence for reluctance. She sweetened the deal.

"How about, say, a Mazda," said Nasrin.

"Are you being ironic?" Mozhdah narrowed her eyes. "That's only been my school nickname since we got to Vancouver."

Nasrin smiled. "No, it's a good car."

"Okay," said Mozhdah. "But it has to be red."

Nasrin turned away to hide her delight, checking needlessly on her client under the dryer. The secret to raising children, she thought—bribery.

THEN, THE WORLD changed. On September 11, 2001, Mozhdah was awoken by what sounded like the announcers on her
clock radio describing the latest action film. Out of the depths
of sleep, she caught snatches of conversation: "Twin towers . . .
planes crashed . . . can't believe it . . ."

What have I woken up to? she thought, sitting upright.

The radio hosts weren't talking about a movie. This was
real life. She flung on a housecoat and hurried into the living room, where Bashir and Nasrin were watching television.
Nasrin gasped as fiery footage showed two Boeing 767 airlin-
ers crashing into the World Trade Center's Twin Towers. As
black smoke poured out of the fractured buildings, and debris
and gray ash rained down upon Brooklyn, Nasrin, Bashir, and
Mozhdah wept.

Several weeks later, American authorities connected the
terrorist organization Al-Qaeda, a militant Sunni Islamist
group co-founded by Osama bin Laden, to the 9/11 attack,
which killed three thousand people and wounded six thousand
more. Members of the North Atlantic Treaty Organization (NATO) reacted swiftly and forcefully. An international
coalition led by U.S. president George W. Bush attacked
Afghanistan—where bin Laden was believed to be hiding.

On October 7, 2001, at 16:20 Greenwich Mean Time, the
U.S. and Great Britain launched bombs and missiles at Afghanistan from the Indian Ocean. A grave-looking President Bush
addressed the world. "On my orders, the United States military
has begun strikes against Al-Qaeda military training camps
and military installations of the Taliban regime in Afghanistan. These carefully targeted actions are designed to disrupt
the use of Afghanistan as a terrorist base of operations and
to attack the military capability of the Taliban regime," Bush

intoned. Canada, Bush continued, was one of several allies that had pledged to support the invasion. The same day as America began dropping bombs, Canada announced it would contribute sea, land, and air forces to the operation.

The attack came in the dark of night in Afghanistan, though it was early morning on a Sunday in Vancouver. Grainy footage was broadcast on television screens, showing Tomahawk cruise missiles soaring through the air, and fire and explosions in Kabul. Bombs were dropped by B-52s, B-1s, and B-2 stealth bombers onto Al-Qaeda and Taliban air defense systems, bunkers, airfields, and war planes around Kabul, Jalalabad, and Kandahar. Osama bin Laden responded by video, pledging retaliation against the American people.

The U.S.-led military campaign was called Operation Enduring Freedom. Media outlets reported that its ultimate objective was to facilitate U.S. Army Special Forces entering Afghanistan to root out Osama bin Laden and Al-Qaeda.

Mozhdah and her family watched in stunned silence.

"Everyone will be killed," Nasrin said in a stricken voice, staring aghast at the blurry, fiery explosions on television.

"There was no other way to get rid of these terrorists," Bashir said quietly, as the city they once called home was bombarded.

"But Afghans are being killed! Just look—whole areas of Kabul are in flames!" Nasrin exclaimed.

"How else to get rid of the Taliban?" Bashir replied, his voice hard. "Afghanistan has no future under their control. But with the Canadians going, I can return to Afghanistan and help rebuild. They will need interpreters—people who know the country," Bashir said.

"I want to go too," said Mozhdah.

Bashir said grimly, "Afghanistan isn't now, nor will it be anytime soon, a country for women."

"Bashir is right, Mozhdah," Nasrin said in a frightened voice. "This is all-out war. There was nothing for Afghans before this attack, and there will be less than nothing afterwards."

"We'll see," Mozhdah said boldly. She felt strangely flushed, her breathing quick. She felt sickened by the destruction, but a flicker of hope had been ignited. Could the Americans drive out the Taliban? Could things change for the better? Canada was now involved. She was both Afghan and Canadian. If Canada was going to volunteer its military might and its soldiers, surely she had some obligation to help. But how?

The invasion by the United States and its allies brought massive changes. Watching the news was like being on a never-ending rollercoaster ride. Mozhdah and Nasrin listened as America's First Lady Laura Bush declared the war in Afghanistan a "fight for the rights and dignity of women," and the U.S. State Department condemned the oppression of women and children by the Taliban and Al-Qaeda. Taliban members were being forced out of their strongholds, including Kabul. Mozhdah watched Western television journalists deliver their reports in flak jackets, faces grimy with dust. That should be her standing there, she thought. She'd be good at it. Because she knew Farsi and was familiar with the culture, she would be able to unearth stories Western reporters couldn't. A thought took root in her mind. Could she become a foreign correspondent?

Following graduation from high school, Mozhdah opted for college rather than university, taking courses that interested her most, like philosophy and political science. These would provide a good foundation for a law degree, which she was still weighing as a future course of study.

She was accepted into Kwantlen University College in Richmond, a short drive from their home in Vancouver. When school started in September, she fell in love with the small classes and the friendly instructors, who had time for questions and discussion after lectures. Mozhdah reveled in her philosophy courses, the lectures on ethics and political philosophy, obsessed with thoughts about the existence of evil and why there was such suffering in the world. Why did Afghans suffer so much, generation after generation? Why did they seem doomed to endure interminable war and violence?

Kwantlen was considered a feeder school—an institution that prepped students for more rigorous university studies. Mozhdah set her sights on the University of British Columbia (UBC) and, as she neared the end of her college studies, visited the sprawling, 988-acre, leafy green campus. But as she peeked into the huge, intimidating classes filled with hundreds of students being taught by aloof-looking professors, she felt overwhelmed.

One day after classes at Kwantlen, she was at the salon helping Nasrin, who was cutting the hair of one of her regular clients, Rory O'Flynn. Over the years, Rory and his sister, Susanne, who was also a client, had come to know Mozhdah well. Nasrin had recently invited them to hear Mozhdah sing at her first concert, held in one of the banquet halls at Vancouver's Hellenic community center.

Mozhdah was seated in the salon chair next to Rory. "I just don't know what to do," Mozhdah told him. "I was thinking about attending UBC, but I'm not sure that it's for me."

Rory, a former government worker who now owned his own contracting business, nodded sympathetically. "UBC," he said, "is a competitive, research-focused university. The best people," he continued, "often come from the colleges or technical schools, which give students practical skills. In my experience, a university degree often means little more than an individual has the ability to write a twenty-page essay. And what good is that in the real world?"

Mozhdah looked at Rory, startled. She hadn't thought about post-secondary education from this perspective. A university degree had, in her parents' eyes, always been a priority. The war in Afghanistan had prevented Bashir from pursuing a PhD. Perhaps his focus on university was because of his own thwarted aspirations? Maybe Rory was right; unless Mozhdah planned to pursue law, was a university undergraduate degree the path to follow?

Rory looked keenly at Mozhdah. "Have you ever thought of broadcast journalism?" he asked. "You're articulate, well read. You're up on current affairs, and I bet you'd look terrific on camera. But what really makes you special," Rory continued, "is your ability to sing."

"What?" Mozhdah said, slightly incredulous.

"I can imagine seeing you on TV, singing, doing something like hosting your own show," said Rory.

Mozhdah laughed. "That's crazy," she said.

Maybe it wasn't crazy, she thought later. Rory's words affirmed her earlier ambitions about becoming a correspondent. She could return to Afghanistan as a broadcast professional and help her country this way. As she lay in bed that night, too excited to fall asleep, she promised herself: *Yes, I'm going to do it.*

2

Mozhdah applied and was accepted into the broadcast journalism program at the British Columbia Institute of Technology (BCIT). It felt like home. Over the two-year diploma program, Mozhdah volunteered for extra hours in the control rooms and working the cameras. As she practiced interviewing people live on camera at places like city hall, questioning politicians about public policy, Oprah's calm but firm delivery of sometimes-prying questions would flash into her mind. It took courage to ask such questions, Mozhdah realized.

The BCIT program was technically demanding. About one-third of the class of thirty were women, and their number dropped to four by second year. For Mozhdah, it was an advantage being in the minority. Mozhdah didn't find BCIT's male-dominated program intimidating, thanks to Bashir telling her from an early age that she was as good as any man. Generally, Mozhdah found her fellow students thoughtful and considerate, as they learned the fundamentals of broadcasting: directing newscasts, operating a camera, handling video and audio, as well as working the main control room. There was a close camaraderie among classmates; if she, or anyone else, needed help, they only had to ask a fellow student. But it was challenging and demanding, and the workload, at times, was overwhelming.

"It's too much," said Mozhdah one night, after getting home late from BCIT after editing a television feature. Nasrin was warming a plate of leftovers in the microwave. "I can't believe they expect us to do all this work. I put in another twelve-hour day."

Nasrin spun around, not looking sympathetic, as Mozhdah expected, but angry. She glared at Mozhdah. "Why are you complaining?" Nasrin snapped. "Look at Oprah. She has her own television program, despite everything she endured growing up—abuse from her grandmother, poverty, neglect, sexual abuse by relatives, pregnant at fourteen. Everything conspired against her. And look where she is today—one of the most powerful women in the world. Do you think she complained about twelve-hour days? If you don't get somewhere in life, Mozhdah, with everything—*everything*—your father and I have given you, then there's something wrong. Oh, and another thing. You know who else puts in twelve-hour days?" Nasrin said, pulling the plate of hot food out of the microwave and dropping it in front of Mozhdah so hard that rice grains bounced onto the kitchen table. "I do. And I do it six days a week, in addition to running this household! And I've done it for years. Without complaining! Now eat!"

Dumbstruck at her mother's outburst, Mozhdah began quietly eating Nasrin's spicy potato-and-lentil-stuffed *bolani* flatbread and rice, muttering, "Why you gotta be *sooooo* perfect, Oprah?"

MOZHDAH CUT BACK on singing lessons during the most demanding times of her studies at BCIT, though she still undertook one-hour sessions three times a week with Wahid Omid. She continued putting her poetry to music, developing modern-sounding songs woven with Afghan melodies and instrumentation. Mozhdah would also sing traditional Afghan folk songs that were updated with a modern tempo and Wahid's guitar or keyboard mixing. Re-creating old Afghan music was enthralling. Mozhdah began to dream of singing the songs in front of Afghans, showing them that, if their music could be renewed, so could their country.

There was one song in particular, one of Mozhdah's favorites, a traditional, upbeat song that had often been sung by the famous Afghan singer Najib Haqparast. It honored women and their beauty, and was so melodic and full of joy that Mozhdah felt it captured better than any other song the spirit of the people of Afghanistan before war.

One day, Mozhdah asked Wahid: "Could we take this song and change the lyrics? I want to sing something for Afghan boys and men—all the traditional songs are sung by men about women. Why can't there be a song honoring the boys and men of Afghanistan?"

Wahid was enamored with the idea. Such a song, he told her, would have to be sung by a woman. And who better than Mozhdah?

"Bring me some new lyrics and we'll figure out how to put them to this melody," he told her.

Excited, Mozhdah went home and spoke to Bashir. She thought that because he wrote his own poetry, he would bring a special skill to rewriting the ancient song and making it modern—a song to honor the men, young and old, who had tried to protect their families while fighting for peace. Mozhdah was confident that her father could rewrite the song in a way that would speak to both young and older Afghans. It would reference different provinces within the country and be an anthem of hope—bolstered by the changes that began in 2001, when America and the coalition forces launched the mission to drive the Taliban and Al-Qaeda out of Afghanistan.

For the next week, Bashir and one of his Afghan poet friends, Ishaq Sana, worked on the words, imbuing them with a lyricism that could only come from someone brought up among Afghanistan's indomitable people, who would always protect their country's vast, craggy landscapes. When they finished, Mozhdah, eyes gleaming, brought them to Wahid, who began murmuring the words softly in Farsi. Mozhdah had given the song a new title, *"Shir Bacha-e-Afghani,"* or "The Brave Afghan Boy."

"Afghans will love this song—especially these two verses," Wahid said, reading aloud:

You are from Kabul or Mazar
From Paktia or Kunar
In manhood and bravery
You are second to none.
You are from Herat or Ghor
From Ghazni or Badakhshan
You are cool and proud
If you are from Kandahar

Over the next several weeks, Mozhdah and Wahid worked on the music. Wahid, who had embraced the new platform YouTube to disseminate his music to the Afghan diaspora, then made a remarkable suggestion: Why not make a music video? He would gather some musicians and direct and film it with his cameras.

Mozhdah was thrilled. What would she wear? In keeping with the patriotic theme of *"Shir Bacha-e-Afghani,"* Mozhdah, with advice from Wahid and Nasrin, decided to wear outfits representing the traditional Afghanistan as well as the new, emerging nation. She picked several Afghan dresses, in the colors of the Afghan flag: black, green, red, and white. Mozhdah ultimately selected several outfits that incorporated modern as well as traditional Afghan style, including a long red dress with bare arms, accessorized with a black floppy felt summer hat and black tie draped around the neck, along with a red waist-length jacket. She also wore three Afghan women's outfits, including one especially spectacular *firaq partūg*, a long flowing embroidered garment of pink, green, and purple. Gold embroidery covered the front, like the breastplate of ancient armor. As befitted the modern young Afghan woman, Mozhdah decided to forgo the traditional chador headscarf, selecting instead a jeweled headband. Afghan women, thought Mozhdah, should have the choice whether to cover their heads, rather than having to bow to religious, cultural, or familial pressure.

Wahid secured the use of a stage at a friend's banquet hall in Vancouver and brought in several musicians to play both modern acoustic and traditional Afghan drums as well as electric guitar. A male dancer in traditional flowing *khet partūg*, or *shalwar kameez*, with silver-embroidered vest, was also in the video.

Much to Mozhdah's surprise, the video took less than two hours to film. It had taken longer to dress the stage, draping chiffon in Afghanistan's colors for a simple but evocative backdrop.

After editing the video, Wahid gave both CD and DVD copies of *"Shir Bacha"* to Mozhdah, who slipped them in her dresser at home, thinking how fun it had been to experiment with shooting a music video. Then she forgot about it.

Several days later, Wahid called Mozhdah. "Check out You-Tube," he said.

"Why?" she asked.

Wahid admitted that he had posted *"Shir Bacha"* to YouTube a few hours ago, without her permission.

"What?" Mozhdah exclaimed. "Why would you do that? You should have asked first."

"Sorry, Mozhdah," Wahid said sincerely. "But I knew you'd say yes. You should know," he paused for effect, "five hundred people have viewed it in the past two hours. Just think," he said excitedly, "your first song, being heard around the world!"

"I have to see this!" Mozhdah exclaimed.

Cordless phone in hand, Mozhdah sprinted upstairs to her bedroom and opened her laptop, waiting impatiently as the screen awoke from sleep mode. She Googled *"Shir Bacha-e-Afghani"* and watched eagerly as YouTube appeared on-screen. Then—there she was, with the band. It felt weird seeing herself on the internet.

"Oh Wahid, I love it!"

Mozhdah wondered who the people were who were clicking the "like" icon under the video. They soon let her know. Mozhdah was inundated with messages on Myspace, the global social networking site later supplanted by Facebook. She also received requests from Afghanistan television and radio stations to air the video and play the song. The Jamalzadah private home number somehow became public and strangers began calling the house, asking if Mozhdah would sing at concerts. It was thrilling, overwhelming, and just a bit frightening.

Nasrin and Bashir were amazed too, and Nasrin slipped effortlessly into the role of music manager. Nasrin was friends with the Los Angeles–based singer Habib Qaderi, who had risen to international stardom among the Afghan diaspora as well as in Afghanistan following the 2001 release of his album *Golden Dream.*

Nasrin reached out to Habib, who was touring. Would he, she inquired, consider letting Mozhdah open at some of his concerts? Habib responded enthusiastically. Why not help a young, talented Afghan woman just finding her footing in the music industry? He flew Mozhdah and Nasrin down to San Francisco to rehearse for an upcoming concert. Mozhdah would sing two songs in English: Madonna's "Take a Bow" and Vanessa Williams's "Save the Best for Last." Mozhdah was slightly abashed when Habib decided that her Farsi wasn't good enough to sing more traditional Afghan songs, and she promised to work on the nuances of Farsi pronunciation.

The rehearsals did not go well, with Mozhdah almost throwing up from nerves. When concert day came, waiting to take her turn onstage, Mozhdah fought waves of nausea. She was nearly struck dumb by the huge, noisy audience and wanted only to flee to the airport and never sing again.

This isn't me, Mozhdah thought frantically. *I can't do this. I'm not a performer.*

Mozhdah somehow got through the two songs in a haze of fear.

"The crowd really liked you," Habib said over the phone a few days later, after Mozhdah and Nasrin had returned to Vancouver. Mozhdah had sparked a buzz among Afghans, who wondered who the talented young singer was. "Can you fly down and sing those two songs again as my opening act?" Habib asked. The venue this time would be the small intimate City National Grove of Anaheim in California. Still nerve-racking, thought Mozhdah, but slightly easier to handle.

A few months later, Nasrin organized a concert for Habib at Vancouver's Hellenic community center. Mozhdah would, once again, open, singing the Madonna and Vanessa Williams songs, in addition to the 1968 folk-pop classic "Those Were the Days," sung by Mary Hopkin. It had been a global hit and rerecorded in more than twenty languages. Ahmad Zahir, Afghanistan's most revered singer, known as the "Elvis of Afghanistan," had translated the lyrics into Farsi.

Afterwards, the requests from concert organizers changed. Would Mozhdah consider headlining her own concerts?

Mozhdah glared at Nasrin. "Don't you dare say yes."

BASHIR HAD BEEN away for six months, working as a cultural adviser with the Canadian Armed Forces, which had sent troops into Afghanistan in January 2002, just a few months after Al-Qaeda's 9/11 attack on American soil.

He took a cab home from Vancouver International Airport, struggled through the front door, and gratefully dropped his bulky military backpack in the foyer. Then he walked stiffly up the stairs into the living room, to be enveloped in hugs by Nasrin, Mozhdah, Safee, and Masee.

He was exhausted, having slept little on the long journey, hopscotching from Afghanistan to Europe and then to Toronto, enduring long dull connections between flights.

"I have something I want to show you," Bashir said to Mozhdah after Nasrin's welcome-home dinner.

He went to his backpack and opened a side pocket, bringing out a journal that was always with him, filled with reminders, email addresses and phone numbers, and bits of poetry. He tore out several pages covered in his thin, elegant Farsi writing and handed them to Mozhdah.

"What's this?" she asked.

"While I was with the Kandahar Provincial Reconstruction Team in the south, something terrible happened just before I was about to leave." He paused.

Mozhdah looked at him, waiting.

"I was packing when I was informed about an attack on several schoolgirls at Mirwais Nika High School on the outskirts of Kandahar."

"What kind of attack?" Mozhdah said, her eyes widening.

"It was the Taliban," said Bashir. "They attacked the girls with battery acid. At least two of them might have been blinded."

Mozhdah stared in horror at her father's strained, weathered face. "How did it happen?"

"Two men, on a motorcycle. The girls were walking to school and the men used water pistols to spray the acid," Bashir said. "I just can't get the image out of my mind—these deranged men attacking innocent girls." He paused, and then said quietly, angrily, "Their lives are probably destroyed."

Mozhdah looked at her father, tears in her eyes.

Bashir took a big breath. "I wrote a poem on the plane ride home. For the girls. I've titled it '*Dukhtare Afghan.*'"

"Oh," said Mozhdah softly, "'Afghan Girl.'" She looked at the travel-stained, torn pages and began to read in Farsi: "I'm a girl, an Afghan girl, a girl from the land of the braves / Don't break my wings, don't break my crown..." She stopped, overwhelmed by emotion and the poem's powerful simplicity. "This will make a brilliant song," she said, eyes bright with tears.

"That's what I thought too." Bashir nodded.

This time, Mozhdah sought the help of Milad Faqiri, a talented eighteen-year-old musician who was the son of a family friend, to help write the music. Despite Milad's youth and inexperience, Mozhdah was enamored with his initial compositions, which sounded effortlessly melodic. The score he eventually wrote was modern yet distinctly Afghan—a haunting dirge that seemed to encapsulate the suffering of the country's women.

"Dukhtare Afghan" was released on Afghan radio. Shortly afterwards, while Mozhdah and her parents were contemplating whether they could afford to fund a music video for the song, Afghanistan's recently launched private Ariana Television Network (ATN) approached Nasrin. Their offer was: ATN would fund and sponsor a video, if the station was given exclusive rights to air it. The video would be made by Habib Durani, who directed much of the station's crop of edgy, diverse news and dramatic programming. It was Habib who selected the location, a place reminiscent of Afghanistan's rugged terrain—the Mojave Desert in Nevada. A top crew was hired, and Mozhdah was put up at Mandalay Bay, a luxury resort and casino on the Las Vegas Strip, for the duration of the shoot.

The Mojave Desert has a raw, bleak beauty; the early dawn light turns the sandstone cliffs red as blood. In the video, Mozhdah wore a filmy white chiffon dress, designed and sewn by Nasrin, which the desert wind whipped around her body. She also wore a deep green, embroidered *firaq partūg*. There were no musicians featured in the video for "Dukhtare Afghan"—just Mozhdah, her long hair lifted by air currents, surrounded by hard soil and blood-red rock, as if the earth itself mourned the savage attack.

Citizens of Afghanistan watched the music video for "Dukhtare Afghan" on ATN; the Afghan diaspora caught it on YouTube. Most people loved it, while a small but vocal minority hated it. Mullahs, men, politicians, some women, and even a few younger Afghans were astonished and offended that a female singer would dare to speak out so boldly on behalf of women. Others thought Mozhdah's flowing, opaque chiffon gown, backdropped by the dawn light, was provocative and highly offensive. Culturally, Afghan women would never wear such garments. Simply forgoing a hijab, or headscarf, could draw accusations of being a prostitute. Others perceived the video to be male bashing. But their criticisms only served to raise the song's profile. Many were deeply moved by the courageous message of the video, which began with a quote from Shamsia, one of the acid-attack victims: "I won't stop going to school. I'm studying to be able to build our country."

Mozhdah was astounded by the video's divisiveness. Was it possible, amid such polarization, to create any long-lasting positive impact? Would it change the hearts and minds of men? Certainly there were men who praised her, who came to her shows and wept during the song. But it was the women Mozhdah wanted to reach, hoping to give them just a bit more courage as they faced a violent and threatening world.

PART 3

The Mozhdah Show

2009–2011

CHAPTER 9

Nasrin's Bold Move

A FEW MONTHS LATER, while Mozhdah was reading at home, her beloved cat, Mittens, curled up next to her on the couch, the phone rang. It was someone calling from Afghanistan, asking for Mozhdah.

"Hello. This is Massood Hashimi," said the stranger, the telephone line crackling with static, the voice remote, as if the call were from the other side of the world. "Is this Mozhdah Jamalzadah?"

"Yes?" Mozhdah said tentatively.

"I am with 1TV in Kabul."

What was 1TV? "Never heard of it," she replied.

Massood began to speak rapidly in stilted English: the producers of the television network wanted her because she was a perfect fit for 1TV: young, controversial, and unafraid to challenge Afghan social conventions. Because of her music video, she was wildly popular among most Afghans. And, Massood continued, there was a new show being planned...

Mozhdah cut him off. "Can you please speak to my manager, Nasrin Jamalzadah? She's right here," she said, handing the phone to her mother.

Nasrin looked quizzically at Mozhdah and put the phone to her ear.

"Hello?"

Mozhdah watched as her mother frowned, listening to Massood struggle to speak English, and asked him to speak in Farsi. The phone call lasted a few minutes, with Nasrin asking several brief questions before saying goodbye. She rolled her eyes.

"What was that all about?" Mozhdah asked.

"Something about a new television station being launched by someone named Fahim Hashimy—they are planning a talent show and want you to host it. They asked for a publicity shot and résumé. I'll send them that, but I told him to get an actual producer to call me," Nasrin said.

"And the station is called 1TV? I've never heard of it," Mozhdah said.

"Neither have I," Nasrin responded.

About a week later, Nasrin fielded another phone call from 1TV.

"Who was that?" Mozhdah asked Nasrin.

"A head producer from 1TV called... her name is... " Nasrin looked closer at the piece of paper where she had scribbled notes, "Siobhan Berry. They want you to host a reality show called *Afghanistan's Got Talent*, based on *Britain's Got Talent*."

"Why me?" Mozhdah asked curiously.

"Well, your music videos, your songs, your broadcast education," Nasrin replied. "What other Afghan has your talent and training?"

"When do they want me to start?"

"December," said Nasrin. She walked into the kitchen and began dinner preparations while Mozhdah went to the fridge to grab some juice. Suddenly, Nasrin stopped what she was doing and spun around to look at Mozhdah.

"There are more Taliban bombings than ever before. I don't know if a show like this would be worth risking your life for," Nasrin said worriedly. She ticked off several of the latest attacks. Just that past August, the Taliban had exploded a suicide car bomb outside NATO headquarters in Kabul, killing at least seven and injuring a hundred. Only ten days later, just after the first results of the presidential elections were announced, a massive car bomb shook Kandahar, killing at least thirty. This was followed a few months later by U.S. president Barack Obama's announcement of the deployment of an additional thirty thousand troops to help battle the growing Taliban violence. The Taliban's reaction: step up the violence even more.

Mozhdah looked at her mom. "1TV wouldn't invite me if they thought I'd get killed," she said casually. "And this is something I would love to do. This is something that I've trained for: to be on television. I was meant to return to Afghanistan, to help out somehow. This is the beginning. I just know it."

Nasrin didn't answer. The germ of an idea was taking root in her mind. She would mull it over with Bashir before suggesting it to Mozhdah. The idea involved taking her copy of

The Oprah Winfrey Show—20th Anniversary six-disc DVD collection to Afghanistan. It was about time, thought Nasrin, that Afghanistan got used to powerful women.

IN DECEMBER 2009, Mozhdah arrived to begin preproduction on *Afghanistan's Got Talent.* She flew straight to Kabul from Hamburg, Germany, where she had attended Ariana Television Network's fourth annual music award show, created the year of ATN's launch in 2005 in Afghanistan. The awards recognized and celebrated Afghan musical talent, from traditional to modern-day hip-hop. A splashy affair, the gala drew guests from the Afghan diaspora around the world, the women garbed in cocktail dresses and sparkling jewels, the men in suits and ties. Mozhdah found the evening nerve-racking and remained poised on the edge of her seat as her name was called out four times. She was up for Best New Female Artist, and *"Dukhtare Afghan,"* or "Afghan Girl," received three nominations: Best Lyrics, Best Patriotic Song, and Best Light Song. She won the latter. It cemented Mozhdah's growing reputation as one of the most celebrated and famous Afghan female pop artists to have emerged in the past thirty years, ever since the Soviet invasion drove the country into ruination and the Afghan people into despair. Mozhdah felt torn by the award. She was happy for Bashir, whose poetry had inspired such powerful music. But she was saddened by the act of cruelty that had inspired the grieving verses.

When she arrived at Kabul International Airport, Mozhdah was startled by the presence of a camera crew from 1TV and four uniformed guards, armed with AK-47s, who stood waiting for her and Nasrin at baggage claim. Two young men approached and politely greeted the women. One man introduced himself as Fahim Hashimy's secretary, the other as Asil, who would be Mozhdah's assistant. While the television camera rolled, Asil handed Mozhdah a bouquet of roses and she gave a short interview, saying how excited she was be back in her native country and working for iTV.

When several men grabbed their luggage, Mozhdah whispered to Nasrin, "I could get used to this."

With the guards surrounding the group, keeping watch for anything suspicious, Nasrin and Mozhdah were escorted to a waiting armored Toyota Land Cruiser. Asil explained that they would be driven straight to the iTV guesthouse, their permanent new home.

Kabul is laid out on a grid, with the center protected by what is called, somewhat pretentiously, the Ring of Steel, a series of twenty-five Afghan National Police checkpoints. Whole sections of the city are cordoned off into little fiefdoms where embassies and government ministries hide behind concertina wire and blast walls. These areas of safety usually have heavy metal barriers and large concrete roadblocks protected by armed guards who require identification from people who want to get through. Because so many roads are cordoned off, the city's thousands of commuters are bottlenecked into a few major roadways, creating time-consuming detours. Mozhdah and Nasrin looked out onto the traffic snarls through the tinted windows of the Land Cruiser. They were comfortable; the air conditioning was on high, but the effluvium of human waste seeped into the vehicle from the open sewers and trash pits lining the rutted, potholed streets. Mozhdah stared at a vagrant woman in a dirty blue burka, standing in the middle of the road, one arm limply outstretched, palm up, pleading for money. Mozhdah felt her heart thump in horror as she glimpsed the filthy face of a tiny child peek out from the crook of her mother's arm.

The vehicle began to pass enormous, multistory houses, painted in garish confectionary colors, with huge balconies, domes, pillars, and elaborate tile designs, the "poppy palaces" of Kabul, facetiously referred to on occasion as "narco-tecture."

"Why poppy palaces?" Mozhdah asked Asil. They were built, Asil explained, by the people who profited from the Afghanistan opium trade.

Mozhdah turned to Nasrin, incredulous: "And I thought everyone in Afghanistan was living in mud-brick huts. Not even homes in the posh areas of Vancouver are this extravagant."

Mozhdah turned again to Asil. "So people are living here, in these ostentatious mansions, versus jail, where they ought to be?"

Asil smiled slightly. "Afghanistan," he said, "is very corrupt. Not only does corruption go unpunished, but it is rewarded, as it buys influence with government officials. It is very hard for the Afghan people to trust their government because of this," he said.

This was disturbing, thought Mozhdah, as she turned to look out the window at her surroundings: the thin beggar women in burkas, the children standing in the middle of traffic, swinging dented tin cans with thin trails of smoke wafting from them.

"What are they doing?" Mozhdah asked.

"These children," Asil said, "are called *spandis*. Their cans contain an herb that, when burned, is supposed to ward off evil. The children approach vehicles in traffic to bless them with the herb, and in return, they are given a tiny amount of money. Many of them do this to help feed their families."

Such a strange superstition, Mozhdah thought. Most people, she assumed, realized that these children were using the burning herb cans as a prop to beg. But some people probably believed in such myths, or at least thought it better to be safe than sorry.

There was silence in the vehicle, Mozhdah and Nasrin staring out the windows, slightly overwhelmed, breathing air that was heavy not only with the odor of raw sewage but also the metallic tang of the AK-47s being held by the guards.

"Where, exactly, are we going?" Mozhdah asked.

"District ten, in the northern part of Kabul," said Asil. "It's called Wazir Akbar Khan. You Americans say it's like Beverly Hills in Los Angeles—full of rich people. Many foreign embassies are located here," Asil said.

"I'm Canadian, not American," Mozhdah responded.

Asil made no response to her correction but went on to explain that Mozhdah's residence was located across a laneway from the 1TV station, close to the street where the German embassy was.

"That's good isn't it?" Mozhdah asked. "That means it's safe."

Asil paused before answering. "It is well protected."

The Land Cruiser bumped over potholes—some seemingly large enough to swallow one of the diminutive Toyota Corollas favored by Afghans—making Mozhdah appreciate the vehicle's excellent suspension system. Near their destination, they turned onto a road with traffic barricades. The impediments forced vehicles to slow to a crawl, theoretically deterring a suicide bomber from roaring close to a target and detonating. There were three check stops with armed security, and the driver rolled down his window at each stop to show identification and speak tersely to the guard, who glanced briefly inside, face expressionless, at Mozhdah and Nasrin. At one stop, another guard walked around the vehicle with a mirror on the end of a long handle to check the undercarriage for hidden explosives.

"I don't know whether to feel safer with this level of security—or less safe because these precautions are necessary," Mozhdah whispered to Nasrin.

"They wouldn't do it unless they had to," Nasrin nodded.

Finally, they rolled up to the guesthouse, which had huge heavy gray iron gates that were opened by guards on the inside. The vehicle stopped on the expansive tiled driveway and the guards who had accompanied them jumped out of the Land Cruiser first, then opened the doors for Mozhdah and Nasrin to disembark. Mozhdah stepped out gingerly in her high heels onto the smooth tiles, surprised at the chill in the air, looking around admiringly at a landscape of ornamental trees and flower gardens.

Asil led the pair towards the huge wooden double doors and opened one, allowing the women to step inside. Mozhdah gazed around in wonder. The foyer was an expanse of white-and-gray marble leading to a wide double staircase, also marble, with gilded banisters with elaborate scrolled designs. They moved into the living room off the foyer, where three people sat, awaiting their arrival. They stood up as the women entered the room. When Siobhan Berry introduced herself, Mozhdah and Nasrin hugged her like old friends. Siobhan commiserated with Mozhdah and Nasrin about their long journey and how exhausted they must feel.

Mozhdah smiled and nodded. "Yes, we're tired. I don't sleep well on planes."

"Let me make introductions," Siobhan said. "These two expats are Vicky McCluskey and Christopher Clark. Vicky is the art director and senior designer of 1TV's graphics, and Chris oversees the audio as well as doing the trailers and creating the news themes—he's our go-to sound guy."

Smiling, Mozhdah and Nasrin shook their hands.

Siobhan briefed them on the schedule. It was expected that Nasrin and Mozhdah would want to sleep and recuperate from the long flight. She nodded towards a boy off to the side, who smiled shyly.

"This is Mousa," Siobhan said, "he will show you to your rooms."

There was food and drink in the dining room that they could help themselves to. Siobhan would try to join them later for dinner, as she lived in the house as well. Tomorrow would be their first meeting, at 9:00 AM sharp in the 1TV studio. She would escort Mozhdah and Nasrin there. Siobhan added that the compound was well guarded, and there was no need to worry about safety.

"What will we be doing tomorrow?" Mozhdah asked, stifling a yawn.

The meeting would include Fahim Hashimy, the owner of 1TV, as well as CEO David Reid. Siobhan smiled and remarked how much they would like David, who also resided in the guesthouse.

"Looking forward to it," Mozhdah replied.

After chatting a bit more, Mozhdah and Nasrin were escorted up the staircase by Mousa. Mozhdah entered the bedroom, noting that her luggage had already been brought up. Golden light filtered through the high stately windows onto a room just as elegant and well appointed as the rest of the house, with an expansive bed and matching headboard, dresser, nightstand, and vanity, as well as an en suite bathroom with marble floors and thick towels. She happily noted the lock on her door. *They are spoiling me*, Mozhdah thought— *not that I'm complaining.*

Jet-lagged and bone-tired, Mozhdah unpacked and lay down for a snooze. She slept through the evening and awoke well before dawn, read a book in bed, then dressed carefully for the morning meeting. When she heard stirrings from the other houseguests, she ventured downstairs for breakfast. Famished, Mozhdah had several helpings of toast, hard-boiled eggs, and coffee with Siobhan, Vicky, Christopher, and Nasrin.

"I'll fill you in on a few details about 1TV that you might not know, to prep you for this morning's meeting," said Siobhan, sipping coffee. "I've been here for a while. Fahim, 1TV's owner, headhunted me from MTV Asia Pacific in Bangkok to train one hundred and fifty young local Afghans up to the broadcasting standards that you'd see in the West."

"You look so young to have so much responsibility," Nasrin exclaimed.

Siobhan laughed. "Thank you! I needed help, obviously, and brought in some great colleagues to be director of photography, graphic designer, audio director, and production manager. You've already met two of them: Vicky and Christopher," Siobhan said. "Another staff member, who you haven't met yet, is Australian Mick Demontigny. He's the director of photography and is teaching the camera operators how to hold a camera and getting them up to speed on lighting, framing, and camera movement."

Siobhan continued: "1TV's programming is in Farsi and Pashto and encompasses news, dramas, and entertainment programs, as well as reality, game, children's, and cooking shows. Our vision is to use television to help change and improve the conditions of Afghans. Not all Afghans are fans, obviously," Siobhan said.

"The Taliban?" Nasrin said worriedly.

Siobhan nodded. "Fahim won't let me go anywhere without an armed guard."

"We were under heavy guard just driving here from the airport," Mozhdah said.

"Don't expect that to change," Siobhan said dryly.

Siobhan briefed the pair on the background of the CEO, David Reid. An American, David had been involved in broadcasting management for decades and came to Kabul at the request of Fahim from Turkey, where he had been general director of Fox Television in Istanbul. David arrived in Kabul on October 3, 2009, and 1TV aired two weeks later, on October 17, 2009.

"The first broadcast was chaotic," said Siobhan. "That morning, there was a suicide bomb attack on the Indian embassy in Kabul, about a third of a mile away from the station. The blast killed seventeen people, and dozens were wounded. One of our news reporters grabbed a camera and ran out the door at the sound of the blast. So our first news report showed footage and exclusive on-scene interviews, along with analysis," she said with satisfaction. "We showed we are a legitimate competitor in the industry—equal to anyone."

After freshening up in their rooms, Mozhdah and Nasrin were escorted by Siobhan across the guesthouse compound, through the high iron gates and across the lane, past another well-guarded, high metal gate into the 1TV compound. Mozh-dah had dressed for the meeting in stylish, pale pink capri pants, a white blazer, and cream-colored high heels. Nasrin, dressed in a black blazer, black pants, and red heels, carried a large roomy handbag. Both of them wore chiffon hijabs draped loosely around their heads. Siobhan answered questions about Kabul's social life—Mozhdah was pleased that there actually was one—during the short walk across the compound, then across the road into the studio. She pointed out the cavernous sets with cycloramas and tracking that allowed for a variety of backgrounds, as well as studio cameras and teleprompters. To one side, Mozhdah spied a large production control room, currently dark, with multiple banks of screens.

Siobhan turned down a concrete hallway to the boardroom, the click of their heels echoing loudly. Mozhdah could hear muted voices off in the distance.

The door to the boardroom was ajar, and Siobhan pushed it open. There were numerous people seated around the table. David Reid was distinguishable right away, being the oldest in a group of men and women in their late teens and twenties. Fahim introduced himself. Mozhdah was shocked. She was expecting an older, wealthy-looking, heavyset guy. Here was this keen-eyed, charismatic, slender young man, carrying a subtle but distinctive air of authority. Staff associated with the production of *Afghanistan's Got Talent* were present, as was an administrator named Kardaar. Everyone introduced themselves, and Mozhdah and Nasrin leaned across the table to shake hands.

"*Sobh bakhair,*" Fahim said to Mozhdah.

"*Sobh bakhair,*" she replied.

Fahim began to speak rapidly to Mozhdah in Farsi. She understood what he was saying, but... he spoke so quickly. She stopped him several times. *"Lotfan takrar konaid"*—"Could you please repeat that?" Once or twice she was forced to respond, *"Man in ra namedanam"*—"I don't understand."

Fahim's face was inscrutable. Then Mozhdah noted two people, the ones who had introduced themselves as *Afghanistan's Got Talent*'s director and producer, Mukhtar and Saber, whispering.

Fahim directed his next comment to them. "Is there a problem?"

"Can we speak outside the boardroom?" the producer asked.

Fahim smiled and looked at the people seated at the table. "We'll just be a moment."

The three stepped into the corridor, and Fahim closed the door. Their voices rose to normal conversational volume. The thin walls of the boardroom allowed everyone to overhear.

"She can't speak Farsi!" Mozhdah heard Mukhtar say. "How can we have a show with a host who can't speak the language?"

Mozhdah heard a murmur from Fahim.

Mozhdah couldn't bear to look at anyone, her face hot with embarrassment.

The three stepped back into the boardroom and took their seats.

"You're not quite as fluent in Farsi as we hoped you would be," Mukhtar piped up in English as he took his seat at the table.

Fahim threw him a warning glance.

David looked at Mozhdah and said kindly, "Ah, Mozhdah, I suspect that you speak what Afghans refer to as 'sweet Dari.'"

Mozhdah looked at David, puzzled.

"'Sweet Dari,'" repeated David, "is the Dari—or Farsi, if you prefer—spoken by the children of the Afghan diaspora who grew up outside of Afghanistan. It is workmanlike but perhaps needs a bit of polish."

"Oh," said Mozhdah, feeling her stomach drop.

"It's not good enough for broadcast," the producer said.

"Fahim," David said, ignoring the comment, "couldn't we get Mozhdah some tutoring in Farsi?"

"Yes," Mozhdah said, relieved. "I'd love that."

Fahim looked curiously at Mozhdah. "Do you think you can learn to speak fluently in a few months?"

Mozhdah nodded. "I will speak perfect Farsi in very short order," she said. "Trust me."

"Well, this delays things a bit," said Fahim. "But we'll work on the premise that your Farsi will improve with tutoring. In the meantime, you can attend rehearsals and work with the producers."

Mozhdah said thank you, reiterating her determination to speak perfect Farsi soon. "I have a question," she said. "What are the dress policies for female on-air talent? Do you insist on headscarves? I didn't wear one in any of my music videos, except for 'Ya Sakhi,' of course, which honored Ramadan."

There was silence around the table as the producers glanced at one another.

"Not wearing a hijab will offend some viewers, as well as people in the government," Siobhan said, adding that it was doubtful that the station would be flexible on this policy.

David cleared his throat. "When I was general director at Fox TV in Istanbul, this issue came up as well. The religious conservatives said it was imperative that all women wear a hijab. But some of the younger staff pointed out that when

Muhammad himself said women should cover up, he wasn't referring necessarily to covering their heads. He was referring to women covering their jewels, like rubies or diamonds, if they had them. I understand that women are expected to be modest, but at a modern station like 1TV, why make Mozhdah wear a hijab?"

The producers began talking over one another and Fahim broke in. The issue, he said, wasn't negotiable at this point. But he was open-minded and would discuss it again in the future. In the meantime, he said, there were more pressing things to talk about, such as how to get *Afghanistan's Got Talent* on the air.

The production meeting continued until lunchtime, when Nasrin, Mozhdah, and Siobhan returned to the guesthouse for a simple meal of vegetable soup, cooked vegetables, fried eggplant, naan, and tea.

"I'm going to speak up this afternoon," Nasrin said to the other two at the dining room table.

"What about?" Siobhan asked.

Nasrin looked at Mozhdah, and the pair smiled conspiratorially. "You'll see. It will be a bit of a surprise, I think."

"Can't wait," Siobhan said cheerfully.

They returned to the studio an hour later. There were only a few more items to address, and as the meeting wound down, Nasrin sat up straight in her chair, cleared her throat, and said, "I have something to say."

Surprised, everyone looked at Nasrin, who had, until now, largely been silent. Nasrin plopped her large black handbag on the boardroom table, unzipped it, and pulled out the six-disc DVD set of *The Oprah Winfrey Show—20th Anniversary Collection* that she had brought with her from Canada.

"Who has heard of Oprah?" Nasrin asked.

The Afghans shook their heads, looking puzzled. David and Siobhan's eyebrows shot up in disbelief.

"I've heard all of you talk about this musical reality show, and as Mozhdah's manager, I'm not too sure whether *Afghanistan's Got Talent* is right for her."

The producer glared.

"I am suggesting," Nasrin replied, speaking in Farsi, "that you watch these DVDs after the meeting. They are in English, but from what I can tell, you all know enough English to understand what's going on. Oprah is a talk show host in the United States. She has helped change race relations in America, and she has enlightened people about child abuse, domestic abuse, and sexual abuse. She has helped people understand one another, as well as themselves. She has taught people how important empathy, kindness, and understanding are. She has educated people about things like mental illness. Year after year, she has changed people's lives for the better.

"This is the kind of show that 1TV should be broadcasting— not *Afghanistan's Got Talent*—because this is what Afghans need," Nasrin said boldly. "Mozhdah is the perfect person to host such a show."

Everyone in the room stared in shock at Nasrin. Mozhdah was careful to avoid looking anyone directly in the eye—she could sense the heated glower of the producer. *Go, Mom!* she thought to herself.

"You," Nasrin continued, unperturbed by the shocked faces, "have homework to do. Take these DVDs, watch them, and let's meet back here tomorrow to discuss."

There was silence while everyone waited for Fahim's reaction. It felt like all the oxygen had been sucked out of the room.

Mozhdah realized she had been holding her breath and took a gulp of air.

Fahim looked amusedly at Nasrin, holding her gaze, then directed his attention back to the producers. They should, he said, spend the evening watching the DVDs Nasrin had brought. Tomorrow, they would report back to him. Fahim then wished everyone a good evening and, grabbing his notebook, strode from the room, expression opaque.

"I didn't catch what you were saying in Farsi," David said to Nasrin. "What's just gone on?"

"I told Fahim and the producers that Mozhdah's not going to do *Afghanistan's Got Talent*," Nasrin said firmly. "Fahim's going to give Mozhdah her own show—inspired by *The Oprah Winfrey Show*."

David sat speechless, a smile slowly breaking on his face. Siobhan grinned broadly. Mozhdah looked at them both, relieved, then winked at Nasrin, who zipped her handbag shut. Both cheerily waved goodbye before walking out the door and down the hallway, their heels clicking on the concrete, the sound of loud, breathless chatter breaking out behind them.

CHAPTER 10

An Explosive
Welcome

B Y THE TIME Mozhdah and Nasrin came down
for breakfast the next morning, Siobhan was
already at the studio. They spoke in muted
tones, in English, so that Mousa, the houseboy who served
them their eggs, toast, and tea, wouldn't understand what they
were saying.

"I'll bet they're still in shock at 1TV," Mozhdah said. "I can't
believe you told Fahim that his show wasn't good enough. You
were so . . . composed."

Nasrin smiled. "Why have a talent contest when an intelligent talk show would help address the social ills of this
country?"

Mozhdah laughed. "No contest! I have so many ideas! I know
I can make a difference. We could make it fun—entertaining.
I could sing, we could feature different Afghan musicians, we
would have so many discussions—everyone would watch!"

Nasrin took a sip of tea and placed the cup down on the table before answering. "Yes, Mozhdah *jan*, I agree."

After breakfast, the pair strolled across the courtyard, nodding a greeting at the armed guards dotting the perimeter, then walked across the street into the 1TV compound and studio. Footsteps echoing sharply in the cavernous space, they spied Siobhan in the distance, heading towards the boardroom, a cup of coffee in one hand, files tucked under the other arm. Siobhan waited for them at the doorway.

"Ready for this morning's meeting?" Siobhan asked.

"Sort of," Mozhdah said nervously.

The boardroom was humming with energetic chatter as they walked in. A chorus of good mornings—some in English, some in Farsi—greeted them. That was a good sign, Mozhdah thought. If the word had come down from Fahim to send her and Nasrin back to Canada, the atmosphere wouldn't be so cheery.

Siobhan started the meeting. David, she told them, sent his regrets, but had another meeting he had to attend. But he wanted everyone to know that he was supportive of a talk show based upon *Oprah*.

"Did you get a chance to watch the *Oprah* DVDs last night?" Siobhan asked.

There was a pause as everyone looked at each other.

"I *love* this woman!" exclaimed Saber.

Everyone burst out laughing. Mozhdah felt a wave of relief.

Mozhdah responded: "We love her too. We've spent years watching her show while working in Mom's hairdressing salon at home in Vancouver."

Siobhan then asked Mozhdah, Nasrin, and the staff how they might envision such a talk show for an Afghan audience.

They discussed the length of time—everyone agreed to an hour-long time slot—and how they might meld entertainment with more hard-hitting, difficult, or even taboo subjects. As Mozhdah knew from her journalism training, it was important that experts help people address their personal and familial problems, guiding the dialogue. The format would feature an individual, several individuals, or even a family discussing personal experiences related to the day's selected topic. Mozhdah would facilitate this setup, acting as moderator. It was important that any expert she might have on the show, be they a physician, teacher, or psychiatrist, had academic or industry credentials and the ability to present objective analysis. As she spoke, Mozhdah thought back to the young *spandis*—trying to earn a bit of money by waving a burning can of herbs to bless motorists—and suggested that this was a social problem that should be investigated. Why were they on the street? Wouldn't these children rather be in school? Looking into the lives of *spandis* would make them relatable to a public who dismissed them as beggars. The circumstances that created the existence of *spandis*—poverty, illiteracy, and child labor— would be addressed as part of the investigation, Mozhdah suggested.

"Can you give another example?" Mukhtar asked curiously.

"How about domestic abuse?" Mozhdah said. Despite the fact that Afghan women were entering the workforce, running for office, and becoming educated in greater numbers, they were still the victims of violence, inflicted mainly by male relatives, Mozhdah told them. She had been reading the extensive reporting on this widespread social problem, and less than a year ago, in August 2009, Afghanistan's government had introduced the Elimination of Violence against Women law. "The

United Nations Assistance Mission in Afghanistan is monitoring whether the law is being implemented," Mozhdah said. "It will be important for us to report upon their findings. Remember what the Taliban used to say when they were in power? 'A woman's place is only in the home or in the ground.' We have to address this still-prevalent attitude."

Mukhtar interjected: "How do you do that when such things are so deeply integrated into Afghan tradition—even our religion?"

That's the central question, Mozhdah thought to herself. "One of the ways to address such traditions is through education," she explained, choosing her words carefully. "This is why it helps to bring in experts who have studied family violence and can speak to the consequences of physical abuse. Children who are spanked or beaten," Mozhdah continued, "tend to have low self-esteem. They feel shame, as well as fear of their parents. They are more likely to be violent towards their siblings, as well as other children and animals. Also, if they see their father beating or berating their mother—calling her names—they might grow up to become abusers as well. We could bring families onto the show and have a psychologist explain to them alternative ways to discipline and control their children," said Mozhdah. "Some experts say that childhood punishment is the root of violence in the world. For a country like Afghanistan still trying to overcome decades of war, this makes the issue of domestic violence really important. How we treat our children," Mozhdah said firmly, "affects our future—the future of this country."

There was an uncomfortable silence. Mozhdah wondered if the 1TV staff were reflecting upon unhappy circumstances in their own families—their own lives.

Mukhtar piped up. "Such things need to be discussed but never are. It would be impossible to get a family to agree to come on the show and admit they beat their kids."

Siobhan interjected. "What if," she said, "the show had actors who *pretended* to be a family—Mom, Dad, kids—and were given a scenario to act out? Perhaps the boy had stolen some food meant for dinner and was caught and hit by a parent. An expert could provide alternative disciplines to corporal punishment. It would be easy for viewers to envision themselves in such a scenario," she said.

Mukhtar said, "But what about that new law, the Elimination of Violence against Women? Some people have denounced it as 'un-Islamic.' You know that the Quran grants men the right to beat their wives. Shows like this might be too controversial."

Mozhdah flushed with anger. Although she considered herself secular, she was fascinated by religion and its effect on people and was well versed in the Quran from reading English translations. She had heard men repeat what she considered an abhorrent misinterpretation of verse 4:34 in the Quran, giving them the right to beat or strike their wives if they were disobedient or defiant.

"These are the kinds of things we need to address and challenge," said Mozhdah, careful to keep her voice even. "In Afghanistan, is spousal abuse more cultural, or does it occur because it is religiously sanctioned? According to my understanding of Islam, striking a woman is unacceptable."

There were low murmurs around the table. Assent or dissent? Mozhdah wasn't sure. Afghanistan, she thought, had a long way to go.

Everyone began chatting at once, suggesting additional scenarios that could impart a lesson about family dynamics.

Siobhan looked up from the notes she was fiercely scribbling. "I'll run them past David when I see him later," she said.

The group broke for lunch, and Siobhan walked with Nasrin and Mozhdah back to the guesthouse for a meal of *Kabuli palaw*, a rice dish with raisins and carrots.

"I really think that Fahim and David are going to love these ideas," said Siobhan. "There's nothing like this in Afghanistan right now. And, as you said, it is sorely needed. When so many people are illiterate, what better way to introduce new concepts than on television?"

After lunch, the production crew gathered again to discuss additional topics and ideas for shows. Mozhdah could conduct interviews with experts and government officials, as well as interview Afghan celebrities: actors, directors, musicians, and authors. They would incorporate music into every show, possibly with a house band. Mozhdah could sing her hits, or new songs, as well as traditional Afghan folk songs. Although it would not be a variety show, the mix of issues, entertainment, and interesting people would appeal to a broad audience.

"Thinking along those same lines," said Siobhan, "when is the best time to run this? What do you think about prime time—Thursday and Friday night?"

In Muslim countries, Thursday is the end of the workweek—equivalent to Friday in the West. There were nods around the table; the weekend was the best time to attract a large audience.

Siobhan remarked that she supported taking on some of the more controversial issues, but slowly, adding that the audiences at home needed to get to know Mozhdah first, learn to like and trust her.

"We have to make the show an integral part of people's lives so that when controversial topics come up, viewers think about what they saw—even if they don't agree with it—rather than calling for the show to be banned," Mozhdah responded.

No one disagreed.

THE NEXT MORNING, Mozhdah breakfasted alone with Vicky McCluskey, the two leisurely sipping their morning tea. Mozhdah was settled in Afghanistan and Nasrin had clients to attend to at the salon, so she had returned the previous night to Canada.

"I'm so excited about this show," Mozhdah said to Vicky. "Everything is coming together so quickly. There's a sense of synergy and energy—the 1TV producers just seem to *get* it."

Vicky nodded. She began, "It's as if..." but was cut off by a sudden explosive boom.

The house shook from the roof to its foundations. The glass in the windows trembled. Ripples appeared on the surface of their tea.

"What was that? Has someone crashed a vehicle into the house?" Mozhdah exclaimed.

The cook, Bibi Haji—Bibi meaning "lady of the house"— rushed into the dining room from the kitchen. "A bomb!" she cried.

"Where did it hit?" Mozhdah asked, trying to keep calm.

"I don't know," Bibi replied, panicked.

Mousa came running into the dining room, out of breath. "A rocket!" he exclaimed. "A rocket. On the corner... the TV station..."

"What?" exclaimed Mozhdah. "The station's been hit?"

"No, no," Mousa said agitatedly. "The building. Where the guards stay."

Mozhdah heard someone thundering down the stairs from the second-floor bedrooms. It was David Reid, carrying an AK-47. "Is everyone okay?"

"David!" exclaimed Mozhdah, startled at the sight of this normally composed man awkwardly holding the menacing weapon. "We're okay." What was David thinking, running around with such a weapon in response to a missile hit? Mozhdah hoped he had the safety catch on.

"The blast was huge, just outside the TV station," David said, his voice shaking.

His cell phone rang. His tense, clipped responses made it clear he was being apprised of the extent and damage of the blast. "Uh-huh. Anyone hurt? Yup."

David sighed and sat down heavily on a dining room chair, his shoulders slumped, as if the adrenalin and energy in his body had vaporized. The AK-47 lay across his lap. Mozhdah could hear the high-pitched wail of approaching emergency vehicles. "None of the guards, or anyone from the station, was hurt," David said.

"Thank God," said Mozhdah.

"But the windows are blown out, and there is glass in the compound and inside the studio. Please don't go outside today, and stay away from windows. We're going to have to install some kind of protection—mats or something—in the windows here in the house."

He looked at Mozhdah, sadness and worry making the lines in his face more prominent. "I don't think we're going to get much work done on your show before everyone leaves for the Christmas holidays," he said apologetically. "It's going to take a few days to get everything cleaned up and new windows put in."

"Don't worry about that," said Mozhdah. "What's important is that no one was hurt."

David smiled wanly at Mozhdah. "On a lighter note, Fahim, Siobhan, and I have had a chance to go over some of the ideas that you and the producers came up with. Some of the ideas are great, and Fahim has agreed to the name, *The Mozhdah Show*. It'll be a bit like *Oprah*, except we'll have a stronger entertainment element. You'll sing, and there'll be guest singers and musicians, as well as something for kids. Fahim has decided to put *Afghanistan's Got Talent* on the back burner for now."

"That is phenomenal news!" Mozhdah exclaimed. "Thank you so much. I'm so excited!"

"It *is* exciting," David responded. "And it's thanks to you and Nasrin that this is happening. You had the courage to come here and challenge Fahim about a critical programming choice that would have given 1TV a huge national presence. You showed us something even better. Something..." David paused, seemingly too emotional to speak. When he did, it was in a quiet, thoughtful voice. "I think, Mozhdah, that you'll show Afghan women and girls how much potential they have, if only they were given support and opportunity."

Tears came to Mozhdah's eyes and she nodded. Things could be—should be—so different for Afghan girls and women, for all Afghans who faced the daily threat of bombs and violence.

David cleared his throat, smiling. "I have some more good news. A friend of mine, who used to live in your home city of Vancouver, is coming here in January to help me get the station's advertising team up and running. His name is Steve Comrie." Steve, David explained, would be taking a hiatus from his position as a general manager at a Fox TV station in California. He was an expert in building technology companies and telecommunication networks and had immigrated to the U.S. to help David start a company in Seattle that provided telecommunication networks for large phone companies. "So, the good news is: we'll get advertising support for *The Mozhdah Show*. This station is going to throw its support behind you. Your show will be amazing," said David.

"I know it will be, thanks to people like you," Mozhdah said, using enthusiasm to mask her fear and horror over the nearby explosion. She wondered if the rocket had been meant for the 1TV station. How surreal, she thought, to be speaking calmly about her talk show with her CEO shortly after a rocket attack. And she wondered, not for the last time, whether she had done the right thing in coming to Afghanistan.

EARLY THE NEXT morning, Mozhdah ventured out of her compound, crossing the hot, dusty paved road to the 1TV grounds to look at the damage to the station. About fifty yards away lay a jumble of concrete where the rocket had hit. It was terrifying seeing the destruction from this distance, and she didn't dare go any closer. Inside the 1TV compound, workmen with large brooms brushed chunks of glass from shattered windows into a pile on the concrete.

David, who was supervising, noticed Mozhdah and shooed her back to the guesthouse. "I'll come and talk to you later today," he said. "I think you should leave Afghanistan early. We have too much work to do to get the station back into shape."

Mozhdah returned to the house and, after going through

the gates into the compound, was surprised to see a cow with a rope around its neck, standing near the house. An elderly man in a knee-length shirt and trousers called *peran tomban* held the rope as the cow sniffed at the green leaves of a rosebush. Mozhdah spied a large machete hanging from a belt around the farmer's waist.

Mozhdah walked quickly inside the house, loudly calling: "Bibi Haji! Mousa! Why is there a cow in our compound?"

Mousa trotted out of the kitchen. Mozhdah could hear the thud of someone coming quickly down the stairs leading to the foyer. It was Vicky, who stopped and looked curiously at Mozhdah and Mousa, who were speaking in Farsi.

"I think that Mr. David has ordered it for *khairat*," Mousa told her.

"Explain it to me," said Mozhdah, who knew about *khairat* but realized there might be different interpretations.

"*Khairat* is something you do when a great danger has passed," Mousa said. "The rocket attack could have killed us. Only by the will of Allah are we alive today. In exchange for Allah's goodness, we must help the poor."

"How does the cow fit into this?" Mozhdah asked.

"We have to slaughter it and give the meat to the needy."

"Here?" Mozhdah asked incredulously. "You can give thanks to Allah in other ways, by giving away money, clothing, anything. You don't have to slaughter an innocent animal." She turned to Vicky. "Please, Vicky, go get David. Quickly!"

Vicky nodded and strode out the door.

Mozhdah went back outside. "You can't do this," she said in Farsi to the farmer, who stared at her, confused. She flashed back to a horrific day in Pakistan when she was a child and a lamb had been killed for a *khairat* sacrifice in their backyard.

The terror in the tiny, frail animal's eyes, the agony as its throat was cut, the struggle to get away—the limbs waving back and forth—the bright gush of arterial blood, the final rasping gasps. This was not going to happen here.

About five minutes later, David came running up, breathing hard, followed by Vicky. "What's going on?" he demanded.

"This cow is going to be sacrificed, because the rocket didn't hit us. It's not by Allah's will over anyone else's that we weren't hit. This cow won't change anything. If this animal is killed, I'm going home and I'm not coming back," Mozhdah said in a choking voice. "I mean it."

"I'm sorry Mozhdah. I thought it would be a way to help people get over the shock. I'll take care of it, don't worry. I didn't realize you would be so upset."

David disappeared to find someone who would speak to the farmer with him.

Vicky put her arm around Mozhdah. "Let's go into the house," she said. "David will make sure that poor animal isn't killed."

"He'd better," Mozhdah said angrily.

The next day, her suitcases packed, her plane out of Kabul scheduled for later that afternoon, Mozhdah walked over to the 1TV compound to bid farewell to David and the 1TV staff. She said hello to the guards standing at the gate, and they returned the greeting.

One, however, in a cold voice, said: "That was not good what you did yesterday—sending the farmer away and saving the cow. There will be repercussions. You will see," he said, ominously.

Mozhdah rolled her eyes at him and crossed the road to the 1TV studio.

CHAPTER 11

The Oprah of Afghanistan

FTER SAYING HER goodbyes at 1TV, Mozhdah returned to the guesthouse, deciding to use the free time to reply to a cache of neglected emails before she left for the airport. She sat on the bed, perusing the subject lines, deleting those she wasn't interested in reading, opening messages from friends in Canada, the United States, Afghanistan, and other parts of the world, typing brief, friendly replies. Her finger hovered momentarily over the delete button when she came to an email with "White House" in the subject line, but then she realized it was from her friend in Washington, D.C., Tim Nusraty, an adviser to President Barack Obama. She clicked it open and read it. She read it again, and again.

"Oh my God!" she shrieked.

"Are you okay?" Vicky exclaimed, sticking her head through the doorway of Mozhdah's room.

"Read this," Mozhdah said excitedly.

Vicky looked over Mozhdah's shoulder at her computer. She scanned the email, then read it out loud. Mozhdah was being invited to the White House to sing "Afghan Girl" on International Women's Day in front of President Obama and his wife, First Lady Michelle Obama. Tim had put forth Mozhdah's name as a musical guest. Vicky gave Mozhdah an excited hug.

"I've always imagined meeting Barack Obama," Mozhdah squealed. "I can't believe this is happening! I've watched every speech he's ever made! What should I say in my reply to Tim? 'Dear Tim: Thank you for making a dream come true.' That's a bit undignified," she said, and burst into laughter.

The December holiday season went by in a blur. Mozhdah spent part of the month in the Netherlands, where she was a headliner, along with other Afghan singers, at a concert for the Afghan diaspora. In the decade leading up to 2002, the Netherlands had been the second-most-popular destination in Europe, behind Germany, for Afghan asylum seekers, and nearly forty thousand people of Afghan origin were living in the nation of 16 million. Rather than return home to Vancouver for the holidays, Mozhdah stayed in Europe visiting relatives. It was a working holiday, with a constant exchange of emails with 1TV producers about programming, set design, music, outfits, and other minutiae. Mozhdah occasionally voiced her opposition to wearing a hijab on the show. It became clear that the producers would not compromise on this issue.

The thought of singing at the White House was a happy distraction from work concerns. Mozhdah emailed Tim about proper protocol, etiquette, and how formal, or informal, an event it was. She had met Tim, an Afghan-American attorney with the U.S. National Security Council, after performing at the Afghanistan embassy in the nation's capital the previous August to celebrate Afghan Independence Day. They had become friends; Mozhdah was impressed by his kindness, intelligence, and love of music. In turn, Tim was impressed by Mozhdah's talents and warmth and what an excellent ambassador she was for Afghanistan.

After the sold-out concert in the Netherlands, and relaxing family visits with meals of traditional Afghan food, Mozhdah returned to Kabul, excited to dive into show production, trying to push the thought of future rocket attacks out of her mind. She immediately began Farsi tutoring with Dr. Mohammad Zaman Rajabi, who had studied psychology at the University of Philadelphia and been booked as *The Mozhdah Show*'s regular guest psychologist. As Nasrin put it, Dr. Rajabi would be Afghanistan's version of Dr. Phil. Oprah Winfrey had been behind the creation of the talk show *Dr. Phil*, hosted by Phillip McGraw, who doled out blunt and often stern but commonsense advice to people in crisis.

Often, Dr. Rajabi would revert to English during the tutoring sessions with Mozhdah. "This way," he said, "I can practice my English and you can practice your Farsi—it's a win-win!"

Mozhdah smiled to herself, thinking that it rather defeated the point of tutoring lessons. More helpful was the "swear jar" that was placed in the studio for Mozhdah's benefit. If anyone heard her speak English, she was immediately fined five dollars, which went straight into the jar.

While Mozhdah practiced her Farsi, the team excitedly waited for the arrival of Steve Comrie on January 18. If David's stories about his friend were anything to go by, Steve had the experience and skills to turn 1TV into a viable, self-supporting entity independent of foreign aid from Western nations—unlike so many initiatives and projects in Afghanistan.

That day, Mozhdah awoke to hear faint voices: David's and one she didn't recognize, speaking English downstairs. Steve must have arrived safely, she thought, and got up to prepare for the studio workday. But when she arrived at the breakfast table, nobody was there, and since it was Monday—a slow day—she finished a leisurely breakfast and returned to her room to grab her computer, notepad, purse, and sunglasses.

Suddenly, a heart-stopping explosion shook the house to its foundations. The glass in the windows, which had been covered with matting to prevent shards flying into the room, reverberated violently. This time, Mozhdah had no doubt what had caused it—either a rocket or a car bomb had detonated nearby. A surge of panic engulfed her. Should she go downstairs? Mousa was probably already investigating. Certainly a 1TV camera crew would be sprinting out of the studio to cover the blast. Possibly the studio itself had been hit—it felt that close.

After the explosion, there was a period of eerie silence, as if the whole city were waiting for another blast. Mozhdah gulped a lungful of air, realizing that she had been holding her breath. Then her heart leaped in terror, as the harsh, earsplitting staccato of AK-47 gunfire rent the air. Suddenly, David's weapon made sense. What if the attackers got into the guesthouse compound? She was unarmed and completely vulnerable. Was this to be a necessary part of living in Kabul: learning how to handle a machine gun? A day ago, she would have dismissed the thought. Today, with gunfire exploding just outside the walls, she pledged to learn how to fire a weapon.

Mozhdah stayed in her room for an hour after the shooting stopped, then poked her head out the front door. The courtyard guards, tense and vigilant, their weapons ready to fire, agitatedly waved her back inside. She turned on the television set in the living room to watch the news on 1TV, switching between it and the competing TOLO TV channel. Details emerged. The attack was part of a huge coordinated operation involving twenty Taliban fighters, several of them suicide bombers. President Hamid Karzai was swearing in new cabinet ministers that day, and this was the Taliban's demonstration of contempt for Afghanistan's fledgling democracy. Launched at 9:50 AM, the attack focused on the center of the city. Taliban fighters had set fire to a shopping center complex, and a suicide bomber detonated explosives outside the central bank, located next to the presidential palace. Another suicide bomber, driving a van painted to resemble an ambulance, detonated his vehicle outside a different shopping center. Insurgents took over a building beside the Ariana cinema, taking two children hostage. The five-star Serena Hotel came under attack. Preliminary reports estimated the civilian death toll to be low, though dozens of people were wounded. A firefight was ongoing between the Taliban, armed with heavy machine guns as well as other guns and explosives, and Afghan security forces.

Mozhdah was overwhelmed by grief, fear, and rage. The battle had been close to the guesthouse—how close she wasn't yet sure. Maybe she should fly home to Canada. No, she chided herself, she couldn't give in to fear. She had worked hard to get this far, and so many people were depending upon her. *The Mozhdah Show* could prove to be a weapon and a bulwark against the hatred, ignorance, and religious fanaticism behind the rampant violence. And what message would she send to Afghan women if she were to go home? They faced possible death every time they walked out their front door. If she were to be a champion of women, Mozhdah realized, she would have to show just as much courage as the women of this country. Helping forge a path out of war, she was beginning to realize, would be a dark and difficult journey.

Mozhdah could not envision how dark the path would eventually become.

THE NEXT MORNING, as a tense silence hung over the city, Mozhdah went down to breakfast to see Steve Comrie sipping a cup of tea—a genial-looking man but with a pale and drained face. He stood up to shake Mozhdah's hand. "I hope you don't mind if I join you for breakfast," he said with a smile.

"Welcome to Afghanistan. We rolled out the fireworks just for you," she said wryly.

"Yes, you might have given me a bit of warning," Steve said. "It certainly made for an interesting day, and it gave me the chance to see the camera crews and news team in action. They were pretty impressive—they quickly pulled together some remarkable footage for the evening newscast. It helped that one of the attacks took place right beside us," he said lightly. He paused, taking a sip of his tea. "Hopefully this isn't too common an occurrence."

"Put it this way," Mozhdah replied. "It's not *uncommon*."

"Hmm, well, let's talk about something less depressing— your show! What a great concept. David told me how your mom—Nasrin?—instructed Fahim on what he was, and wasn't, going to do at his own station. Wish I'd been a fly on the wall."

Mozhdah laughed.

Steve continued: "A show based upon *The Oprah Winfrey Show*. Remarkable. I know how we can sell this to advertisers and get international media publicity and support from foreign offices here. We'll market you as the Oprah of Afghanistan!"

Mozhdah laughed again. "You're comparing me to the world's most admired talk show host. No pressure. I haven't even started the show yet. What if it's not even popular?"

"Impossible!" Steve replied enthusiastically. "I've seen your tapes, heard your voice. I saw how you were with a test audience. In the television business, when we're trying to engage an audience or create something outstanding, we call that punch-through programming. It's something that really grabs everyone's attention. *The Mozhdah Show* will have that. I've been inside enough television stations to know what will work, what won't, and what will take off. You'll not only be 1TV's biggest star but Afghanistan's biggest star."

Mozhdah opened her mouth, but nothing came out. She flushed with embarrassment. "As I said, no pressure. I'll try to live up to your expectations."

Steve smiled. "I know you will. Luckily, the studio was unscathed during yesterday's attack, so I'd like to call a meeting with the production crew. I'm pulling together an advertising team, and it would be great if you could be there."

The days flew by in a blur of work and preparation, until March came and Mozhdah prepared for the flight to Washington, D.C., for International Women's Day. Nasrin arrived in Kabul from Vancouver with suitcases of clothes, not only for the show but also for Mozhdah to select new outfits to wear in Washington. Mozhdah picked several possible dresses to wear at the White House. One, a flowing full-length green chiffon dress with subtle floral designs and cap sleeves—a perfect spring dress—caught her eye. It was an outfit respectful of a modernizing but still-conservative Afghanistan.

The celebration was to take place in the famous and sumptuously decorated White House East Room, where many receptions, concerts, dances, ceremonies, banquets, and major events—such as Obama's first press conference after being elected the country's first African-American president—had taken place. The room featured two enormous portraits: one of George Washington, America's first president, and one of his wife, Martha Washington.

President Obama and First Lady Michelle Obama had invited students, local residents, public school teachers, and nonprofit workers to honor the day alongside celebrities like Katharine McPhee and Kerry Washington, who hosted the event. Other attendees included former secretary of state Madeleine Albright, venerable civil rights activist Dorothy Height, and a host of Girl Guides from across the country. At the event, twenty women from around the world would be specially honored for their achievements in athletics, science, business, and the arts. Mozhdah was one of two performers; the other being McPhee, who was runner-up in the 2006 *American Idol* contest.

Nasrin and Mozhdah flew into Washington a week before the March 8 event to allow themselves to get over jet lag, go shopping, explore the tourist attractions, and enjoy dinner out with Tim Nusraty and his family. Being able to walk around the city unescorted by armed guards and not having to worry about suicide bombers was an enormous psychological relief. Mozhdah found herself smiling at the smallest things, from budding spring flowers to the smell of cut grass. By now, Mozhdah had spent about three months in Kabul and was beginning to understand the stress of living under

what amounted to constant siege. In Kabul, when she needed
a change of scenery, Mozhdah would leave the guesthouse to
attend a dinner party or go out to a restaurant with friends.
David, who worried about Mozhdah as if she were his own
daughter, tried to discourage her from such excursions. She
couldn't leave without armed guards, and only in an armor-
plated vehicle. David's anxiety and fear about her safety was
a damper on the evening. It was like being in prison, she
thought. And although she tried not to dwell on it, fear of the
next attack was always on her mind. Would suicide bombers
target a Kabul restaurant she was at? Would the next rocket
drop squarely on the 1TV studios or her residence?

As International Women's Day drew closer, Mozhdah
grew more nervous. The night before her performance, she
lay sleepless in her room at the One Washington Circle Hotel,
imagining forgetting the words to "Afghan Girl." She finally
fell asleep about 3:00 AM but awoke two hours later. Nasrin
was in a double bed in the same room, and Mozhdah quietly
ordered breakfast. Afterwards, Nasrin helped Mozhdah get
ready, using a curling iron to give her hair some wave and
tying it back with a purple flower. They debated which ear-
rings went best with Mozhdah's simple, pretty green dress. It
was warm and sunny—no rain, Mozhdah was relieved to see,
with the day promising to reach sixty-four degrees, according
to the hotel TV weather channel.

"So you've memorized what you're going to say today?" Nasrin asked.

"I'm just going over it in my head. It's not much more than a
thank-you, really," Mozhdah said, pale from nerves and lack of
sleep. "I still can't believe I'm going to meet President Obama
today."

Later that morning, Mozhdah waited in the hotel lobby for the limousine, sent by the White House, to pick her up. Upon arrival, the first priority was a sound check, but once that was out of the way, Tim Nusraty took Mozhdah on a quick tour of the East Wing, visiting the three Blue, Red, and Green state parlor rooms, with their sumptuous theme-colored draperies, painted walls, and enormous chandeliers. As the time for the actual event came closer, Mozhdah got a text message from Nasrin that she had arrived. Mozhdah peeked out the door, looking out upon the southeastern side of the White House grounds. A crowd had gathered and Mozhdah recognized a few luminaries, picking out Dorothy Height, thanks to her extravagant wine-red brimmed hat, right away. Dorothy was the godmother of the civil rights movement and had led the National Council of Negro Women for forty years. At age ninety-eight, though tiny and stooped, she was still very much a part of the struggle for equal rights. She still looked ready to march, Mozhdah thought.

As the crowd of mainly women and girls entered the reception room, a marine band played. Mozhdah took in the surroundings, determined to commit to memory every detail: the chandelier light posts, rich gold curtains, huge mirrors, and polished floors. Tim found Nasrin and led her to a chair at the front. He had wrangled it so that Nasrin would sit next to the president and the First Lady during the ceremony.

When Michelle Obama arrived, dressed in a tailored dark brown sheath dress, her hair in a smooth, short bob, Mozhdah, who wasn't in the audience but waiting in an adjoining room for her turn to sing, peeked out to watch. By Michelle's side was President Obama, elegant in a black suit, white shirt, and royal purple tie. Michelle opened the event with

a short speech, standing behind a lectern with the presidential seal on it. Mozhdah felt goose bumps as the First Lady
spoke: "We honor women who refused to listen to those
who would say that you couldn't or shouldn't pursue your
dreams. And we honor women who may not have had many
opportunities in their own lives, and we all know women
like that: women who poured everything they had into making sure that their daughters and their granddaughters could
pursue their dreams, women who, as the poet Alice Walker
once wrote, 'knew what we must know without knowing it
themselves.'"

Mozhdah felt the burden of those words, knew that she was
responsible for taking that message back with her to Afghanistan; somehow she must channel that same courage and spirit
into her show.

President Obama also gave a short speech, introducing the
emcee, actress Kerry Washington, as well as the two singers for the event: Katharine McPhee and—Mozhdah held her
breath—"Mozhdah Jamalzadah." She felt like her heart had
stopped, and she could barely draw breath from excitement.
How could she possibly sing? As President Obama addressed
the many advances that women had achieved globally and
in the U.S., he also decried the work that still needed to be
done. "Full gender equality has not yet been achieved." Still,
there were many things to applaud. These included, Obama
said, a new Violence against Women initiative that advocated
for affordable child care and parental leave, the special efforts
being made to recruit women into fields like engineering,
as well as the promotion of health care for women around
the world. Such progress was because of the work of "daring,
indomitable women," he said.

As Mozhdah forced herself to breathe slowly and calmly, Obama continued in his signature rhythmic cadence: "We lifted what is called the global gag rule that restricted women's access to family planning services abroad. We're pursuing a global health strategy that makes important investments in child and maternal health. We sponsored a UN resolution to increase protection for women and girls in conflict-torn countries, to help make it possible for more women like Mozhdah, who traveled from Afghanistan to join us here today, to reach for their dreams."

Mozhdah flushed, hearing Obama say her name a second time, and the buzzing in her ears made her miss the next few lines of his speech. Then she heard "... promoting women's empowerment is one of the best ways to promote economic development and economic success. We are doing it because it is the right thing to do."

I feel like ... Obama has my back, thought Mozhdah. *What a strange—and powerful—feeling.*

Twenty minutes into the event, Katharine McPhee sang a song she had written, titled "Surrender." At the half-hour mark, it was Mozhdah's turn to sing "Afghan Girl." She walked up to the podium, glanced down at her mother, seated next to Michelle, the president sitting beside his wife. Nasrin looked pleased and relaxed, as if sitting next to the presidential couple was the most ordinary thing in the world. Mozhdah began by thanking President Obama and acknowledged Michelle's contributions and leadership as a role model for women. "I came here from Kabul, Afghanistan, and I'm trying to do all that I can for the women of Afghanistan. My father and I wrote this song for the acid victims of Kandahar city. A few young girls were trying to make their way home from school when they got attacked by acid, and I thought I had to do something for them."

Mozhdah sang "Afghan Girl" in Farsi, nearly stumbling over the lyrics when she saw Michelle Obama take Nasrin's hand. When she had finished, Mozhdah said, "Thank you, thank you very much," smiled at the people in the room, and nodded her head shyly at the outbreak of loud, enthusiastic clapping. Kerry Washington then went to the podium to thank the attendees and the Obamas for hosting the event. Kerry mentioned that Mozhdah had translated some of the lyrics for her from the song, and she paraphrased them for the audience.

Gratitude swept through Mozhdah and she felt the power emanating from the youthful energy of the girls in the room, who were inheriting a world of gender inequality but were heirs to something so much more important: the bold, unshakeable, principled spirit of people like Dorothy Height and Michelle Obama. This occasion, Mozhdah thought, wasn't just about acknowledging the accomplishments of these women and the movements they were leading; it was a way to gather energy for the next grueling battle in the struggle for women's rights. Mozhdah also realized that every person in that room, from President Obama to Madeleine Albright, Dorothy Height, and Kerry Washington to the Girl Guides, supported her and believed in her struggle. She wasn't alone; there was an army behind her, and even though they wouldn't be with her physically when she returned to Kabul, their courage would bolster her own. *That's what women are*, Mozhdah thought. *We are all part of the same struggle. We fight together on a battlefield that spans the globe.*

In that moment, Mozhdah lost whatever fear she had about being in Afghanistan and the trepidation she felt about *The Mozhdah Show*. Whatever happened, she was one of thousands—no, millions—of women who were raising their voices, whether in song, like Mozhdah, or in speeches at the United Nations, or in a classroom in rural Afghanistan. She could not fail—would not fail—because these women trusted she wouldn't. How could she let them down? She thought of two lines from "Afghan Girl": "Don't break my wings, let me fly / Don't break my crown, let me think." She blinked rapidly to stop the tears that suddenly sprang to her eyes. *Women have a superpower, and it's their voices,* she thought. *The more we raise our voices, the more we raise each other up.* And she swore a pledge to the women and girls of Afghanistan: never, ever would she stop speaking out for them or stop fighting for them.

THE MOZHDAH SHOW began taping in Kabul a few weeks later, at the start of the Persian New Year. Still exhilarated by her visit to the White House, Mozhdah focused all her energy on the final production details, overseeing scripts and guest selection. She chuckled inwardly at the final set design: fuchsia walls and floor with matching guest couch and hostess armchair—catering to Afghans' love of bright colors—and a highly stylized "Mozhdah" written in Farsi on the back wall in large letters. Such a striking set necessitated equally dramatic dress, and Mozhdah opted for a consistent silhouette: high heels, leggings or fitted pants, tailored jackets, and ornate jewelry, her long hair covered in as understated a hijab as the producers let her get away with. This was her show, and Mozhdah's wide smile and take-charge attitude made that clear.

Production behind the scenes was not quite as smooth. During early strategy meetings, Mozhdah insisted on control over which topics would be addressed, causing some heated discussions with the producers. As they determined the show's first season lineup, Mozhdah frequently called Bashir to ask for advice. Because of his time in Kandahar as a cultural adviser for the Canadian Armed Forces, he was well versed in what conservative Afghans would tolerate. Mozhdah wanted to jump into the things that mattered to her most: Afghanistan's shocking rates of domestic violence against women, the need for Afghan society to allow women to initiate divorce proceedings in the case of spousal abuse, and child marriage.

"Not yet," Bashir said.

"Why?" Mozhdah demanded. "The statistics are horrifying."

Bashir explained that if Mozhdah were to dive headfirst into such controversial topics, the men—the decision-makers of the family in Afghanistan—would feel threatened and forbid their wives and children to watch the show. Viewers would be alienated. What Mozhdah could do, Bashir suggested, was slowly introduce the issue of family violence by first looking at child abuse. Mozhdah, said Bashir, had to get viewers to love her show and, more importantly, like and trust her. Then they would accept discussions about more difficult and controversial issues. Any criticism of Afghan customs and beliefs had to be presented so that viewers didn't perceive it as being an attack on the culture of Afghanistan itself, said Bashir.

"First," said Bashir, "get into their hearts. Then you can get into their minds."

"WHERE'S MOZHDAH?" Neelofar Neda, the producer of *The Mozhdah Show*, asked a nearby crewmember, who shrugged ignorance. "Go find her," said Neelofar. He spun around, looked about desperately, and sprinted off.

Mozhdah was still in the 1TV dressing room with makeup artist Khoshahmadi. They had finished Mozhdah's makeup but were still struggling with the hijab. Mozhdah refused to let it frame her face and hide her hair, as hijabs are supposed to do.

"That's not how I want it," Mozhdah snapped. "It has to be away from my face and off my hair as much as possible."

Khoshahmadi clucked his tongue in frustration and looked nervously at his watch. "We're supposed to be on set in a few minutes, Mozhdah. *Please* let me fasten your hijab."

"We would be on time if it wasn't for these stupid scarves. Attach it to the back of my hair like this," Mozhdah said, grabbing a pin. "I want my hair to fall in the front," she added, pulling her long wavy locks forward.

Khoshahmadi relented, securing the prettily embroidered chiffon hijab well away from her face, then tossed brushes, compacts, and lipsticks into his makeup case and clicked it shut. The two rushed out of the dressing room and down the hall to the door outside the studio. Mozhdah knew her tardiness would be causing stress among the producers. The only thing to do was emanate an aura of cool calm.

"Really, Mozhdah?" Neelofar said, standing just outside the door to the studio, pacing in her anxiousness. "You haven't pre-interviewed your guest singer. You really need to be on time from now on. You're on in five minutes."

"But someone has pre-interviewed him with the questions I'll be asking, right?"

"Yes," Neelofar said, handing Mozhdah the interruptible feedback earpiece, allowing one-way communication. Mozhdah's Farsi was still imperfect, and the earpiece allowed

Neelofar to whisper a word or phrase to Mozhdah when she sensed an impending verbal stumble.

"Then he'll be fine," said Mozhdah, adjusting the earpiece and smoothing her hair over it. "Let me have a quick look at the questions so I don't have to rely too much on the teleprompter, and please get me my mic. Where's my mic?"

The studio door swung open and Rameen, director of *The Mozhdah Show*, strode out, his face contorted with stress and anger. "Get into the studio, Mozhdah, now!" he snapped.

"I'm waiting for my mic. I certainly can't go in without my mic, can I?" she retorted. "And don't you dare yell at me!"

"I'm about to cue the audience." He glared at Mozhdah, who glared back. He ducked into the control room, and Mozhdah could hear him cue the audience in Farsi, "Okay, everyone. It's time to begin *The Mozhdah Show*! We want you to show how excited you all are! Let's hear a round of applause." The audience clapped loudly, followed by Rameen exclaiming, "We need more excitement! Let's take it to the next level!" Not until the whistling, cheering, clapping, and stomping became ear-splitting did he cue Neelofar to send Mozhdah into the studio.

Neelofar whispered to Mozhdah, "Three, two, one... go," and opened the studio door to reveal a crowd of about 250 people, who had received special invitations from 1TV to be part of the audience. "Good luck!" Neelofar whispered, grinning.

Mozhdah walked out into a wall of noise, which grew louder as she came onto the stage. She noted how much more subdued the women and girls in the front of the audience were. Habituated since childhood to suppress their emotions, they were careful not to display any feelings.

"Hello!" Mozhdah said brightly in Farsi. "How is everyone today?"

The audience responded with more whistling and cheering. She spied David Reid sitting off to one side. Five huge television studio cameras, including a crane camera, faced her from different angles. Mozhdah was nearly overwhelmed by the boisterous energy in the room, and she thought how momentous this must be for all of the audience members, who had never been inside a dim studio, where it was cool, safe, and fun, where they could listen to live music and hear interesting discussions. It was, she thought, like a parallel universe, and wondered if it was also creating a fantasy that, for Afghans, could never come true. She pushed the thought out of her mind.

"We have a wonderful show for you today!"

CHAPTER 12

Making Television History

T HE MOZHDAH SHOW was broadcast twice a week—every Thursday and Friday in prime time. Both shows were taped on Friday: the first at 10:00 AM, the second at 2:00 PM. The producers followed the same format for each show: rev up the audience, and then Mozhdah would walk onstage, thank everyone for coming, greet the viewers at home, and present the show's agenda, including the special guest. Sometimes, the producers would keep the special guest a secret, to build audience anticipation.

Mozhdah was bent on addressing family abuse, especially violence against women, but followed Bashir's advice that she ease into these contentious issues by focusing on the challenges of rearing children and the use of corporal punishment in the home. Afghanistan has long been regarded as one of the worst places in the world for women, but children also suffer because of the extreme poverty, lack of proper medical care, and violence. Mozhdah constantly undertook online research and combed the latest reports from international NGOS and bodies like the United Nations. She shook her head at statistics from the United Nations Children's Fund (UNICEF) showing that Afghanistan's under-five mortality rate was 257 deaths for every 1,000 live births—the third worst in the world behind Angola and Sierra Leone. Reports from NGOS found that 90 percent of Afghan children were abused in some manner, including physical violence, sometimes as harsh as choking or kicking. Mental abuse consisted of insults and being sworn at. Parents, relatives, elders, or teachers usually perpetrated the abuse.

Mozhdah decided to focus on different aspects of child abuse over several shows. As she had planned, each show would incorporate an expert's viewpoint on the day's topic. Dr. Mohammad Zaman Rajabi, who had tutored her in Farsi, was her regular expert guest. A clinical psychology adviser at Kabul Mental Health Hospital, Dr. Rajabi was a rarity in the country—a child psychologist—and was well known and trusted. His hospital, located on the outskirts of Kabul, treated children traumatized by war and experiencing the nightmares, depression, and anxiety of PTSD, or post-traumatic stress disorder.

Each show began with Mozhdah posing questions to Dr. Rajabi. After a commercial break, several actors would put on a skit, presenting an everyday Afghan scene. An example would be an Afghan family enjoying tea together on a rug. One of the children might do something annoying or naughty, and the father would try to physically discipline the child. All too familiar with his parents' disciplinary methods, the youngster would sprint off. The father, growing ever more furious, would chase the child around the stage while the audience erupted with laughter. Eventually, Dad might grab the child and pretend to swat him, and the skit would be over. Mozhdah and Dr. Rajabi would then analyze what happened, and how the incident could have been approached differently. The messaging included speaking to the child, with the objective being to find alternative ways to modify behavior without inflicting physical harm.

Just before another commercial, Mozhdah would alert the audience to the next guest, often a singer. Following the break, the singer would be formally introduced and launch into their song. Afterwards, Mozhdah would interview the guest. She might get the individual to comment about the topic of the skit. If it had been child abuse, Mozhdah would ask them whether they had ever been hit as a child, and their thoughts on corporal punishment. This might lead to a discussion about the long-term effects of physically disciplining children and suggestions from the guest about other options.

The interview was followed by another skit, where the same actors would dramatize a different way to mete out discipline. Afterwards, Dr. Rajabi would analyze what had transpired, reaffirming the lesson being presented.

The final segment was usually a competition between two kids from the audience. Neelofar would devise an easy game: throwing balls into a basket or solving brainteasers. Both of the kids received prizes. The winner would get a larger prize, and depending upon which advertiser agreed to sponsor this segment, it could vary from toys to smartphones. Then the show would often end with a final song from the guest singer.

Because of the security measures necessary to film such a controversial show, none of the audience members who were staying for the second taping were allowed to leave the studio, so they were fed lunch. Often, an advertiser would sponsor the meal, and this generosity was acknowledged on the show. One of the studio favorites was KFC, which stood for Kabul Fried Chicken, a knockoff of Kentucky Fried Chicken. Kabul had various outlets, which had been opened by two competing rivals and copied the North American signage, including the iconic face of Colonel Sanders. Rather than milkshakes or fries, these KFC impersonators offered kebabs and pizza, as well as the usual fried chicken. The audience loved it, and Mozhdah sometimes wondered if one of the reasons people wanted to watch the filming was the promise of a free meal.

After each filming, Mozhdah stayed behind to chat with audience members and hear their feedback. After one show, a stout woman, with brown eyes and heavy eyebrows, her face worn, her clothes old but clean, wearing a green hijab, shyly introduced herself as Atefa. Mozhdah shook her hand, feeling the calluses from a lifetime of hard work.

"My family and I came all the way from Mazar-i-Sharif," Atefa said.

Mozhdah quickly calculated that it would have taken the family about six hours to drive to the studio, up to ten hours if they had taken the bus.

"Thank you for coming," Mozhdah responded.

Atefa struggled to find words, and Mozhdah waited patiently. Tears began to trickle down the woman's sun-browned skin. Then she grabbed Mozhdah in a hug and wouldn't let go.

What is making this woman so emotional? Mozhdah wondered, hugging her back.

Atefa released Mozhdah but kept hold of her hand. "I wanted to tell you," she said. "My husband doesn't beat our children anymore. And it's because of you and your show."

Mozhdah didn't say anything, afraid that she would burst into tears in front of the rest of the audience members still waiting to chat. The two women looked into one another's eyes, and Mozhdah knew that she didn't have to say anything at all.

ONE OF THE final shows of season 1 addressed an issue of great personal importance to Mozhdah—the power of positive thinking. Mozhdah had embraced the idea after reading *The Power* by Rhonda Byrne, who wrote that thoughts and feelings—good or bad—reflect back on a person like an echo. Mozhdah felt that she had experienced this phenomenon, accomplishing her goal of hosting her own talk show in Kabul. Afghans, she thought, tended to dwell on the negative, which, she conceded, given the decades of war, poverty, and violent death that two generations had now endured, made sense. But a sea change was happening in the country. Her show was a part of that. Her music was a part of that too, and Mozhdah endeavored to make her melodies and lyrics uplifting, and the songs that were politically charged empowering—especially for women.

Ever since the 2001 invasion by American-led coalition forces, the international community had made enormous efforts to help Afghans rebuild. The year before Mozhdah's show started, in June 2008, eighty donors at the Paris Conference in support of Afghanistan pledged more than $20 billion to bolster the nation's development strategies and promote human rights, socioeconomic advancement, and political and economic reform. But although people's lives were slowly changing for the better, the decades of war had taken their toll mentally. People lacked optimism and hope for the future. As Mozhdah told Neelofar one day, after rosebushes had been planted along the medians of Kabul city streets, "people see only the brown dust covering the roses, rather than the rose-bushes themselves."

Whereas some rural areas of Afghanistan were little better off than they had been under Taliban rule, Kabul was thriving, and Mozhdah wanted the citizens to acknowledge and celebrate the changes, which meant that positive things could happen in their lives too.

"For example," Mozhdah told the studio audience, "if you stub your toe getting out of bed in the morning, do you allow this to set the tone for the rest of the day? Or," she continued, "do you say, 'Oh, forget this, I'm going to have a great morning, and I'm not going to let this bother me.' To enhance positive feelings, you could play some music that you love, and dance around the house—just have a good time," Mozhdah said, "and your day could go a whole different way. If you try to be positive, you will experience positive change."

The audience tittered at the toe-stubbing example, and Mozhdah sighed inwardly. *They think I'm joking*, she thought. She hoped there were people in the audience who actually absorbed what she was saying. *It's real*, she thought, *and it will make a difference in their lives.*

Another issue that Mozhdah confronted was the runaway cost of marriage. After years of repression under the Taliban, which forbade dancing or listening to music, Afghans enthusiastically embraced their freedom by hosting huge elaborate weddings. Kabul alone had seventy vast wedding halls that could hold thousands of people. Marriage was a passage into adulthood, as well as the legitimization of sexual relations. With sex before marriage forbidden in Islam and considered a moral crime in Afghanistan, young men and women were eager to wed. A wedding also brought large extended families together. Unfortunately, hosting such an event for hundreds, sometimes thousands, of relatives meant that the groom and his family, who were responsible for the nuptial celebrations, went deeply into debt to pay for them. Wedding bills would run as high as $20,000, $30,000, or even $40,000, an astronomical amount for people who might earn, on average, $1,200 a month in Kabul, where salaries were higher than in the rural areas because of the influx of foreign money. Mozhdah's producers arranged a skit to show the absurdity—and fallout—of such extravagance, with an actor playing the father of the groom, running and hiding whenever family members came to the door to collect money owed that had gone towards wedding expenses. The audience roared. Mozhdah joined in the laughter while posing a challenge to her studio and home audiences. Often, the bride's family would pressure the groom's family to spend vast amounts of money, not realizing they were condemning their daughter to penury and insolvency. Why couldn't weddings be smaller?

Mozhdah looked around at the audience, who looked stunned. Were they insulted, Mozhdah thought worriedly, by the suggestion of smaller, more sensible wedding celebrations? Excited chatter broke out, and Mozhdah caught snatches of conversation. "Why *can't* weddings be smaller?" "Why do we need to invite relatives we haven't spoken to in years?" "The cost of weddings is ridiculous!" At least with this issue, Mozh-dah thought, she had gotten through to her audience.

AS THE SEASON hummed along, David Reid called a 9:00 AM meeting of *The Mozhdah Show* producers. Several people were late because of Kabul's notoriously snarled morning traffic, a post-Taliban phenomenon when Afghans returned in droves to the capital from other provinces and from abroad, many bringing capital with them and buying vehicles—thousands more than the streets of the city were built to accommodate. Steve Comrie and the advertising staff were there on time, as was Mozhdah. Sipping chai and chatting, or texting on their smartphones, they waited for the few stragglers.

Finally, the meeting began.

"Thanks for joining us today, everyone," David said. "We want to brief you on how 1TV, and specifically *The Mozhdah Show*, is doing in terms of advertising."

David handed the meeting over to Steve, who launched into his presentation. He had good news—great news, in fact—for the station. He turned his attention to Mozhdah, saying that they knew that companies would be open to advertising on her show but didn't realize it would be quite this popular. All the advertising slots were sold out for not only *The Mozhdah Show* but several other original 1TV programs as well.

"Congratulations, everyone. I'm so impressed," Mozhdah said.

David explained that the advertising team was still finess-ing final details with companies like Azizi Bank, which had been using Mozhdah in their ads for a while and was prom-inently featured on *The Mozhdah Show* as soon as it began broadcasting.

Rahim Gardizi Company, Afghanistan's biggest steel company, which was involved in metals extraction and mining, had also come on board as an advertiser, and the Coca-Cola Company was making ads specifically tailored to the Afghan market to debut on 1TV. The Gardizi Company didn't need to advertise, since it was already selling steel to governments and NGOs, but nonetheless wanted to showcase via a 1TV ad the role the company wanted to play in Afghanistan's future.

Steve also described the relationship that had been cultivated over the past several weeks with Etisalat, a multibillion-dollar telecommunications company headquartered in Abu Dhabi that had cellular networks throughout the Middle East. The company had already built towers and started to establish a network in Afghanistan. David and Steve had attended a meeting with some members of their executive and management teams—men educated at Harvard and Cambridge universities.

David laughed. "They couldn't understand why two Americans would want to be here risking their lives. We said we're here to do what we can to help idealistic young Afghans try to create a better life for their families and rebuild their country."

David described the discussion he and Steve had with the Etisalat executives, who felt that the Taliban had misused Islam to legitimize their violence, thus hijacking the spirit and intent of the religion. As a result of years of such misrepresentation, the Quran—its true words and meaning—had been corrupted. They believed that the only way to properly understand the Quran was to have it read aloud in the original Arabic by an imam.

"As part of our agreement with Etisalat, we will give an imam half an hour every morning to read Quranic passages.

We're calling the show *The Reading of the Quran*. It will be translated into Farsi, and Afghans will know this is the correct interpretation—not some adulterated version cooked up by the Taliban." David paused for effect. "Etisalat won't be sponsors of *The Mozhdah Show* but will still pay us $20,000 a month. And our marketing department will create ads for the company too."

"Some other advertisers on *The Mozhdah Show* are spending similar amounts," Steve interjected. "But, generally, we're charging from $400 to $500 a minute."

But the big news, Steve told them, pausing for effect, was the bidding war for a spot on Mozhdah's show between Afghanistan's biggest cellular companies: MTN and Roshan. MTN made the higher bid. "So they get the spot," said Steve. "It's the first commercial bidding war to secure an advertising spot in the history of Afghan TV, isn't that right, Dave?"

David nodded. "We're making television history in Afghanistan."

Steve described how the advertisers were all drawn to the unique programming being done at 1TV. "Our flagship show is the news division—it's hard-hitting, independent, and objective news reporting," Steve continued. "But the buzz—the punch-through event, as we say in America—is *The Mozhdah Show*. It's the first television program featuring a woman that has women producers and is intended for families: toddlers, kids, moms and dads and grandparents. It is a fresh, independent, and controversial voice."

Furthermore, Steve said, 1TV was on target to bring $2.5 million in advertising revenue into the company, based upon eight hours of original programming a day.

"That's incredible," Mozhdah gasped.

David smiled. "It is, isn't it? But, of course, we're working under the shadow of the Taliban, who don't like our programming, and who will like it even less as we head into shows that tackle more controversial topics, like domestic violence, as Mozhdah is planning to do."

David continued in a more somber tone and revealed that Fahim Hashimy, the 1TV owner, had recently met with representatives of the Taliban and offered them payment in return for not blowing up the station's transmitters.

David threw Steve a glance. Everyone murmured in shock.

"There will be no compromise on the coverage of Taliban atrocities," David continued, "but 1TV needed some assurance that it would continue to exist."

"What if the Taliban take that money to finance their suicide bombing?" someone asked hesitantly.

David nodded his understanding. They had debated it, he told them, and it was a difficult decision, but they thought it was better to be on the air than not. "If there is a monetary price to pay to preserve the station's hard work, then we have to accept that," David continued. "Perhaps covering Taliban atrocities on the news will make the government negotiate harder with their leaders to secure a peace agreement or commit more military resources to controlling insurgency."

Steve interjected that 1TV would also use satellites to broadcast all over Central Asia and even into the Middle East so that the influence of the station, and, of course, its advertisers, would be felt across these two huge regions. "It is," he said, "an enormous accomplishment."

There was a spontaneous smattering of applause and an outbreak of chatter. Mozhdah felt thrilled to be part of such a momentous undertaking, but disturbed. Had 1TV shaken hands with the devil?

David moved on to the next agenda item. Television advertisers require audience measurement systems that compile data showing how many people see their messaging, the ages of the viewers, and their purchasing capabilities. David told them that he had hired university students to go door to door in Kabul, Jalalabad, Mazar-i-Sharif, and Kandahar to interview people and find out what they were watching. This gave 1TV hard data to show advertisers.

"Are there any questions?" David asked, scanning the room.

"I don't have any questions," Mozhdah piped up. "What I do want to say is congratulations to all of you." She paused. "Thanks for including me in this meeting—but I have to run. I am taking some children—orphans—out for lunch. I'm not sure if I have enough supervisors for the group, so if anyone wants to join me and help keep control of a bunch of excited kids, lunch is on me," she said.

Everyone laughed, and there was a chorus of excuses. "Too much work to do today." "Sorry, Mozhdah!" "Bring me some leftovers." "Best of luck!"

MOZHDAH'S FRIENDSHIP WITH orphans had begun in an unexpected way. Earlier that year, when she was in Kabul preparing to debut *The Mozhdah Show*, she had received numerous requests from businesses wanting her to appear in their ad campaigns. These included the country's two top private financial companies, Azizi Bank and Kabul Bank. At the beginning of 2010, rumors were swirling about rampant corruption at Kabul Bank, which handled the salary payments to the Afghan National Police and Afghan National Army. Azizi Bank, however, was highly reputable. It had been launched by Mirwais Azizi, a lawyer and businessman who had fled Afghanistan in 1988. Mirwais went on to create what would become a multibillion-dollar company, Azizi Group. Based in Dubai, Azizi Group invested in banking and finance, oil and gas, tourism and hospitality, real estate development and construction, trading and charity works in the Middle East, as well as in emerging markets like Afghanistan. Azizi Bank approached Mozhdah, who accepted their offer, knowing that they were a big part of a new, emerging, modern Afghanistan. Azizi Bank's first commercial on 1TV, filmed with Mozhdah as spokesperson, coincided with the debut of *The Mozhdah Show* in March.

Filmed over a period of two days on the grounds of the Inter-Continental Hotel in Kabul, the ad featured Mozhdah wearing a bright red dress with glittering gold medallions and gold embroidery that paid homage to the clothing of Bashir's home province of Herat, while she sang "Afghan Girl" in her alto voice, a timbre different from Asian women's traditional high-pitched registers, a subtle signal of modernization that countered her traditional garb. At the beginning of 2010, around the time when the first 1TV ad aired, there was a boom in business at Azizi Bank, and people said that Mozhdah brought luck to the financial institution. People also deluged the bank with requests to know where Mozhdah got her dress. Before her show made her famous, Mozhdah had become known as the Azizi Bank Girl, launching a relationship with the company that included commercials for the sister company Onyx Construction. With the support of Mirwais Azizi, who wanted his commercials to represent a modern

Afghanistan, Mozhdah didn't wear a hijab, a departure from how women were garbed in other ads on TV.

Mirwais kept an office in the Azizi Bank headquarters, in the exclusive district of Wazir Akbar Khan, close to the 1TV studio and guesthouse. Mozhdah's meetings in his air-conditioned office, often with Nasrin at her side as her manager, were conducted over chai. At the end of one meeting, Mirwais, gray-haired, with a moustache and stocky build, dressed in an impeccable bespoke suit, walked Mozhdah and Nasrin to the exit.

He turned to Mozhdah and said, "There is a good reason why you are here. I sense that you truly want to help people."

Mozhdah nodded, pleased by his observation. She thought back to when she was a teenager, watching reports on television, desiring to be a part of the change that was happening in Afghanistan after the 2001 invasion—wanting to be a foreign correspondent, or somehow help the millions of people, especially children, who had been born into war, who fled to refugee camps, or who lived under Taliban brutality.

"I especially want to help orphaned children. I want to help abused women," Mozhdah replied. "But other than addressing these problems on my show, I'm not too sure how to help out."

Mirwais looked thoughtful, and then asked if Mozhdah would like to work with the Azizi Foundation. He explained that 20 percent of the company's net profits in Afghanistan were funneled into such initiatives as the Marastoon Orphanage, located on the southwest outskirts of Kabul.

"I don't want to go there to visit as some sort of a photo op for Azizi. I really want to be involved," Mozhdah said.

Mozhdah and Mirwais discussed what might be the best way for her to help orphans. She agreed to twice-monthly visits to the orphanage, a schedule that would fit her work demands. After her visits, she would let Mirwais know what the children needed, be it clothing, sports equipment, art supplies, or simply the chance to go on a field trip to experience the outside world.

At the time, about 2 million children in Afghanistan had lost either one or both parents to such things as war, violence, disease, and poverty. Many were in orphanages because their mothers had lost husbands. As single parents, the women often couldn't afford to feed their children. Many kids ended up on the streets, highly vulnerable to sexual abuse or forced prostitution, possibly becoming *spandis*. The orphanages were often run by the Afghan Red Crescent Society, which relied upon financial assistance from civilian donors, businesses, and foreign governments. Some orphanages were funded and overseen by NGOS, providing excellent support for their young charges. Others were understaffed and overcrowded and provided the bare basics of shelter, sustenance, and schooling, offering little in the way of proper education or trades skills training.

Marastoon Orphanage held 255 girls and boys, toddlers to teenagers, many of whom had spent their entire lives at the facility. None of the children had proper shoes or clothing, and Mozhdah contacted the Azizi Foundation to ask for new tracksuits and running shoes for all the kids.

The new outfits were beautiful: black tracksuits with a pink stripe down the leg for the girls and a blue stripe for the boys. The next time Mozhdah visited the orphanage, she was surprised to see the children wearing their old worn, torn clothes. Where were the tracksuits and running shoes?

"They took them away," one child told her—"they" meaning orphanage staff. Mirwais had warned Mozhdah that this might happen; anything new was often confiscated and resold, thus lining the pockets of facility managers. When Mozhdah found out, she alerted the deputy chief of the Azizi Foundation, Haji Ali Akbar Zhoandai, who lambasted Marastoon Orphanage staff. They never confiscated anything that Mozhdah brought into the facility again.

Mozhdah made sure that the children received backpacks, books and pencils, soccer balls and volleyballs. Despite the low standards of skills training and schooling, Mozhdah realized that the girls had more freedom and independence than many their age in Afghanistan. Rather than being given away in marriage as a child or young teen, they did sports, such as soccer and Tae Kwon Do, alongside the boys. It was important, thought Mozhdah, for her to inspire in these girls the ambition and drive to pursue education and training once they left the confines of the orphanage, in order to take care of themselves as adults.

In Mozhdah's most ambitious undertakings, she would escort the children—all 255 of them—on field trips, such as boat rides. Sometimes, she would walk with the children through the grounds of some of Kabul's sumptuous grand hotels, showing them the outdoor pools and the vast marble foyers with chandeliers—unimaginable luxuries. They would take over entire ballrooms for meals, where traditional rice dishes and lamb kebabs would be served. Mozhdah would walk around opening soda cans for the children, as most had never seen one in their life. One little boy stuffed cans of soda into his pockets.

"Why are you doing that?" Mozhdah asked.

"These are for my sister and my mom. Sometimes they come visit me, and now I have something to give them," he responded.

"That's a wonderful thing to do," said Mozhdah, thinking how unhappy the mother must feel to be unable to care for this thoughtful, bright child.

Mozhdah wondered what the boy's future was: Would he ever be reunited with his family, would he receive the training or education that would allow him to build a career in sectors like business or technology that were part of a modernizing Afghanistan? Such excursions, she thought, at least allowed the children to begin to dream about a better life for themselves after they finally departed the brick-wall enclosure of the orphanage.

Mozhdah Jamalzadah as a newborn in Kabul, Afghanistan, with her mother, Nasrin, and father, Bashir.

Nasrin and Bashir show off newborn Mozhdah to the family, including cousins, aunties, and grandmother Tafsira, in Kabul.

Mozhdah as a toddler with her father, Bashir, in Kabul.

← Nasrin and Bashir Jamalzadah with their children Masee and Mozhdah in Kabul. The youngest, Safee, is yet to be born.

↓ Mozhdah, Masee, Bashir, and Safee show off their new winter attire in their home in Oshawa, Ontario.

A Jamalzadah family portrait.

Mozhdah's sixth-grade photo.

Mozhdah on the set of an Azizi Bank commercial.

Businessman Mirwais Azizi at a media conference with Mozhdah.

Mozhdah on a field trip with kids from the Marastoon Orphanage.

Mozhdah at Bagram Airfield, north of Kabul in Parwan province.

Mozhdah sang to the troops at Bagram Airfield, the main United States air facility in Afghanistan.

Mozhdah posing with troops at Rish Khor U.S. army base after a performance.

A soldier at Rish Khor U.S. army base teaches Mozhdah how to shoot a tank-mounted machine gun.

Mozhdah being interviewed by an American journalist on the set of *The Mozhdah Show.*

Mozhdah with Dr. Mohammad Zaman Rajabi, who was *The Mozhdah Show*'s regular guest psychologist.

Mozhdah and her mother, Nasrin, (in white jacket) with crew, band, and guests on the set of *The Mozhdah Show*.

Mozhdah sings her hit song "Afghan Girl" for President Barack Obama and First Lady Michelle Obama on International Women's Day at the White House in Washington, D.C.

To Mozhdah — Thank you for your wonderful performance!

Michelle Obama

President Barack Obama and First Lady Michelle Obama thanked Mozhdah with a signed portrait.

THE WHITE HOUSE

March 15, 2010

Ms. Mozhdah Jamalzadah

███████████
███████████████████████

Dear Mozhdah:

Thank you so much for joining the President and me at the White House for International Women's Day. It was such a pleasure to hear your beautiful voice, and we truly appreciate you traveling so far and taking the time out of your schedule for us and our guests.

The stories of women who work each and every day to make our world a stronger, more vibrant place are so inspiring, and I want to thank you for helping us celebrate their lives. It was so lovely hearing you sing, and I know it will be a vivid memory for all of us for a long time to come.

Sincerely,

Michelle Obama

First Lady Michelle Obama's letter thanking Mozhdah for her performance at the White House.

← Mozhdah and several of the children from the Marastoon Orphanage in Kabul on a field trip.

↓ Mozhdah and the kids from the Marastoon Orphanage would travel by bus on their field trips around Kabul.

As a special guest, Mozhdah had a reserved seat at *Surprise Oprah! A Farewell Spectacular* at the United Center in Chicago in 2011.

Mozhdah debuts two new feminist anthems at an outdoor concert at Khurshid TV in 2015.

CHAPTER 13

Kafir

F
ALL 2010 WAS the end of the contract for the expat team responsible for training the young 1TV staff. As the departure of Siobhan, Vicky, and the others neared, it felt like a little piece of *The Mozhdah Show* was dying, and their going-away party was as sad as it was celebratory of the show's success.

But there was a more disturbing development. CEO David Reid was leaving too. Consummate professional that he was, he gave no reason for his departure. Rumors, however, circulated that he had clashed with Fahim Hashimy over the 1TV owner's poor treatment of staff.

Mozhdah, careful to avoid Kabul's bubbling gossip cauldron, considered it none of her business. At David's bittersweet farewell, she thanked him for his hard work, his mentorship, and his unwavering support of her vision.

David encouraged Mozhdah to keep pursuing the issues that she was passionate about. "Be true to what you believe in," he said. "The girls in your audience live vicariously through you. They watch you. I've seen them close their eyes while you sing, and I can tell that they are imagining themselves being as free as you are."

David's words overwhelmed Mozhdah. She didn't know what she would do without him. David's friend Steve Comrie had also left, after training the advertising team at 1TV. Mozhdah's social circle diminished noticeably. Luckily, she was close with Neelofar Neda, the show's producer. And there was her friend Brishkay Ahmed, an Afghan-Canadian Mozhdah had met back home in Vancouver, when she performed at Brishkay's brother's wedding as a gift to the family. Here in Kabul, Brishkay was co-directing a police drama titled *Between You and Me*, and the two got together whenever possible.

Following the filming of season 1, Mozhdah took a short, rejuvenating holiday in Vancouver, spending time with friends and her cat, Mittens. She was eager to begin season 2, which would start filming in Kabul in March 2011, a time when green buds emerged from their winter dormancy and the evenings were still cool but the afternoons warm enough for social gatherings on the top deck of the guesthouse. Brishkay would sometimes drop by, and Mozhdah, Neelofar, and a few other friends would discuss all manner of things, from the Afghan broadcasting industry to local actors, to the state of the government and the country, as well as the latest Taliban attacks. Mozhdah was filled with a sense of purpose, brimming with new ideas for her show. She *must* be making a difference, she thought. She was bringing music into the homes of Afghans and creating dialogue about controversial, taboo topics. Her clothing choices—her tailored outfits and small light headscarf—modeled what women, especially those in the professions in Afghanistan, could aspire to.

But the threat of Taliban violence loomed over her enthusiasm, and that of her coworkers at 1TV, like menacing storm clouds. Although an international contingent of soldiers continued to try to rout out Taliban insurgents, the results were disappointing. The same month that season 2 filming began, the United Nations released its report on civilian deaths in 2010. In all, 2,777 people died, most by Taliban bomb and suicide attacks, an increase of 28 percent from 2009. On the positive side, schools and roads were under construction, and teachers, police, physicians, and engineers were being trained. Mozhdah was one of the voices of this evolving society, speaking to Afghans in their own language, showing how life could be better for men, women, and children by challenging conservative ways of thinking. She was throwing down the gauntlet to the Taliban.

Mozhdah's stature in Afghanistan had risen following her performance at the White House. She received invitations from embassies in Kabul as well as prominent citizens and politicians to attend parties and dinners and sing. One invitation, which she happily accepted, came from Bagram Airfield, the largest American military base in Afghanistan, located near the ancient city of Bagram in Parwan province, forty miles north of Kabul.

A more recent invite had come from Rish Khor U.S. army base just south of Kabul, close to the town of Rish Khor-e Bala. The area was arid, barren, and hilly—good terrain for training soldiers in military operations and combat readiness.

Mozhdah agreed to the invitation; the base commanders wanted her to sing "Afghan Girl," as well as a few other songs. They had planned a packed afternoon, starting with lunch with the troops, followed by a surprise event. Mozhdah wondered what it could be. A flyover? A military parade with a band? A display of combat training? What could a group of soldiers devise that would be entertaining?

On the day of the visit, several U.S. army vehicles stopped outside the front gates of her house—she had moved out of the 1TV guesthouse into a sprawling home in Kabul's Wazir Akbar Kahn district that was leased for her by Mirwais Azizi. For company, Mozhdah had an Afghan-Canadian friend from Toronto, Touba, move in, and the pair adopted two kittens rescued from the streets of Kabul.

Mozhdah received a call on her cell phone that they had arrived, and she stepped outside her guarded compound to see two American soldiers in gray camouflage uniforms holding machine guns. Another soldier waited by the door of a tan armored high mobility multipurpose wheeled vehicle, or Humvee. She was escorted by Matt, an employee at 1TV, as well as one of the studio's guards. The three piled into the back.

It was chilly enough for a coat, and Mozhdah had chosen to wear an olive, light wool military-style jacket with gold-colored buttons, as well as black leather boots and a leopard-print chiffon hijab. With the combat-net radio crackling with unintelligible communications, they roared off, churning up street dust. Mozhdah watched, amused, as drivers of the ubiquitous dented, rusted, and exhaust-spewing Toyota Corollas refused to move off to the side to let the huge vehicles pass, despite the soldiers tailing their bumper by a hair's breadth. It was a tiny— and annoying—act of defiance against the American soldiers.

Once they'd made it out of the crush of vehicles—horse- and donkey-drawn carts as well as cars—caught in the Gordian knot of Kabul traffic roundabouts, the Humvees sped up, arriving at Rish Khor U.S. army base in short order. The area had once been a Russian paratrooper base, the driver casually informed Mozhdah as they entered the front gates.

Mozhdah's vehicle slowed to a stop and a soldier stepped up smartly to open the door, holding out his hand to Mozhdah as she jumped cautiously out into the bright sunlight. There was a long uneven lineup of people dressed in variations of gray camouflage and a low level of animated chatter. All looked expectantly at Mozhdah as she walked towards them, escorted by the soldier who had opened the Humvee door. The first part of the lineup consisted of various officers, who were introduced according to rank. They included several generals, as well as a captain, major, lieutenant colonel, and colonel. Mozhdah smiled and shook each of the men's hands, murmuring variations of "Nice to meet you," trying to remember everyone's name. A lineup of Afghan army officers was next, and Mozhdah greeted them in Farsi.

The crowd made its way to an enormous mess hall for lunch. Mozhdah, Matt, and the 1TV guard were shown to the head table with the generals. Soldiers noisily took their places, and in the bedlam, Mozhdah's table went up first to the buffet-style food counter, which offered a mix of Afghan dishes like rice and kebabs and fresh naan, in addition to Western fare like pizza and fried chicken.

Mozhdah nibbled her food, conscious of the flutter of nerves in her stomach. The army base had provided a band of Afghan musicians to accompany her, and she wondered how good they would be. She had been assured that they had practiced the music to her songs.

After lunch, as Mozhdah sipped her tea, a general walked up to the stage and spoke into the microphone. "Let's give a big American welcome to Mozhdah Jamalzadah—Kabul's reigning talk show host—who sang her hit song 'Afghan Girl' in front of our commander in chief, President Barack Obama, at the White House one year ago."

Accompanied by clapping, whistles, and whoops, Mozhdah walked gracefully onstage, smiling shyly at the earsplitting welcome, took the proffered microphone from the general, and then thanked everyone for inviting her to the base. She briefly outlined the songs she would sing to the troops that day: two in Farsi and one in English. The first would be "Afghan Girl." The next was the traditional Afghan song "*Damane Sahra*." The third was "My Love," which Mozhdah had written for the orphans of Afghanistan and would sing in English.

The band had indeed practiced, and the acoustics in the mess hall, thanks in part to its many hard surfaces, were reasonable. As she sang, Mozhdah watched the war-hardened young men and women nod their heads to the rhythm. For the English song, the ode to orphaned Afghan children, she could see them listening intently to the words:

I'll hold your hand
When you can't find your way
I'll help when you
Can't make it through the day
I'll be your guide
When you're too far from home
And no one hears a word you say

As soon as she finished "My Love," Mozhdah placed the mic back onto its stand, smiling and nodding at the audience.

The applause was deafening, and Mozhdah could only wave her thanks and leave the stage.

An army photographer took pictures of Mozhdah with some of the soldiers, and then she was escorted outdoors once again. She was led a short walk away to a huge table covered in a white cloth, which was laden with a variety of weapons.

"What's this?" Mozhdah said incredulously.

A soldier stood at the table in gray camouflage uniform, tactical boots nearly white with dust, and dual drop leg thigh holsters for holding a handgun and a knife. Slightly heavy-set, he had black hair and a dark, closely shorn beard. He introduced himself with his full name and rank, adding that Mozhdah could call him Antonio. He was going to teach Mozhdah how to shoot.

"I like guns," Mozhdah admitted with a smile, thinking back to days at the annual Pacific National Exhibition summer fair in Vancouver. As a teen, she had loved spending time at the fair's arcade games, honing her sharpshooter skills and often winning stuffed animals.

Antonio told Mozhdah to first get a feel for each gun—hold it in her hand and see what felt good.

Mozhdah picked up every weapon, feeling the weight and power, a bitter scent of metal filling her nostrils.

"This one," she said, holding a small, light, black gun that fit snugly in her hand.

"This is a U.S. military standard-issue semiautomatic Beretta M9 pistol," said Antonio.

"It's easy to hold," Mozhdah said, scrutinizing the weapon in her hand.

Antonio showed Mozhdah how to disengage the safety and prepare the weapon for firing by releasing a round into the chamber. To aim, he told her to close one eye and look down the pistol barrel. To strike a target, she should hold the pistol as still as possible and focus on the sight, then hold her breath and deliberately squeeze the trigger.

"If you pull the trigger too quickly, the bullet will miss the target," Antonio instructed.

Mozhdah nodded, held the gun in two hands, and stared down the barrel of the Beretta at the human silhouette shooting target, focusing on the center of the chest. She held her breath and squeezed. The echoing explosion of the shot hurt her ears, but she peered with satisfaction at the small hole in the target—virtually a bull's-eye. Smiling slightly at the cheering behind her, Mozhdah squeezed the trigger several more times, making sure to hold her breath to prevent the gun from moving up or down. The bullet holes erupted in the center of the target. When Mozhdah finally ran out of bullets, she turned around, a huge grin on her face, and reluctantly returned the gun to Antonio.

"You've done this before," he joked.

"Beginner's luck," replied Mozhdah.

Mozhdah and the entourage walked a short distance to where two enormous tan armored tanks sat, like dusty slumbering dinosaurs. On top of one tank was a turret-mounted Browning .50 caliber machine gun with a long ammo belt of hundreds of armor-piercing bullets. Antonio scrambled to the top of the tank and put a hand out to help Mozhdah climb up. The huge weapon, Antonio explained, was called a fifty cal and had a range of more than two thousand yards. He instructed her to grab the spade grip, or handles, and point the barrel straight at the mountain. "Then push the trigger here," he said, pointing to a mechanism on the grip.

After slipping on a heavy set of earmuffs, Mozhdah tentatively pushed the trigger, feeling the resulting boom as much as hearing it. The power of the massive machine gun reverberated through her body, and the pressure crushed the air out of her lungs, making it hard to draw breath. She pushed the trigger again. Growing more confident, she kept it pressed down, letting the gleaming bullets rip from the weapon and hit the distant landscape with a dusty spatter.

Next, Antonio led Mozhdah to an adjacent tank. This one, he explained, was an automatic grenade launcher, and rather than pushing the trigger mechanism for rapid firing, Mozhdah should press once and wait for the grenade to explode when it hit its mark. Far off in the distance, Mozhdah spied her target— the remains of a burned-out tank. She crouched down, aimed, and pressed the trigger, feeling her body absorb the powerful burst of the weapon. She waited to see where the shot would land. Then—a huge blast right next to the burned-out target. *Nearly a bull's-eye*, she thought with satisfaction.

At the end of the day, as Mozhdah was saying farewell to her hosts at Rish Khor, Antonio strode up to her with something in his hand.

"This is our gift to you," he said. He handed her the Beretta M9 that she had used for target practice, as well as a magazine of ammunition. "Hopefully," he said, "you'll never have to use it."

Mozhdah looked at him gratefully. "Thank you so much. I hope I never have to use it either," she said.

She dropped the weapon into her purse, where it settled to the bottom. The added weight made her feel safer, more secure. She would keep it with her every time she went out, she decided—just in case.

A VARIETY OF issues had dominated the first season of *The Mozhdah Show*. For the second season, Mozhdah was determined to go beyond discussions of child abuse, the expense of weddings, and the power of positive thinking to something more hard-hitting: domestic abuse of women. One phenomenon was especially horrifying to her: the self-immolation of Afghan women who set themselves on fire, often using cooking oil, as a final desperate escape from a forced marriage that had reached levels of abuse so severe that life had become intolerable. The Ministry of Women's Affairs had statistics on how many women—103—had set themselves ablaze between March 2009 and March 2010. The number was believed to be the tip of the iceberg, since families hushed up such tragedies. "We have to address this," Mozhdah told the production team, "and the reasons behind it."

Even more controversially, Mozhdah wanted to discuss divorce—especially women's inability to initiate divorce proceedings—in light of the abusive marriages many women were in. During production meetings, Mozhdah emphasized how this controversial topic could be approached with sensitivity and diplomacy. "Starting off, we could do a few shows about the effect of violence between the mom and dad on children, as well as the effect on the family in general," Mozhdah suggested. Once again, they would use Dr. Mohammad Zaman Rajabi as their psychology expert to advise them on the myriad emotional and physical ramifications children who witnessed abuse suffered, such as depression, anger, bedwetting, and headaches.

Mozhdah and the producers assessed audience reactions as they took the show in a more serious direction. During her meet-and-greet after every show, female viewers constantly encouraged Mozhdah to continue the discussions of domestic violence. Sometimes their voices were pleading, and Mozhdah shuddered to think how many of these women, many in arranged marriages, endured violence at home.

The show's producers contacted organizations like the Afghan Ministry of Women's Affairs and the United Nations Development Fund for Women to gather statistics from reports like the Global Database on Violence against Women. As Mozhdah read and took notes of the statistics on kidnapping, forced marriage, emotional and physical abuse, rape, polygamy, marital rape, and the confinement of women to the home, she thought angrily how, for some women, little had changed since Taliban rule.

Part of the problem was prevailing attitudes towards domestic abuse, especially when studies showed that many women believed beatings were justified for such supposed transgressions as neglecting the children, going out of the house without permission, arguing with the husband, refusing sex, or burning a meal. Combing through the reports, she realized that it wasn't just a lack of awareness but a lack of education behind such regressive beliefs. The Taliban destroyed the education system, banning girls from school and allowing only religious education for boys. Rebuilding the education system and training teachers was a massive undertaking requiring years of international and national investment. *Let my show be part of the education that women receive*, Mozhdah thought. Even if these women and girls are isolated in their home or rural community, at least they can be introduced to the notion that violence is never justified—nor can it be legitimized—by cultural or religious beliefs.

Despite all Mozhdah's research and determined passion, the show's producers resisted adding divorce to the programming. Mozhdah argued that if divorce were to become acceptable in Afghanistan for women, they might leave untenable situations and begin a new life, rather than resorting to the horror of self-immolation.

"But where would these victims go?" Neelofar countered. "Back to their families? There is a saying in Afghan culture that when a girl marries, she only returns to the family of her birth in a body bag." Neelofar paused and looked hard at Mozhdah. "There are other things to consider," she said. "Few divorced women will ever marry again, as it's considered a disgrace, both to herself and her relatives. The attitude is that the woman failed to protect the marriage."

"Even if the relationship ends because of abuse from the husband?" Mozhdah said indignantly.

"Yes," said Neelofar.

"But that's what we're here to do—change these outdated attitudes," Mozhdah insisted. "That's the problem with this country. If something bad happens to a woman, it's her fault, no matter if it's rape or a beating. And it means that the men of this country never take responsibility for their actions. And if you don't take responsibility for your actions, how can you evolve?"

Neelofar sighed. "Some people," she said carefully, "have begun to accuse you of being a kafir."

"What's that?" Mozhdah asked.

"It means 'unbeliever,'" Neelofar said. "It's the name for a bad influence—someone who wants to change the minds of the younger generation and make them non-Muslims."

"Then I guess I'm a kafir," Mozhdah said.

Mozhdah refused to give up. This was her show, after all, and she would address women's right to divorce. Eventually, she wore down the naysayers, and a show on divorce was planned.

The studio audience wasn't forewarned of the subject matter, and when Mozhdah began with the words, "Today's topic is divorce," she sensed disappointment. Dr. Rajabi, who supported divorce for women experiencing any abuse, appeared as a guest to offer his professional insights.

Mozhdah began by acknowledging how important family honor, dignity, and reputation were to Afghans. The behavior of women—wives, mothers, daughters—affected a family's social standing. Marital separation can destroy a woman's reputation and bring shame on her family.

Mozhdah argued that a sister's or daughter's physical and mental well-being took priority over family honor. Men could legally divorce a wife without her permission, yet a woman couldn't divorce unless she had her husband's consent. How was that fair?

"I'm not promoting divorce," Mozhdah continued cautiously. "But if your daughter or sister is contemplating suicide to escape a marriage, you should think first of that family member, rather than the family's reputation."

Interspersed with Mozhdah and Dr. Rajabi's discussion were "streeters"—1TV called them vox pops—segments where a small camera crew goes into the streets to ask people their opinion on issues. For this show, random citizens were asked whether divorce should be allowed in the case of familial abuse. Most of the people interviewed were both aware of and deeply sympathetic towards the many young Afghan women trapped in abusive marriages and agreed that divorce should be available in such situations. Some stated that, in such cases, religious or cultural edicts opposing divorce should take a back seat to protecting loved ones. However, there were a few people—both men and women—who remarked that a husband should be allowed to beat his wife if she deserved it. The producers decided not to air these opinions, however.

As the segment neared its conclusion, Mozhdah took time out, as she always did, to ask the audience for their comments or questions. To her surprise, she was met with a wall of silence. The audience was clearly uncomfortable with—even disapproving of—the subject, as well as Mozhdah's approach.

As she walked out of the studio and handed her mic to Neelofar, Mozhdah muttered, "I don't think I got through to anyone."

The day after the show aired, Mozhdah was told by the producers that 1TV had been inundated with anonymous threats to bomb the station. Since *The Mozhdah Show* started, the station had received occasional bomb threats, and these were generally ignored. When told of the new raft of threats, Mozhdah was angry at the cowardice, the inability of some to listen to new ideas.

"What are you planning to do?" she asked her producers.

They chuckled. "We wouldn't work at all if we were constantly scared of what might happen," said one. "We just get on with the job."

Nonetheless, an edict on the topic of divorce was circulated by Kardaar, a 1TV administrator. No matter how desperately society needed to address Afghanistan's complex and often oppressive social customs, the subject was forbidden for future shows. Divorce, for Mozhdah—as it was for the women of Afghanistan—was off limits.

ABOUT A MONTH later, Mozhdah's cell phone rang.

"*Salaam*... Oh, hi Kardaar," she said genially.

She listened. "American journalists? They want to interview me? Here at the studio? No? That's fine."

She paused, listening. "Sure, I can do it today," Mozhdah said. "It's my day off, so I'm pretty open. What time? You'll be there? Okay. And you're sending a driver? Fine, I'll be waiting," she said and hung up.

Ever since her visit to the White House, and especially in the wake of the show on divorce, Mozhdah's popularity had soared. The controversy she had stirred up—as well as her courage in continuing her show following the threats—was especially appealing to foreign media. Mozhdah appeared on ABC's *Good Morning America* with George Stephanopoulos, CNN, Indian and Chinese television, the BBC, and CBC. Print publications like *Time* and Canadian publications like *Maclean's* magazine and the *Vancouver Sun* and *Calgary Herald* also did stories on "the Oprah of Afghanistan." Afghan media outlets requested interviews too. Competing Kabul station TOLO TV was even more aggressive, trying to woo Mozhdah away from 1TV, inviting her to host its popular reality singing show *Afghan Star*, which was modeled on *American Idol*.

Mozhdah prepared for the interview with the American journalists, dressing in pants and a button-up blouse and stiletto heels, accessorizing with a long string of pearls. Kardaar hadn't mentioned if it was an on-camera interview, though she assumed it was. She grabbed a hijab, then realizing she had left her sunglasses in the 1TV dressing room, walked quickly over to the studio, where she ran into Matt, one of her escorts on the recent trip to the Rish Khor U.S. army base.

"Where are you going in such a hurry on your day off?" he asked.

"Kardaar has arranged an interview with some journalists somewhere in Kabul," Mozhdah said, slightly out of breath.

"Why aren't they coming here?" Matt asked.

"I asked the same thing. I don't know."

"Don't go," he said.

"What do you mean?" Mozhdah stopped and look at Matt, confused.

"It sounds ... off," he said.

"That's crazy. It's some journalists from the U.S.," Mozhdah said, irritated.

"Journalists would want to film you in the studio where you actually do your job. They have to get B-roll, interview some of the station staff ... you know how this works. It sounds ... suspicious," he said.

"But it's Kardaar," she said.

"That's exactly what makes me suspicious," Matt replied. "I've heard things ... "

"Don't be silly," Mozhdah cut him off and, sunglasses in hand, strode off.

She returned to the guesthouse to await Kardaar's driver. The guards let the vehicle, a shiny armor-plated suv, through the gates. The driver parked, stepped out, and walked over to greet Mozhdah. She was polite but irked that he was alone.

"Where are the guards?" she asked.

The driver nodded towards the vehicle, where an armed guard had just disembarked.

"There is nothing to worry about," he assured Mozhdah.

He opened the passenger door, nodding to her to climb in.

She did, and the heavy door closed with a thud. The guard climbed into the front, machine gun in his lap.

Mozhdah settled into the back, slipped her sunglasses on, and pulled her hijab closer around her face, despite the tinted windows. It would not do to have anyone—like a Taliban sympathizer—recognize her during the drive and possibly follow them.

The driver wove his way through traffic to one of Kabul's more exclusive districts, home to the influential and wealthy, from former warlords to politicians and those who profited off the poppy trade. The SUV stopped in front of a gate that was opened by guards bearing machine guns and drove up to an opulent house. The driver got out and opened the vehicle door for Mozhdah, then led her to the huge wooden front door and opened it, allowing her to step inside the cool interior, with its marble flooring and high ceilings. She followed the man down a wide, curving staircase.

"Where are we going?" she asked.

"Downstairs."

I can see that, she thought, annoyed. "This is where the news crew is?"

He didn't respond. *Maybe he doesn't know*, Mozhdah rationalized.

The man opened a door at the bottom of the staircase and beckoned to Mozhdah to step through. She did, and the door clicked shut behind her.

Mozhdah took her sunglasses off to stare at the interior. There were pool tables and a bar. Disco balls, glittering in the dim light, hung above two stages. Security cameras were mounted in the corners. This enormous room, Mozhdah realized, was some kind of private nightclub. Whose house could it possibly be? She couldn't imagine Kardaar owning such a lavish, and somewhat tacky, home.

Someone was seated at a table, a cocktail glass in front of him, and she squinted in the dim light. "Oh, Kardaar, I didn't see you there when I first came in—*salaam.*"

"*Salaam,* Mozhdah," Kardaar said. "How are you today?"

"Fine, thank you," Mozhdah said. "Where are the journalists?"

"Oh, they're coming. Have a drink with me, Mozhdah."

"No, thank you," Mozhdah said sharply. She was annoyed. Why would Kardaar ask her to do something so unprofessional before an interview?

"Come and sit beside me," Kardaar said, patting the seat of the chair beside him.

Mozhdah didn't say anything, repulsed by Kardaar's gesture. She moved towards the table, placed her white shoulder bag on top, pulled out a chair opposite Kardaar, and sat down.

"I see what you're doing—playing hard to get," Kardaar said.

"Excuse me?" Mozhdah said angrily. How dare he speak to her like that?

"You're feisty," Kardaar continued. "It's why your show is so good. You don't care who you ... piss off, do you?"

Mozhdah was incensed. Kardaar, obviously, was drunk.

"There are rumors going around," Kardaar said, his eyes narrowing.

"When aren't there?" Mozhdah said, sitting straighter in the chair and crossing her arms. "And every single one of them is false."

"There's one that could prove especially bad for your reputation," Kardaar continued. "You," he paused for dramatic effect, "have a boyfriend. You know what will happen if the public finds out—your show will have to be taken off the air. You'll never work in Afghanistan again."

Mozhdah flushed red with growing rage. What the hell was going on? "I'm leaving," she snapped, standing up. "I didn't come here to be insulted—and threatened—by you!"

Kardaar got up from his seat and moved quickly over to Mozhdah's side. She glared up at him and backed away several steps. He reeked of liquor.

"I can make those rumors go away," he said, greedy eyes traveling down Mozhdah's body.

Mozhdah felt like someone had grabbed her by the throat. "I'm out of here," she said in a strangled voice. She moved to sidestep Kardaar, who viciously pushed her backwards.

"You're a liberated woman from the West," he said, then hissed, "What's your price?"

"What? I'm not a prostitute," she snapped. "You, you..." Mozhdah stuttered in rage and growing panic. "You're disgusting!" She shoved Kardaar, trying at the same time to grab her purse, perched on the table.

Kardaar grabbed Mozhdah's hair, pulling her towards him, shoving his face into her neck. He started to kiss it. She screamed.

"This room is soundproof," Kardaar hissed into her ear. "You're wasting your breath."

He forced Mozhdah around to face him and tore at her blouse with his right hand. The pearl necklace broke, and the beads went bouncing wildly across the marble floor. Mozhdah's Tae Kwon Do skills kicked in, and she shoved and punched Kardaar, who retaliated by twisting her hair so tightly her knees buckled in agony.

Mozhdah screamed, "Don't do this! Please don't do this!"

With Mozhdah's hair twisted in his fist, tightening it more and more, Kardaar had total control, though she continued landing punches and kicks, making him grunt with pain. He threw Mozhdah up against a wall, then swung her across the room, where she landed, front first, on the pool table, her hair still in his fist. She screamed in agony.

"Stop!" she shrieked.

Kardaar twisted Mozhdah's hair again and yanked her around so that she was facing him, their noses almost touching. His face was red, eyes gleaming with malice.

"Shut the fuck up," he said, and slapped Mozhdah hard across the face. She tasted blood. It felt like the smack had loosened teeth. One thought came into her terrified brain like a lightning strike—the Beretta handgun. It was in her purse.

The thought that she could save herself gave Mozhdah fierce energy. Let Kardaar rip out her hair, if that's what it took. Where was that damn purse? She saw it on the table out of the corner of her eye, as Kardaar twisted her hair even tighter. Pushing and shoving, stomping on his feet with her heels, using Tae Kwon Do hand strikes to deliver body blows, she managed to move closer to the table.

"Let go of me!" she screamed, as he twisted her hair again. She was certain her scalp was being torn off. *Just a bit closer*, she thought desperately.

Mozhdah pushed and shoved, slipping on the pearl beads underfoot. Kardaar was swearing. Suddenly, he let go of her hair and threw an arm around her neck, immobilizing her in a headlock. His lower arm pushed against her mouth, and Mozhdah bit down into the flesh as hard as she could, grinding her teeth down to the bone.

"You bitch!" Kardaar shrieked.

Mozhdah twisted away and shoved Kardaar as hard as she could, then leaped towards the table with the purse on it. She flung herself on the handbag, fingers scrambling to undo the clasp, and plunged her hand deep down to the bottom, feeling the touch of cold metal. She grabbed the Beretta, pulled it out, and wrenched around to face Kardaar.

"I'll shoot!" she yelled. The gun shook in her hand.

Mozhdah grabbed her purse and started moving towards the door, gun pointed at Kardaar, who followed her like a predator, step for step. "Don't come any closer!" she said, choking on sobs.

She reached the door, twisted it open while still gripping the purse, and began running up the stairs, praying she wouldn't stumble in her high heels and fall. Hair in disarray, blouse torn, mouth bloodied, she raced past the suv, startling the driver, a gardener, and guards, who gaped in shock at her swollen, bloodied face and smeared makeup. She screamed at the guards to open the gate.

Mozhdah ran until she reached a busy thoroughfare, where she flagged down a dented yellow-and-white taxi that was burping black exhaust. She had never taken a street cab before in Kabul. She gave her address to the driver, who eyed her with alarm in his rearview mirror.

She kept her hand in her purse, gripping the Beretta like a drowning person clings desperately to flotsam. It wasn't even loaded; the ammo was in the bottom of the purse. She was sorry for that. Because, right now, she wished that Kardaar were very, very dead.

PART 4

A Woman's Power

2011–2019

CHAPTER 14

A Bitter Farewell

HOW LONG HAD she slept? Mozhdah's body ached so badly she wasn't sure that she would be able to move. She inched painfully towards the edge of the bed and slowly swung her legs to the floor, one at a time. She had slipped on a tank top and yoga pants, but even these loose garments hurt. The torn blouse, pants, and high heels were in a heap by the dresser—they looked obscene, like an animal carcass at the side of the road.

Mozhdah tasted iron. She carefully ran the tip of her tongue around her mouth to check if there were any loose teeth, then touched the inside of her swollen upper lip, wincing. She inspected the left side of her face—swollen and hot. She noted several broken fingernails.

Her neck ached, and she could only turn it slightly left or right. She grabbed the edge of the mattress to push herself upright, making her head spin and stomach heave.

Water. She was desperately thirsty. There was a water glass in the bathroom.

She walked slowly, stiffly. The glass was on the sink under the mirror. Would she look? What would she see?

The question of how the attack could have happened screamed in her head. What had she done to bring this on? She grabbed the water glass, catching a glimpse of her face in the mirror. As she ran the tap, she stared, curiously detached, at the image: red eyes, smeared makeup, face swollen on one side, upper lip split, crusts of black dried blood around the mouth. She tentatively touched the back of her throbbing head. It too was hot and swollen, the hair matted and dry like sun-burned grass.

This person staring back at her was, at least, alive. But she had rage for eyes and pain for a body. Mozhdah was gone. Who was this person staring back?

Why did he do this? Based upon her brief encounters with Kardaar at 1TV, Mozhdah knew him as cosmopolitan and well traveled. He had worked with enough expats in Afghanistan to know what was acceptable behavior towards women. She had discussed gender violence on her show! She kept looping back to what she might have done wrong. Had she led him on somehow in the past? Did he misinterpret a smile? Did he view the courtesy of a greeting or an inquiry about his health as a come-on? Despite projecting an air of modernity and liberated thinking, was Kardaar so deeply immersed in the cultural attitudes towards women that he had come to view her as a threat? A woman who had to be knocked down a peg, who had challenged the power and privilege of Afghanistan's patri-archal society beyond what was acceptable? Had she risen too high in the eyes of many Afghans, as well as the international community, that she had to be punished for her audacity to presume equality with men?

She was humiliated. Sickened. It felt like punishment for her hubris in coming to Afghanistan—for thinking she could change things. What a fool she was. Mortified by her own naïveté, she felt tears run down her face. *Idiot. Idiot. Idiot.* The word circled her brain like a boa constrictor, strangling all other thought.

Mozhdah gulped four glasses of water, one after another, trying to drown the nausea. She ran a facecloth under the tap and dabbed at the dried blood. The water was cool, and she held the cloth against her face. It brought momentary relief. As she rinsed the cloth, mascara washed down the drain in gray rivulets. Mozhdah gingerly rubbed cream into her face and smoothed her hair into some semblance of order, gathering it into a low ponytail.

Suddenly, she was famished. What time was it? What did it matter? Her show was over. She had to quit. There was no alternative. She had to walk away—no, run—from 1TV. She had to get away from Afghanistan. She couldn't bear the thought of seeing Kardaar again. She trod gingerly down the winding marble staircase in bare feet, grateful for the floor's coolness, and continued into the foyer, turning towards the kitchen at the back of the house.

Her roommate Touba was seated at a stool at the kitchen island, drinking tea and flipping through a magazine. "You slept in," Touba said casually, continuing to peruse the magazine without looking up.

Mozhdah didn't respond, walked over to the fridge, and opened it. Touba glanced up, curious at Mozhdah's silence, and gasped.

"What the hell happened? Were you in a car accident? Good God, Mozhdah, you're black and blue!"

Mozhdah stood in front of the fridge and gratefully closed her eyes as the cold air soothed her swollen face. She grabbed a carton of juice and turned around.

Touba gasped again. "Your face! Your arms! Your... oh my God, Mozhdah, what happened?" She burst into tears and jumped up to approach her friend, stopping an arm's length away, afraid to get too close.

The bruises on her pale skin, Mozhdah realized, stood out in the sunny kitchen so much more than in the muted light of the bathroom. She stared at her arms, covered in constellations of speckled purple and blue, mixed with orange and red—the result, she realized, of being thrown against the pool table and wall.

Mozhdah had planned not to tell anyone. Should she say it had been a car accident? Touba would want details. Mozhdah wasn't mentally capable of concocting a plausible story.

"Mozhdah, what happened?" Touba insisted quietly, reaching out to gently touch her friend's hand. "Tell me."

How could she describe the terror? Haltingly, piecemeal, Mozhdah told her.

Tears streamed down Touba's cheeks. She didn't move, didn't make a sound, as Mozhdah described how Kardaar had lured her to a house for the purpose of coercing her to have sex, and then, when she refused his demands, violently assaulted her. It was only because of the Beretta, Mozhdah said in a small, choking voice, that she wasn't raped—or worse.

"Too bad it wasn't loaded," Touba said.

Mozhdah smiled slightly at Touba's response. "Too bad," she echoed.

"A professional! Someone from the station! It's beyond shocking," Touba said hotly. "You should get out of Kabul," she continued. "Go to Dubai. Stay in a hotel where you can rest and sleep. You need to get away. I will come with you."

"That's a good idea," Mozhdah responded. "But I need to go alone. Stay here and take care of the cats. I'll be okay."

"I'll book you a flight to Dubai a few days from now," Touba said. "You're too much of a mess to go out in public right now. You need to let the swelling on your face go down." She paused and wiped tears off her cheeks. "And I'll make you some breakfast. A bit of toast and tea. Sit down. I'll take care of you," said Touba, squeezing Mozhdah's hand gently.

"Thank you," Mozhdah said. "Thank you."

FOR NEARLY A week, Mozhdah lay in her Dubai hotel bed and ordered meals in. She watched endless television shows and movies that she didn't later remember, took long baths, and watched her blue bruises slowly turn yellow. She continued to agonize. Was the attack her fault? What had she done to cause it? Why would Kardaar do that to her? The questions were like a never-ending drumbeat, reverberating in her brain.

Kardaar called Mozhdah several times on her cell phone while she was in Dubai. She didn't answer, felt bile rise when his number appeared on her iPhone. She sensed he was panicking. Few Afghan women would report such an attack to authorities, in order to protect the family honor. But Mozhdah's international stature, and her Western upbringing, made it more likely she might expose his crime. Mozhdah wrestled over what to do. Should she report Kardaar to the police? Should she take the story to the media? The thought of doing either filled her with dread. The media would take her seriously, but would Afghans believe her? The cultural consensus was that if a woman was assaulted, she was automatically at fault. Perpetrators basked in the glow of impunity. The Afghan public would never believe that a man of Kardaar's stature would do what Mozhdah accused him of. Whispered salacious speculation would follow her if she went public or reported it to the police. It would be the end of her career in Afghanistan.

She wasn't going to let that happen. She wouldn't let her fear of Kardaar drive her out of Afghanistan. And she refused to give up on a career—a life—that saw her working side by side with fellow Afghans who also dreamed of bringing peace and equality to their country. But how could she return to 1TV? How could she risk running into Kardaar at meetings? What if he came after her in a dark corner of the studio? She couldn't go near a place where she might hear his voice or feel his presence. She thought of the companies that had bought advertising for season 2; if she left, they would demand answers for why the season had ended early. Kardaar might insinuate that she had been fired for impropriety, a lack of professionalism— or worse. Mozhdah had her reputation to maintain. But there *was* a way out of this. It wouldn't look good for 1TV—for her friends who worked on *The Mozhdah Show*—but it would give her a legitimate reason for leaving the station.

She would have to act quickly. Mozhdah called Nasrin in Vancouver from her Dubai hotel room.

"Can you please tell TOLO management that I'm ready to talk with them about co-hosting *Afghan Star*. Tell them I want to take *The Mozhdah Show* to TOLO TV as well."

"You're joking," Nasrin said in a shocked voice. "Why leave before the end of the season? It makes no sense!"

"I no longer want to be at 1TV," Mozhdah said bluntly. "Simple as that."

Nasrin was startled at the anger in her daughter's voice. "But, Mozhdah, you love 1TV. You love the people who work there. The show is doing so well. It is ridiculous that you would leave 1TV for TOLO before the season ends," she said with exasperation.

"Fine," snapped Mozhdah. "I'll do it myself."

Of course Mozhdah loved 1TV and her coworkers. She felt badly for those who worked on her show. There was no one who could replace her. The network would lose significant sponsorship money. It would damage the reputation of the station. Well, she thought, that wasn't her problem.

Masood Sanjar, the creator of *Afghan Star*, was startled when he received a message that Mozhdah Jamalzadah was on the line.

"*Salaam*, Mozhdah," he said, picking up the phone. After exchanging niceties, Masood asked Mozhdah why she had called.

"I've received so many offers to work with *Afghan Star* and decided that now's a great time to join TOLO," Mozhdah said in a casual voice.

"Now?" Masood asked, startled.

"Yes," Mozhdah said. "Why not?"

"May I ask why? Aren't you still shooting your second season?"

Mozhdah forced a laugh. "A few creative differences. What's more important," she said, "is that TOLO will be better for my career. I'd like to talk to you about moving *The Mozhdah Show* to TOLO, as well as taking you up on your offer to be co-host on *Afghan Star*."

"I must say, Mozhdah, this is excellent news. I think that TOLO will be a great fit for your show. Let's arrange a meeting. When are you available?"

Mozhdah flew back to Kabul, meeting with the TOLO management team a few days later. Unwilling to involve a still-baffled Nasrin, Mozhdah undertook her own salary negotiations, coming away with a far more generous salary than she was receiving at 1TV. A rough schedule was drawn up for *The Mozhdah Show*'s relaunch.

Secretly, Mozhdah had to force herself to be enthusiastic, pretending to be excited about the move to TOLO. In reality, she was devastated. All she wanted to do was go home to Vancouver, hug Mittens, and hide away in her room, as far away from Afghanistan as she could get. But she wouldn't, because that would concede defeat to Kardaar.

After all she had tried to do, the daily dangers, the rocket attacks that could have killed her—it felt like not only Kardaar had betrayed her but the country had too. She had stayed, using everything she had—education, hope, talent, imagination, and courage—to try to help women, children, orphans, and families. As time wore on, a sense of outrage towards Kardaar grew. Moving to TOLO would be an act of revenge against him. But was there any real satisfaction in that? She was also betraying the staff at 1TV—people who were her friends.

Mozhdah called Nasrin to let her know she had signed a contract. Nasrin bit her tongue.

"Mozhdah *jan*," Nasrin said from their Vancouver home. "Are you alone? Do you have time to talk?"

"Sure," replied Mozhdah.

"What happened? What made you leave 1TV? You loved it there. You loved the show."

"Yup," said Mozhdah.

"That's not an answer," Nasrin replied.

There was silence.

"Are you still there?" Nasrin asked.

"Yup."

"Tell me, Mozhdah. Were there threats? An attack on the station? Did the government threaten to shut down the show?"

"None of the above."

Nasrin sighed. "So what was it then that has made you so upset?"

"You really want to know?" Mozhdah said.

"Yes, of course I do."

"I was stupid. I was so, so stupid," Mozhdah said, her voice cracking.

"What did you do that was stupid, Mozhdah?" Nasrin asked, trying to keep her voice calm.

"A 1TV coworker, Kardaar, he told me that there were journalists who wanted to interview me at this house and sent a vehicle to pick me up."

"Go on," Nasrin urged.

"There weren't any journalists there."

"Oh?" Nasrin said, confused.

"It was a ruse—a lie—to get me by myself," said Mozhdah. "I was led down to this, I dunno, party room, private nightclub, whatever it was on the lower floor. It had pool tables and disco balls."

Nasrin could hear Mozhdah's rapid breathing. She suddenly felt sick. "Go on."

"Kardaar attacked me."

"What?" Nasrin exclaimed.

"He asked me what my price was—said that because I was from the West these... *things*... weren't a big deal. He assumed that because I was a Westerner, I'd... be... easy," Mozhdah spat out the words.

The story poured out, and when she was done, Mozhdah was overcome with sobbing. "I wish I'd shot him," she blurted.

Nasrin had begun shaking as Mozhdah told the story. "Oh my God, what did we do?" she said, her voice cracking.

"What?" Mozhdah said, shocked. "What do you mean?"

"Your father and I should never have allowed you to go to Afghanistan," Nasrin said. "When I was growing up, Afghanistan was a good place. Women were treated with respect. But no longer. I'm so sorry, Mozhdah. It's our fault, it's our fault," she said through tears.

"It wasn't your fault," Mozhdah said.

"Yes, it was," Nasrin said. "Men consider women property. You're just a lowly woman, like other Afghan women, and men believe they can do anything they want to them. We thought you would be treated differently, because you were brought up in the West. Because you were famous. Because you were doing such good work. But I didn't think. I let you walk into danger," she wept.

Mozhdah hung up the phone. She couldn't listen to her mother's self-recriminations, her railing against men—against Afghanistan. It only intensified the bitter voice echoing inside her head.

DRESSED IN A silvery minidress and black leggings, stiletto leather boots, a long fitted black jacket, silver bangles, and her long hair loose topped with a wide glittery headband, Mozhdah waited in the wings. Ten singers were left in the competition of *Afghan Star*, season 6.

"Tonight," host Omid Nezami announced to the riotous studio audience, "give a huge welcome to our special guest star, Mozhdah Jamalzadah!"

The boisterous cheering continued as Mozhdah came onstage, while the studio lighting deepened to a rich blue with wall designs mimicking constellations.

Under Mozhdah's feet, an enormous pink star the size of the stage glowed, created by lighting under the translucent floor. Walking to center stage, she launched into "Better with You," a new, effervescent pop song that set everyone clapping in time to the music. Mozhdah was a spectacle, but inside she felt only despair. However, the audience had no idea and cheered throughout the song's duration. Even the female audience members, many dressed specially for the occasion in bright pastel colors of pink and blue with matching hijabs, normally so careful to hide any emotions, clapped enthusiastically, smiling joyously.

As she left the stage, Mozhdah flashed Omid an engaging, practiced smile, thinking how surprised he would be to hear next week that she would be his new co-host. Mozhdah had been assured he would be thrilled. Some people would feel threatened, going from host to co-host of the nation's most popular show. She hoped he'd be happy; she wasn't sure she had the strength to deal with male hostility.

An unexpected salve to Mozhdah's wretchedness was a phone call that had come out of the blue a few weeks ago. A producer from Harpo Productions, the multimedia company founded by Oprah Winfrey, had contacted Nasrin at her hair salon asking how she might get in touch with Mozhdah. The producer was calling to invite Mozhdah to *Surprise Oprah! A Farewell Spectacular* at the United Center in Chicago. The producer explained that many celebrities would be on the show to commemorate the end of an era in daytime TV. She said that Mozhdah had come to the attention of Harpo not only because of her White House appearance but also her numerous interviews on American news channels. It was remarkable, said the producer, to hear how Oprah had inspired Mozhdah, resulting in the creation of a talk show that helped educate Afghans about topics that Oprah had also addressed. As a talk show host in the war-torn nation of Afghanistan, Mozhdah symbolized the global impact of *The Oprah Winfrey Show*. They would love for Mozhdah to come to the spectacular—as a *surprise* guest.

"Oprah would be thrilled to meet Mozhdah," the producer said. "But—and this is important," she added, "you can't breathe a word about it to anyone. It *has* to remain a secret!"

Nasrin gave Mozhdah's cell phone number to the producer, then waited until later that evening to call her in Afghanistan, where it was early morning.

"Did anyone from Harpo Productions get in touch with you yet?" Nasrin asked.

"No," Mozhdah said. "But I just turned my phone on. I have messages waiting but haven't checked them yet." She paused. "What do you mean, Harpo Productions?"

Nasrin's words tumbled over one another in her excitement. "One of Oprah's producers called. There's a finale, a show. You're invited. You're a surprise!"

"Mom, talk sense!" Mozhdah exclaimed, laughing.

"You're Oprah's surprise!" Nasrin said excitedly.

"What do you mean?'"

"They're going to surprise Oprah by presenting you and your story about your work in Afghanistan. Oprah knows nothing about it!"

Meanwhile, Mozhdah visited 1TV before the *Afghan Star* segment aired—and before word got out that she was making a permanent move to TOLO. She couldn't leave her 1TV coworkers without saying goodbye, and she had personal items in her studio dressing room to collect.

Mozhdah visited close to midday, when the staff for her show would be around but getting ready for a lunch break. She planned to breeze in and say her goodbyes quickly. Mozhdah had come up with a vague but plausible excuse that her recent absence at 1TV was because of a family emergency in Vancouver that had required her to fly home.

But Mozhdah's hugs were longer than usual, her mood somber.

Producer Neelofar Neda sensed something, whispering accusingly, "You're leaving us, and you're not coming back," while staring hard at Mozhdah.

What could Mozhdah say to that? She couldn't lie to Neelofar, so she said nothing. Mozhdah knew Neelofar had seen too many people leave the station, leave Afghanistan altogether, not to detect the note of finality, resignation, and mourning that came with permanent farewells. This was the way of Afghanistan. People evaporated like ghosts: killed by insurgents, disappeared to other parts of the world as refugees, gone into hiding, or returned home to the West.

"Take care of yourself, Mozhdah," Neelofar said quietly. "Good luck."

After saying her goodbyes and gathering some of her personal items, Mozhdah returned to TOLO. Omid, to her relief, expressed genuine enthusiasm at sharing co-hosting duties, and the *Afghan Star* production crew went out of their way to be kind and supportive of Mozhdah. Unlike 1TV, TOLO allowed Mozhdah to wear whatever she wanted. She could forgo the hated hijab, a move that would make her one of the first Afghan women on television to go without the traditional head covering. (One of TOLO TV's earliest shows, the short-lived *Hop*, similar to MTV's *Total Request Live*, featured female veejays who occasionally bared their heads.)

Ever since its creation, TOLO TV had challenged traditions. Its founder, Saad Mohseni, an Afghan-Australian banker whose family went into exile after the Soviet invasion in 1979, had returned to Afghanistan after the fall of the Taliban in 2001 and founded the media company MOBY GROUP. In 2003, Saad launched the FM radio station Arman, playing Western pop stars like Madonna and Shakira alongside Afghan musicians. It was a revelation following the ban on music and media by the Taliban, who only permitted the operation of the radio station Voice of Sharia, which broadcast religious news. TOLO, which MOBY started a year later, worked to further break down ignorance, illiteracy, and conservatism. Eight out of ten Afghans owned a radio, and four out of ten owned a television, so TOLO TV dramas and news presented a new way of thinking to much of the country. Programs showed women working alongside men as equals. *Afghan Star* was an especially defiant expression of gender equality, where women not only believed they were as good singers as men but competed against them to prove they were better.

In a country where the first presidential elections since the 1979 Soviet invasion didn't occur until 2004, *Afghan Star* was also one of the only times in recent history that Afghans could exercise their voting power. Although the show's four judges—always one female—chose the best contestants for the show, the public would vote for their favorite singers using smartphones. Every week, whoever had the fewest votes left the competition. The cachet of winning *Afghan Star* was long-lasting. For season 6, the winner would take home a new Nissan car, in addition to making a music video with TOLO, possibly kick-starting a viable musical career. This usually meant being a wedding singer, which in Afghanistan was a prestigious as well as lucrative occupation.

Mozhdah and Omid's time on the show was set to be a revolutionary style moment for Afghans. Under the Taliban, men had to dress modestly, with untrimmed beards and loose clothing that covered the arms and legs. Women, of course, became invisible under the obligatory burka. Mozhdah wore short skirts with leggings, high leather boots, tailored jackets, and extravagant jewelry. Omid sported a cool, messy hairstyle, coiffed by a stylist before each show. Once the show began airing, young men throughout the country started to emulate his look.

Mozhdah's move to TOLO didn't deter the Taliban or religious conservatives from directing their bile at her. Individuals, claiming to be Taliban, accused *Afghan Star* of being anti-Islamic on social media and sent threatening messages to the station. But such threats were accepted as part of everyday operations at TOLO, and security guards and staff kept a careful eye out for possible suicide bomb attacks directed at the station. The threats only entrenched TOLO TV's reputation as a force against the Taliban's violent religious extremism, and Mozhdah's dress and confidence showed Afghan women what the freedom to choose could look like.

It was impossible for Mozhdah not to get a caught up in the excitement of *Afghan Star*. The energy she felt backstage, talking to the contestants and working with the TOLO production staff, provided some respite from the darkness that only seemed to grow inside her as time went on. Ever since Kardaar's assault, Mozhdah had spiraled into a depression but also felt a heightened sense of danger, recoiling in distrust when men, young or old, came too close. The sense of self-blame grew in her mind, even though she knew it was irrational. Yes, there were dangers: suicide bombings and kidnappings. But such risks could be mitigated by concrete walls topped with barbed wire, armed guards, tinted vehicle windows, and secret travel plans. But how could you cope when people you trusted, people you had worked with, became the source of peril? Where was safety? Where was any sense of security? Mozhdah's reflexes recalibrated so that normal nighttime creaking jolted her awake. She was only able to sleep by locking the bedroom door, the Beretta within easy reach.

Although she was on high alert, her emotions seemed frozen; she felt little empathy when, week after week, singers were voted off, the losers bursting into tears backstage, to be comforted by equally teary-eyed fellow contestants. She felt a genuine flicker of emotion when one of the young female contestants, dressed in a traditional voluminous *tunbaan*—a long tunic dress with pants that went to the ankles, as well as a heavy hijab—came up to Mozhdah and whispered: "If I had a foreign passport, I would dress like you. You can wear all of this and go back to Canada. But I can't. I'm stuck here. I still have to walk around the streets of Kabul." The young woman's bitterness was something Mozhdah could relate to.

For the show's March 21 finale, Mozhdah debuted another new song, titled *"Afghanistan Watanem,"* or "Afghanistan— My Nation, My Home." The tune, with its buoyant beat and radiant melody, was an exuberant song of patriotism for Afghanistan. *"Afghanistan Watanem"* quickly became the country's number one song, and TOLO played it several times a day. When she saw how much Afghans loved the song, Mozhdah felt a flutter of joy. Such moments of happiness and excitement, however, were rare.

The idealism that had fueled her drive to help others had evaporated too. She gazed dully at the child beggars on the street, filthy from tousled head to barefoot toes, coated in thick beige dirt. It was like they were part of the landscape. She felt powerless. Looking at them only fed her endless ruminations: *How could I have been so stupid to think I could make a difference— that I could help them?*

After *Afghan Star's* finale, Mozhdah returned home to Vancouver. It was a relief to drop the pretense of enthusiasm required for interaction with TOLO staff and *Afghan Star* competitors and simply snuggle into Mittens's purring warmth. She had several months before TOLO would have the new set and production schedule ready for the revival of *The Mozhdah Show.*

One day, while seated on her bed next to a snoozing Mittens, answering emails, a message popped up from Saad Mohseni, TOLO TV's owner. The subject line stated, "Urgent!"

She clicked it open. "Where are you? There are rumors you're dead," the email read.

Mozhdah sighed. Another death rumor. She was about to type a response when Nasrin knocked on her bedroom door and pushed it open.

"Mozhdah, your father just called from Kandahar by satellite phone," Nasrin said. Bashir had continued as a cultural adviser with the Canadian Armed Forces, whose combat role in Afghanistan was slowly winding down. "He has received calls and emails from friends, family members, and colleagues asking if you're alive."

"I just got an email from Saad, saying people are gossiping that I've been killed. I'm just responding now," Mozhdah said, typing a lighthearted response: "Rumors of my death are greatly exaggerated."

She pushed send and continued, "Mom, there are always rumors. It's Afghanistan! Last week, they said I was in a coma following a car accident. The week before that, they said I'd been kidnapped. It's ridiculous. Afghans love gossip—the darker the better."

"People are taking the rumors seriously, Mozhdah," Nasrin said worriedly. "I wonder what's going on."

Maybe word had gotten out that *The Mozhdah Show* was being reprised, Mozhdah thought. That would certainly anger conservatives, religious fundamentalists, and the Taliban— anyone who opposed women voicing an opinion or being in a position of power. Any woman entering the public realm had to steel herself for an onslaught of threats from those with antediluvian cultural and religious beliefs. Mozhdah, by now, was a seasoned veteran.

"Mom," Mozhdah said in an annoyed voice, "It's *normal*."

A few days later, Mozhdah had packed two enormous suitcases full of outfits to wear at the TOLO TV tapings of *The Mozhdah Show*. She was nervous; there wouldn't be the same camaraderie or sense of family that had buoyed tapings at 1TV, that excitement of being trailblazers. She picked up Mittens, who had just turned seventeen, and buried her face in his black-and-white fur. She was reluctant to leave him. Mittens slept most of the time, had lost weight, and was barely able to jump onto Mozhdah's bed.

She kissed the whiskery face. "I'll be back soon, Mitty," she promised.

The flight to Afghanistan from Vancouver had the usual stopovers. First, London's Heathrow Airport, followed by Dubai in the United Arab Emirates, then another plane into Kabul International Airport. During the London layover, Mozhdah switched the SIM card in her cell phone to the one she used in Afghanistan. Immediately, her screen filled with a litany of text messages, as well as missed calls from the Canadian embassy in Kabul, with urgent requests to contact them. Alarmed, Mozhdah punched in the embassy's number. A secretary told Mozhdah that someone would call her back. Several minutes later, Mozhdah's phone rang. She got up from her seat and began walking slowly through the airport, ensuring no one overheard the conversation.

The embassy employee introduced himself, engaged in a moment of polite chatter, and then said, "I'm sorry Mozhdah, there is no way to sugarcoat this, but our intelligence says that you're in danger and there is a direct threat on your life. You're in London? Please don't continue to Kabul. Turn around and return to Vancouver."

"Oh, those are just rumors," Mozhdah said, with a lightness she didn't feel. "I hear them all the time."

"No, Mozhdah," the embassy staff member said. "We've investigated the threats, and they are legitimate. Please, go home—now."

"But I can't," Mozhdah protested. "I have a house in Kabul. I have cats. I have a life there, and my show's about to start."

There was a chilly pause. "Well, you've been warned. If you continue to Kabul, you must be very discreet and very, very cautious. And get out as soon as possible."

"I promise to be careful," Mozhdah said. "Thanks for the warning."

Mozhdah briefly debated whether to return to Vancouver, then berated herself for letting fear get the better of her. She wouldn't be intimidated by anyone, whether they were terrorists—or men like Kardaar.

Stiff, tired, and anxious, Mozhdah arrived at Kabul airport and began to walk with her fellow passengers to the arrival gate to pick up her luggage, looking around for an airport employee to assist her. One came trotting over, exclaiming: "We thought you had died! We heard that your nose and ears and head had been cut off!"

"You shouldn't pay attention to ridiculous rumors," Mozhdah responded sharply.

The encounter did nothing to relieve Mozhdah's unease, which continued until her first rehearsal for her show two days later. TOLO TV sent an armored SUV to pick Mozhdah up from her house in Wazir Akbar Khan. At the studio, she and the producers went over scripts, while crew members made adjustments to lighting, sound, and camera. Afterwards, a staff member asked Mozhdah to follow him to Saad Mohseni's office.

Seated behind his desk, Saad got up to greet Mozhdah, congenially asking her how rehearsal went and inviting her to sit down.

"Well," Mozhdah responded, "there are a few bugs to work out, but it's a solid production team. I'm looking forward to our first show."

Saad nodded, then looked at Mozhdah, saying that he had heard about the phone call from the Canadian embassy, and the dire warning.

"How do you know about that?" Mozhdah said, surprised. She hadn't told anyone about the call but knew that Saad had connections with government officials, diplomats, intelligence agents, journalists, businesspeople, even the Taliban. On second thought, it wasn't surprising that Saad knew about the phone call—he probably knew details about the threat.

Saad looked hard at Mozhdah. "I'm sorry to say this," he said gravely, "but *The Mozhdah Show* is being canceled. Get out of Kabul. Don't lose your life because of this place. It's not worth it."

Mozhdah stared at Saad, her body suddenly tingling with fear. "Okay," she said in a small, shocked voice. She felt, suddenly, like Icarus, plummeting to earth.

But Mozhdah couldn't leave Kabul immediately, as Harpo Productions had bought her a first-class ticket to Chicago to attend the upcoming *Surprise Oprah! A Farewell Spectacular*. The excitement she had felt over the imminent taping was subsumed, however, by despair over her show's cancellation. A welcome distraction was a guest appearance on a TOLO TV music show, which at least put to rest rumors of her death. But a thought grew in her mind: perhaps Afghanistan's religion-fueled misogyny, as much a part of the country as its hard-baked, mountainous landscape, was too powerful a force to fight against. Mozhdah had wanted to help the people of her home country, especially girls and women. She had been given a national platform and the backing of some of the most talented people in media. And she had failed.

As she boarded the plane for Chicago, Mozhdah suddenly realized that she couldn't fight anymore. When the flight attendant, pushing her snacks and beverage cart along the narrow aisle, asked Mozhdah, "Would you like coffee, tea, or a soft drink?" she shook her head, keeping her face turned towards the oval plane window, and let the tears trickle down her cheeks.

CHAPTER 15

Highs and Lows

ASRIN ARRIVED IN Chicago from Vancouver the same day as Mozhdah, who was bone tired from the long trip from Kabul, and hungry. They had a light dinner at the hotel restaurant.

"Remind me again what the Harpo producer told you when she called you at the salon last year," Mozhdah said, trying to distract herself from her bleak thoughts.

Nasrin laughed, recalling the conversation. "She asked me for your phone number in Afghanistan. After you sang in Washington for the Obamas and appeared on American television discussing your talk show, Harpo Productions decided to invite you to Oprah's final TV show as a surprise guest. After nearly twenty-five years, the show was going off the air, and they were planning a huge celebration. But the producer swore me to secrecy. I couldn't tell anyone in the salon—it nearly killed me!"

After Mozhdah had talked to the Harpo producer and told her she was thrilled to appear on the *Farewell Spectacular*, the company had hired a local camera crew in Kabul to interview her about her television work in Afghanistan and the impact of *The Mozhdah Show*. The filming took place at Darul Aman Palace, an elegant and imposing neoclassical stone edifice on the western outskirts of the city. Over the years, the palace survived fires and years of mujahideen violence, when factions struggled for control of the city, blasting entire wings of the structure into rubble with rockets.

There, in the stately and proud building—a symbol of Afghan resilience—Mozhdah answered questions: "What is it like being compared to Oprah?" "In what way has Oprah inspired you?" "Why did you create a show based upon the concept of *The Oprah Winfrey Show*?" "What made you return to Afghanistan to pursue your show?"

On the flight to Chicago, Mozhdah had increasingly felt like a fraud. She was being recognized for a show that no longer existed. The only thing that kept her from sinking into total despair was the thought that she would meet the woman she had looked up to since she was a teen—the spark for *The Mozhdah Show*. Mozhdah was scheduled to meet the Harpo producers tomorrow at the studio, as they wanted to add to the video they had shot in Kabul, and she desperately hoped they wouldn't ask how her show was doing. She couldn't bear to reveal the truth.

THE TAPED INTERVIEW at Harpo Studios was undemanding, much to Mozhdah's relief. For the May 17 filming at Chicago's United Center, Mozhdah wore a navy-blue dress with rhinestones on the front, bought by Nasrin from Bloomingdale's especially for the occasion. Mozhdah arrived early, so a Harpo producer took her on a tour of the building that would soon hold twenty thousand exuberant fans.

About an hour later, stars began to trickle backstage: Tom Cruise, Jerry Seinfeld, Dr. Mehmet Oz, Dr. Phil, Madonna, Tom Hanks, Beyoncé, Will Smith, Jada Pinkett Smith, and other famous guests. Many introduced themselves to Mozhdah, including Tom Cruise. Mozhdah was flattered, as well as awestruck, by these superstars. Hanks told Mozhdah he'd love to be a guest on her show, and she chatted at length with Dr. Oz.

Mozhdah wasn't Oprah's only surprise guest. While Mozhdah waited in the wings among the Hollywood actors, singers, and celebrities, Hanks, who stood next to Oprah on the stage, introduced another guest, a dedicated viewer who was a "hardworking mother of four who says the show means the world to her." When Madonna walked onstage, Oprah couldn't contain herself. "Get out!" she screamed.

"It's no secret millions of people are inspired by Oprah," said Madonna, dressed in a vintage-style black kimono with delicate white cherry blossoms, her blonde hair waved. "I am one of those people," she told the crowd.

When it came time to reveal Mozhdah as Oprah's next special guest, the producers first showed the short video that had been created at Darul Aman Palace and Chicago's Harpo Studios, which included clips from her eponymous show. In the video, Mozhdah explained how the show started in Afghanistan and how much Oprah had inspired its format. Oprah had helped millions of people around the world, and Mozhdah had been inspired to do the same for Afghans.

Then, Madonna came to the mic. "Please welcome this courageous young woman—Mozhdah Jamalzadah!"

Thrilled and excited, Mozhdah didn't even feel her feet touch the ground as she walked towards Madonna, who kissed her on both cheeks. Then Oprah, her glossy black hair pulled into a ponytail, wearing a purple dress, hugged Mozhdah. Enfolded in Oprah's arms, Mozhdah had the curious sensation that she was being embraced by the world.

AS SHE WAS leaving Chicago to return to Vancouver, Mozhdah felt like she had awoken from a dream to find a world robbed of color. That day on *Surprise Oprah! A Farewell Spectacular* had been, Mozhdah thought to herself, the best day of her life. She had forgotten, if only briefly, the attack by Kardaar and the canceling of *The Mozhdah Show* by TOLO TV. Now, returning home, she felt alone and frightened. Like Oprah, her show was over. But what a difference! The *Farewell Spectacular* celebrated everything that Oprah had accomplished. In comparison, Mozhdah's show had been choked out of existence by hatred, by people who wanted to destroy everything she stood for: equality and justice for children and women, freedom from violence, and a love of music. Worse, a respected colleague, who should have supported Mozhdah, had, instead, assaulted her, destroying her sense of self-worth. If it hadn't been for the Beretta...

What would Mozhdah do with herself now? She had no show; she had no purpose. She stopped reading newspapers or watching television news. She avoided social media. She read, slept, and planned nothing.

One day she stood, glaring at her reflection in the mirror in the bathroom of her parents' Vancouver home, and picked up a pair of scissors. Slowly, she lifted the scissors to her long hair and, chunk by chunk, cut it off. Afterwards, her hair around her feet, she gripped the sides of the bathroom sink, forcing herself to look at—dissect—her visage. What did she see? Dark circles under her eyes, a puffy face. Her knuckles whitened. She was so tired. Tired of the person staring back at her, tired of a dreariness that makeup couldn't mask. Mozhdah could feel the sadness emanating from the reflection, like waves of summer heat off black tarmac.

Mozhdah's parents hadn't said anything about the changes in their daughter, sending furtive glances her way as her list-lessness increased and she gained more and more weight. But when Mozhdah chopped her hair off, Nasrin finally protested. "Why?" she demanded sharply.

"It's too much work," Mozhdah said. "I don't want to deal with it anymore."

Nasrin felt powerless. She didn't know how to help her daughter—didn't know what to say—wondered how she could lift Mozhdah out of her despondency and silence. Nasrin knew they should talk about Kardaar but feared that if she initiated a discussion about it, Mozhdah might simply disappear even further inside her shell of melancholy.

Over the months following the cancellation of her show, Mozhdah's sense of failure over the stillborn program grew. She imagined the gleeful faces of those who had threatened her life, their self-satisfaction over the conquest of another mere woman who dared to challenge the religious and conservative social order. Mozhdah wondered if she should have fought harder to re-launch *The Mozhdah Show*. Was she a coward? The thought haunted her, stoking thoughts of self-recrimination.

Then, one day, while Mozhdah was shopping, she received a phone call from her brother Safee. "We're at the vet's," Safee said in a stricken voice. "Mittens had a stroke."

Mozhdah ran to her car and jumped in, driving as fast as she could to the veterinary clinic, cursing Vancouver's snarled traffic. Nasrin was waiting when she arrived and gripped her arm, steering her into one of the examination rooms. Mittens lay on a towel. Her brothers stood in the room, grief stricken.

"He was in pain," Nasrin said. "The vet put him to sleep."

Mozhdah began sobbing hysterically as she picked up Mittens's limp black-and-white body and held it against her chest. Finally, the vet took him away for cremation. Her brother drove her car home as Mozhdah wept.

Mozhdah was inconsolable. It was as if Mittens's death opened up floodgates of pain over all she had lost: her career, her feelings of safety, and her native country, Afghanistan itself. She sobbed, not only for the loss of her pet but for all the hurt and bitterness she had tried to suppress. What was the point, Mozhdah thought, of even being here? What was there to live for?

Mozhdah wondered whether she would ever feel happy again. Kardaar still had her hair in his fist. *I have to escape this man*, she thought. *I have to escape this unhappiness.* But how? How could she extricate herself from Kardaar's control, from the sorrow that consumed her? Yes, Kardaar had attacked her, and the extremists had stopped her show, but why wasn't she fighting back? Until she did, they had won.

But first, she had to figure out why she had been so easily fooled by Kardaar, why she didn't remove herself from the situation more quickly or protect herself better. What were the masks that men wore?

She asked female friends in Vancouver whether they had ever been violated or abused by men. The answer, consistently, was yes. At a party, at work, walking home at night—there were always men who demanded sex, or tried to take it by force, or simply tried to dominate women in the workplace or in the home. It shocked her. Yes, there were many more good men than bad. But the problem wasn't just men in Afghanistan, it was those in Vancouver too, and elsewhere: men who acted upon their worst instincts if they thought they wouldn't get caught. She would never blame her female friends for what these men did, so why was she feeling that she was at fault for what had transpired in Kabul? It didn't matter what a woman did—or didn't do—the threat would always be there. So what could she do?

Never stop fighting, she thought.

Mozhdah stared into the mirror. "Bring it on," she said, with a grim smile. "Bring it on."

AFTER SEVERAL MONTHS, Mozhdah felt ready to grow her hair long again and stop hiding. She would try once again to help better society—she *would* make it better. Music was what had first propelled her to Afghanistan, and music, she decided, would launch her return. Mozhdah had remained in contact with TOLO TV, and when the producers asked her to once again co-host *Afghan Star* alongside Omid Nezami, for 2012's season 8, she eagerly agreed. There was less risk to Mozhdah's safety co-hosting *Afghan Star*, because of its lack of controversy and nationwide popularity. Nonetheless, the ten shows would be taped under tightened security. This time, Mozhdah felt herself buoyed by the enthusiasm and excitement of the contestants, and encouraged them while she was backstage. She especially loved talking to the female competitors, who shyly admitted that, as Afghanistan's biggest female pop star, they expected Mozhdah to be haughty and unapproachable. They didn't expect her to be, so, well, *nice.*

Mozhdah returned to Canada immediately after *Afghan Star* was finished. There was never any talk of revising *The Mozhdah Show.* For Mozhdah, for Afghans, for TOLO TV, it was too great a risk—another Afghanistan dream dashed. Depression seeped into Mozhdah's consciousness once more. She fought against its suffocating heaviness, focusing on her physical needs while taking time for self-reflection, sleep, and conversation with friends. As she had done during those miserable, lonely times during elementary school, Mozhdah read voraciously—self-help books this time—several of them recommended by a therapist she saw occasionally. She reread *The Power* by Rhonda Byrne, which promoted the idea that individuals are capable of controlling the impact of past experiences. She carried it like a holy book, marking pages, opening it up to read, reread, and reread again. The passage "Whether your thoughts and feelings are good or bad, they return as automatically and precisely as an echo" became a mantra.

Mozhdah realized she was responsible for curating her future, trusted that her aspirations held boundless power, and knew that she could envision and manifest her highest ambitions. She faced her irrational self-recrimination over Kardaar's attack. Mozhdah realized that the feelings of hatred, betrayal, and bitterness that she harbored towards Kardaar and those who threatened to kill her had choked her creative energy. *I was attacked once,* Mozhdah thought. *Many Afghan women are attacked by their husbands or fathers or brothers or uncles. But they carry on. I am lucky in a way they aren't. For so many women, home is a war zone; danger comes from those who should protect them. My family life is a place of love and safety. This is my strength.*

While working around the house, Mozhdah would sometimes listen on YouTube to Oprah's past speeches and her interviews from *The Oprah Winfrey Show*. There was one special passage from a commencement speech Oprah gave in 2012 to the graduates of Spelman College in Atlanta, Georgia, that made Mozhdah catch her breath. "You don't worry about revenge, about getting back at somebody, making sure they pay, you just have to do the right thing," Oprah told the women's college grads. They were the right words at the right time, somehow giving Mozhdah that extra push she needed to revive her dreams of bringing change and enlightenment to the world.

Mozhdah began to work on new songs, and searched for lyricists and composers whose work expressed passion and eloquence. Without a talk show, music was now her voice—a voice of rebellion against the cruelty perpetrated in the name of religion. In calling out violence, she would become an advocate for peace.

She was infused with a sense of determination, even joy, and Nasrin resumed managing and promoting Mozhdah's career. In June 2013, Mozhdah started singing at concerts in Afghanistan, as well as Europe, Canada, and the United States—anywhere the Afghan diaspora had settled. She composed a new song in Farsi, with lyrics written by Habib Yosufi, to help launch her comeback. *"Beyshay-e Sheran,"* "The Homeland of the Lions," was a song for Afghanistan. "This nation will never surrender by force and for gold / The history stands witness that this is the thicket of the lions." She flew into Afghanistan to sing at concerts that were taped and televised on TOLO, Ariana, and Khurshid TV stations in Kabul. For the next two years, Mozhdah's home became anywhere there were Afghans to sing to.

MOZHDAH'S LIFE ON the road was a busy and happy one, though she was nagged by the sense that she should be doing more for Afghans. Then, one day in early 2015, Mozhdah's email began to fill up with messages from friends and acquaintances: "Have you heard?" "Is it true?" "Something horrible has happened." "There's an awful video on YouTube." The same was happening on Twitter and Facebook. Mozhdah checked CNN and other online news channels. Nothing. Mozhdah sent out emails to her friends at TOLO, receiving cryptic responses about an attack on a young woman by dozens of men in the heart of Kabul, close to the Shah-e Du Shamshira mosque. It was a place Mozhdah knew well, a congested, busy square full of vendors and tiny shops beside the Kabul River. TOLO reporters were still investigating.

More news trickled in. The woman had not only been attacked but killed—her body then burned. Rumors whirled. Her name, some outlets were reporting, was Farkhunda. She had burned a Quran in a Muslim shrine. An outraged mob of men beat her to death as punishment. Social media users in Afghanistan were self-righteous: killing this woman was the only way to restore honor to the prophet Muhammad. Bystanders had taken footage of the attack on their smartphones and posted it to YouTube. Mozhdah couldn't bear to watch, her mind suddenly hijacked by memories of powerlessness and terror at the hands of Kardaar. Her body tightened with sharp, painful recall.

The story unfurled over the next few days, and Mozh-dah anxiously followed as the details emerged. Farkhunda Malikzada, who was twenty-seven, had not burned a Quran. Rather, this deeply religious young woman, who had planned to study theology at Kabul University, had earlier confronted a caretaker at the Shah-e Du Shamshira ziarat, or shrine. This had been on a Wednesday—a day when only women are allowed into the shrine—and the man was selling *tawiz*, amulets made of tiny pieces of paper with writing on them. *Tawiz* are supposed to bring good luck in love affairs, in health, and to ensure a woman bears male children. Typically, women use them the most, pinning these talismans to their clothing, or hiding them in the home. They cost about a hundred Afghanis, almost two days' wages. Farkhunda confronted the charlatan, chastising him for taking money from these superstitious, unhappy women, telling him that what he was doing was un-Islamic.

Later, on March 19, Farkhunda confronted the *tawiz* seller again. The Shah-e Du Shamshira custodian, named Zain-ul-Din, was there that day. It was Zain-ul-Din who falsely claimed that Farkhunda had burned the Quran. Some said that Farkhunda had taken the amulets and burned them in a trash can, which Zain-ul-Din pointed to as evidence that Farkhunda had burned the Islamic holy book.

Nearby men, loitering in the afternoon sun, heard Zain-ul-Din's accusations and came to investigate. The attack ensued at about 4:00 PM. Two nearby policemen tried to save Farkhunda by dragging her onto a shed roof. But, with men swinging pieces of wood at her, she lost her grip—falling to her doom. Cell phone videos taken by witnesses showed Farkhunda screaming, writhing in pain, and begging for mercy. After she was run over by a car and dragged nearly a hundred yards, Farkhunda ceased to move. Afterwards, her body was set ablaze in the dry riverbed of the adjacent Kabul River. Mozhdah gasped in horror as she read how Farkhunda's attackers used their kaffiyeh scarves to start the fire that burned her body—her own clothes were too blood-soaked to ignite.

It was weeks before Mozhdah found the courage to watch the videos of Farkhunda being beaten to death. News report followed news report—nationally and internationally—and the claim that Farkhunda burned the Quran was quickly refuted. Mozhdah was sickened—outraged. Even if Farkhunda had burned a Quran—so what? "Any religion that elevates a mere book—holy or not—above human life is a belief system that belongs back in the Dark Ages," Mozhdah bitterly told her father.

The atrocity brought the behavior of Afghan men under an international microscope. It also became clear that these were not Taliban or suicide bombers but fathers, brothers, friends, colleagues—ordinary men who walked the streets of Kabul on a daily basis. *Men like Kardaar*, thought Mozhdah, as she wept with horror at the brutality that Farkhunda had endured in her final hour.

Shortly after Farkhunda's murder, an eighteen-year-old Afghan-Australian musician named Eman Rawi approached Mozhdah with a composition and asked if she would like to put lyrics to it. Mozhdah and Bashir listened to the music together, marveling at its haunting power.

"This should be a song for Farkhunda," said Bashir, who was as devastated as Mozhdah over the death. He wrote the lyrics in two hours in Farkhunda's voice, giving immortality to a young woman brutally and unjustly slain. He titled the elegy *"Dokhte Watan,"* or "Tribute to Farkhunda—Daughter of Homeland."

Several years before, Bashir had written a poem titled *"Ghoroore Tu, Shikaste Man,"* or "Your Pride, My Poison," a blunt denunciation of Afghan men's abusive treatment of women. Mozhdah was so impressed by Eman Rawi's first composition that she asked him if he would compose music for this poem as well. He happily obliged, and the result was as fierce and passionate as "Tribute to Farkhunda."

Only a few months after Farkhunda's death, Mozhdah was booked, along with one other Afghan female singer, to perform at an outdoor concert on the grounds of Khurshid TV. The audience of about a thousand consisted mainly of young men. The few women in attendance sat, as they do at public events, in the first few rows of chairs, for safety's sake.

The audience would be expecting the lighthearted, patriotic music that Mozhdah had sung for audiences during her stints at *Afghan Star* on TOLO, *The Mozhdah Show* at 1TV, and her more recent concert tours. She was planning to sing the popular "Afghan Girl," but she also intended to debut Bashir's new dark and haunting songs.

Nasrin worried what the response would be. "They won't like it," she said, in their room at the Serena Hotel, while styling Mozhdah's hair into a high, elegant pompadour with jeweled headband.

A minute ticked by. Nasrin assumed that Mozhdah had ignored her statement. Then Mozhdah blurted out, "You know the real reason Farkhunda was killed?"

"Tell me," Nasrin replied.

"She was killed," said Mozhdah, "because she was a woman standing up to a man. Our society, our culture, says that men can do this—they are allowed to maim, kill, and slaughter women—with virtual impunity. You're right, the audience won't like my new songs. But someone has to stand up for women—let men know that what Farkhunda's attackers did was immoral and wrong."

Nasrin sighed. It was evident from what she'd seen on social media that she had reason to be concerned. A month ago, Mozhdah had posted the lyrics of the new songs in Farsi on her Facebook page. Many followers expressed their support, though others responded with hostility. Someone calling himself Said Nabi Ludin wrote in poor English: "Can you just get over this women bulshit."

Mozhdah, refusing to turn the other cheek to online trolls, typed a quick reply: "NO I will NOT get over what happened to her. Go F yourself."

Nasrin had contacted Khurshid TV about the security, and they assured her it was adequate. She hoped it wouldn't be tested.

The concert started when darkness fell. Mozhdah began with several of her well-known, popular songs, the outdoor arena erupting with cheers, whistles, stomping, and dancing. She then sang "Tribute to Farkhunda" in Farsi, in the voice of Farkhunda, as if she were speaking from the grave. As Mozhdah sang, the boisterous audience quieted, and a frisson of anger tingled in the warm night air.

It is not a sin to be a woman
Don't beat me with sticks and rocks
Don't burn my body and

Don't silence my melody
Now, better being under the dirt
Than living with wild monsters . . .

Mozhdah looked out over the audience and saw that the smiling faces had gone stony, eyes glaring, arms crossed, bodies rigid. The audience clearly hadn't enjoyed "Tribute to Farkhunda." They were angry. Did she dare sing the next song? Yes, this concert would be televised on Khurshid TV—her message would sweep Afghanistan. It was the reason she was here. She couldn't back out now. The band began to play "Your Pride, My Poison," with its slow, ominous introduction and lyrics that were a grief-stricken angry lament, intensified by marching-band rhythms. Mozhdah detected disgruntled mutterings from the audience. The women in the front rows looked alarmed.

I am a woman, sister, and mother;
I'm the one who gave you life.
Don't stone me to death
Don't chain my feet to the ground
I am alive, don't blind me.
Don't darken my world . . .

By the time the song ended, the men in the crowd were glowering. Some got up from their seats. Were they coming towards the stage? No, they were walking out. The remaining audience became louder—but not with cheering.

I'm going to be attacked, she thought.

Smiling to cover her fear, Mozhdah said a few words of thanks to the audience and moved gracefully offstage. She caught the eye of Nasrin, seated in the front row with relatives from Kabul. Nasrin shook her head slightly, looking around surreptitiously at the audience. As Mozhdah reached the safety of backstage, she stood gratefully in the shadows. But her hand shook as she handed the microphone to a stagehand, heart thudding in her chest. Had alienating some of the men in the audience been worth it? Yes, she thought, this was another necessary step in calling out men on their violence. She just wished it weren't so terrifying.

CHAPTER 16

A Dance
in the Dark

E ARLY IN 2016, Ariana Television Network's ATN
Awards organizers contacted Mozhdah. Since
that year marked ATN's tenth-annual celebra-
tion of Afghan musical talent, they wanted it to be especially
memorable. The organizers told her they had commissioned
Afghanistan's most famous singer, Farhad Darya, to write a
song for Mozhdah to debut at the award show, which was
being held in Istanbul, Turkey.

Mozhdah was ecstatic. Farhad Darya had been a musical
fixture in the Jamalzadah home since the 1980s, when he first
began releasing music in exile during the Soviet–Afghan war.
His songs, calling for peace and unity in Afghanistan, mir-
rored the collective consciousness of the diaspora, becoming a
soundtrack, of sorts, for Mozhdah's own growing ambition to
help Afghanistan as she grew up. Mozhdah had been thrilled
when, the year before, at the ninth-annual ATN Awards, held

in Kuala Lumpur, Malaysia, Farhad had personally presented her with the Best Female Artist Award.

Singing a song that this legendary singer had written just for her would be a career highlight. But Farhad was busy touring, and as the days crept closer to the show, set for April 5, 2016, Mozhdah came to the gut-wrenching and panicked realization that Farhad didn't have time to create a song for her to sing at the ceremony.

The ATN organizers were at a loss and asked Mozhdah if she might have a solution.

"Let me go to my producer, Ovi Bistriceanu," Mozhdah told them. "He can write a song in, like, two days. He's a genius."

Ovi and Mozhdah first met in 2009, when he produced "My Love," Mozhdah's song for the orphans of Afghanistan. In the ensuing years, Ovi worked with many other artists, his reputation rising rapidly within the Canadian music industry, largely because of his collaboration with Toronto-based CP Records.

"I need a song for the ATN Awards," Mozhdah said over the phone to Ovi. "Do you have one?"

"I can give you this song I wrote for Massari. It's sitting on my computer," Ovi said.

Ovi had written several songs for Lebanese-Canadian R&B and pop singer Massari, who had numerous hit singles in Canada with Universal Music. The label had hemmed and hawed at one song, finally rejecting it.

"It's just sitting there?" Mozhdah said incredulously. "*Please give it to me!*"

Ovi sent Mozhdah the music and lyrics. Called *"Boro, Boro,"* the Farsi word for "go away," it featured a boisterous Punjabi beat. Mozhdah thought it electrifying. It was also provocative, being a song about a woman who falls in love with a beautiful stranger, knowing that the relationship is doomed. After listening, she called Ovi again and exclaimed, "This song is perfect!"

Mozhdah was puzzled, however, about how Ovi, a Romanian, came up with the Farsi word *"boro."*

"Googled it," Ovi responded, laughing.

"Boro, Boro" was performed near the end of ATN's two-hour award show. It started with Mozhdah singing offstage while dazzling panels of neon kaleidoscopes and strobes lit up the packed auditorium audience. First, the Takadhimi Dance Group came bounding out, dervishes with long hair and red, black, and gold outfits. Then came Mozhdah, in a floor-length, baby-blue dress with floating chiffon sleeves. The dress, Arabic in design, was so laden with gold embroidery that Mozhdah had to hold it up as she moved. Mozhdah sang *"Boro, Boro"* in both Farsi and English, and when she finished, the audience exploded in a storm of cheers, screams, applause, and whistles. When the performance was later uploaded to YouTube, *"Boro, Boro"* quickly garnered 4 million views.

As soon as she had heard the song, Mozhdah wanted to make a music video in English as well as Farsi, and the overwhelming response to her performance in front of the Afghan diaspora reinforced that decision. The world beat song heralded a new creative direction for Mozhdah, and she wanted a fresh, visionary eye to direct the video.

"Boro, Boro" was filmed along Spanish Banks in Vancouver, a popular summer spot for locals as well as tourists, with its sandy beaches, calm ocean waves, and soft blue mountains across the inlet. Mozhdah wanted to cast a bad-boy love interest for the video, so she contacted a high school friend, Jeff Purewal. For years, Mozhdah had urged Jeff to model, but

he was too modest. Mozhdah's new video director, Parisian Audrey Baunez, took advantage of Jeff's long, lean, muscled body and exotic good looks to create a sexual dynamism that had been absent, out of consideration for Afghanistan's conservative culture, from Mozhdah's previous videos.

The theme, about falling in love with someone you know will break your heart, called upon Mozhdah to stretch her visual and physical limits, expressing the desire infused within the lyrics. "I want you, just like the air I breathe / How long before you leave? / When I'm without you, all I can do is dream about you..."

Audrey pushed Mozhdah the day of the shoot. "You have to show at least a little skin," said Audrey, who, as a film director in her home country of France, had a European sensibility when it came to the expression of human sexuality.

As usual, Nasrin was present at the shoot, having provided a variety of sandwiches that she had made early that morning, as well as cookies and chips, to feed the crew and talent. She was helping them comb through a cache of potential outfits.

Mozhdah held up one revealing outfit.

Nasrin's lips narrowed slightly. "Isn't that a bit inappropriate?" she asked. "We need to make sure Mozhdah covers up," she said, turning to Audrey.

"Then I can't film this music video," Audrey responded.

Mozhdah glanced warningly at Nasrin. "Mom's being cautious—conservative Afghans will be offended."

"I understand your concern," Audrey continued. "You don't want to be perceived as simply a sex object. You're an independent woman and a strong voice for women in Afghanistan. But you have to dress less modestly if you want to have international success beyond your Afghan fan base."

Mozhdah laughed. "You're right," she said, looking point-edly at Nasrin. "I made myself a promise to stop censoring myself for the benefit of those Afghans who'd rather women wore burkas."

Nasrin sighed. "Okay, Mozhdah, if you're aiming for a big-ger audience—a more global one—then Audrey's right, you have to be bolder."

So *"Boro, Boro"* showed Mozhdah dressed in shorts and a loose, filmy white summer blouse—something many West-ern women might wear to the beach. Most provocatively for her Afghan fan base, the video showed Mozhdah's character a heartbeat away from kissing the tall striking stranger.

The video for *"Boro, Boro"* debuted on YouTube on October 22, 2016, racking up millions of views within a few months. Other channels uploaded it, and the number of viewers climbed to 15 million. Mozhdah was thrilled. What's more, the song's success gave Ovi the push he needed to approach her about his ambitions to launch his own label, showcasing music interlaced with the melodic and distinctive folkloric instrumentation reminiscent of his Romanian upbringing. "I'd like to sign you as my first artist," he said casually to Mozhdah one day.

With Mozhdah's signing, Ethnobeast officially debuted, carrying a name that would represent modern musical sensi-bilities rooted in faraway places around the globe.

As Ethnobeast's premier artist, Mozhdah maintained an active social media network to promote her music: Facebook, Instagram, Twitter, YouTube, Snapchat, and Spotify, as well as her own website. Her brothers, Masee and Safee, now in their late twenties, as well as Mozhdah's friend Sofia Wahdat, had initially shouldered the responsibility of uploading songs to YouTube and creating posts for her social media pages—a task eventually taken over by the Ethnobeast team. Facebook, however, remained Mozhdah's domain, and one day she declared to her followers, "My Facebook page is one place I can really express myself, and no one can take that away from me."

After the *"Boro, Boro"* video was posted to YouTube, fans, many writing in Farsi, flooded Facebook and YouTube with their reactions. The majority wrote positive comments: "I'm so glad you're doing this. I'm glad someone is doing it." Others wrote in English, their responses heartfelt, if not always grammatical: "You are beautiful Mozhdah. Your mom is good. Your songs is best."

Some women and men chided Mozhdah for pushing the envelope of Afghan modesty, not only in her music videos but also her Facebook publicity photos, some of which were glamour shots in cocktail attire. One woman, calling herself Jamila, lambasted Mozhdah for posting "half-naked" pictures. Jamila accused Mozhdah of causing greater suffering among the girls and women of Afghanistan with the photos, her outfits fomenting further intolerance in the country by showing that women, given the chance, would behave in a way that was little better than prostitutes. Such perverse thinking wasn't uncommon, and Mozhdah reacted quickly: "First of all that is not a half naked picture. It's completely normal in Canadian society... I do not cater to the ones who have destroyed my land and forced people like me out of my home. Radical extremism is a plague that has destroyed my country."

If online trolls thought that personal insults, hidden behind the cowardice of anonymity, could intimidate or scare

Mozhdah—after she had endured rocket attacks, death threats, and an assault—they were disappointed.

"If I didn't have any haters that would be a terrible thing," Mozhdah wrote. "It would mean that I am a people pleaser and people pleasers are weak individuals. To all who have issues with the way I dress, express myself, and run my life I just want to say I'm so sorry if I've offended you. NOT!!! HA!"

Mozhdah's freer, more expressive attitude and look endeared her to a fan base that was growing thanks to the wider appeal of her upbeat new songs. But when she flew to Afghanistan for a concert, she was painfully reminded how freedom of expression was still something most Afghans could only dream about. People she chatted with backstage at concerts in Kabul or at her hotel would quietly confess to her: "I'm atheist. I don't believe in God, but I have to pretend that I'm a good Muslim every single day of my life; otherwise, they'll kill me, or they'll threaten me, or they'll hurt my family." Such comments inspired vivid recall of the barely contained rage she felt from the male members of the audience in 2015, when she debuted "Tribute to Farkhunda" and "Your Pride, My Poison" at the concert at Khurshid TV. The fear, and the threats, were real.

Despite that, Mozhdah decided to push the envelope further by filming a visual condemnation of male violence. She made plans for a music video for "Your Pride, My Poison"—her most ambitious, creative, and controversial video yet.

Authenticity was important to Mozhdah for "Your Pride, My Poison," and filming took place at a military base near Hamid Karzai International Airport, newly named in 2014. Omid Nikzad, an Afghan-Canadian music video producer living in Toronto, who had started his career with Ariana

Television in Kabul, directed the video. It opens with a young woman, played by an Afghan actress in a torn red *tunbaan*, being dragged across the scree of an Afghanistan mountainside by a man in a white *shalwar kameez*. The video is rife with symbolism—white is the color of the Taliban, who would fly white flags on their vehicles as they roared into conquered cities during their rampage across Afghanistan, starting in 1994. The red of the victim's *tunbaan* symbolizes the blood of women spilled by men in Afghanistan.

In the video, Mozhdah stands atop a precipice, a stark, hazy landscape of gray and brown, sharply cut ridges as the backdrop. Her unfettered hair and black dress, as shapeless as a burka, whip in a dusty gale. Two long scarves, one red, one green, colors in the Afghanistan flag, tethered to her wrists like restraints, snap in the wind. Mozhdah holds her head in grief, or stretches her arms out like a sacrificial figure, as she sings: "Don't stone me to death / Don't chain my feet to the ground / I am alive, don't blind me / Don't darken my world." After the taping, Mozhdah admitted to Nasrin that she almost didn't recognize her own anger-filled voice as she sang. Intercut with the stark, powerful sight of Mozhdah singing are photos of Farkhunda and other Afghan women bearing the unmistakable signs of abuse.

Although it is bleak, the video also holds hope. In it, the young woman being dragged across the mountainside escapes her abuser and joins an elite group of female Afghan army pilots, learning to fly military helicopters. "We, together, can transform our nation into a paradise," Mozhdah sings. The meaning is clear: when women are supported in life and in their ambitions, when they are given the opportunity to soar, the country is uplifted as well.

Mozhdah realized that, for many Afghans, songs like *"Boro, Boro"* gave expression to suppressed desires, and songs like "Your Pride, My Poison" articulated the subterranean rage they dared not express publicly. Mozhdah discussed this with Nasrin and Bashir, who had come of age during more liberal times in Kabul, fallen in love and gotten married of their own volition. In modern Afghanistan, an innocent first crush could have deadly consequences. A girl who told her parents that she wanted to marry a particular boy risked becoming victim of an honor killing—the murder of a girl or woman who is perceived to have brought shame on a family, or to have flouted community or religious customs. A boy would be too ashamed to admit to his parents that he desired to marry a particular girl.

"I feel like these videos make my Afghan viewers happier," she told her parents. "I think that the people who watch my videos and listen to my music envision greater personal freedoms in Afghanistan. The messages I get from Afghans on social media—it's like they're giving me virtual high fives all the time."

For Mozhdah, partnering with Ethnobeast had been a blessing. Having always been an independent artist, it was the first time that a record label had backed her career. Over the following year, she and Ovi produced Mozhdah's first album, *Words*, which featured nine original songs, as well as one cover of a traditional Pashto song. Being associated with a label made it easier to receive support from government organizations like Creative BC, which supports British Columbia's music industry. Creative BC funded half the expenses of production, and also funded the creation of music videos for the singles on *Words*. One, titled "Feathers," portrayed the cultural dilemma immigrant and refugee parents and their children often face when the kids are exposed to the freedoms of Western society. This can spark rebellions and familial rifts, with teenagers refusing to dress in accordance with tradition. Worse, they might start dating—something anathema to many Muslims, even those leading a more secular Western lifestyle.

The video for "Feathers," featuring Afghan-Canadian rapper Kresnt, showed Mozhdah in a dress that had been fashioned out of a burka by Afghan-American Sara Assefi, of the design company SShadoow. Covered in elaborate embroidery, the garment was a sartorial counterweight to an emotional visual narrative about an Afghan teenage girl who dares to date a handsome teenager from her newly adopted country. The girl brings her boyfriend home to meet her family. Nasrin plays the role of the hijab-wearing conservative mother, and the furious and disapproving father storms away from the dinner table. Mozhdah sings: "Get me high like an eagle / I want a taste of your freedom / But it feels so wrong." The refrain expresses the discordance and the discombobulating, desperate fumbling for identity and integration that so many immigrants experience:

Trying to keep my head right
But somehow I feel I'm
Drifting all around like
Feathers in the air
Staring at this red light
Feel I'm losing my mind . . .

Words gave Mozhdah new music for touring. Starting in 2016, and continuing through 2018, Mozhdah was a headliner at European concerts alongside such artists as Valy Hedjasi, rapper DJ Besho, Aria Band, and Seeta Qasemie. Like Mozhdah, these singers were part of the Afghan diaspora who had fled Afghanistan's interminable violence and settled in Europe or North America. They maintained their connection to Afghanistan through music, weaving the longing and love for their tragic nation into songs.

Ethnobeast created several more music videos for *Words*. Mozhdah's favorite, however, was for a song that wasn't on her album but a cover of the pop single *"Dernière Danse,"* or "Last Dance," by French singer-songwriter Indila, first released in 2013. *"Dernière Danse"* had been France's number two song and a hit throughout Europe. The song tells the story of a young immigrant woman in Paris who encounters contempt and racism wherever she goes. For Mozhdah, the song was an exquisitely painful metaphor for her own turbulent journey: the brutal attack by Kardaar and the consequential spiral into despair, as well as the onslaught of threats that beset her Facebook and YouTube pages from the earliest days of her singing, through to *The Mozhdah Show* and beyond. She honored the song's origins by singing it in French. The video, filmed by *"Boro, Boro"* director Audrey Baunez, was shot in black and white in a graveyard in East Vancouver. Damp, wintery Vancouver provided the somber backdrop, giving it almost a horror-movie sensibility. Audrey chose Mozhdah's outfit: a floor-length steampunk dress with leather corset and stiff tulle fabric that created an elegant Victorian silhouette.

"Dernière Danse" was a visual expression of Mozhdah's journey, the turmoil of past ordeals, the effort to forget, and the struggle towards liberation, all while being roiled by continual darkness. The epiphany in the song's lyrics is the

understanding that rebirth lies within—if the individual has courage and strength of resolve.

This song, thought Mozhdah, has been the soundtrack of my life ever since Kardaar's assault. I, too, am reborn.

CHAPTER 17

A Mother's Burka

OZHDAH'S *"DERNIÈRE DANSE"* music video pushed her creatively, with Audrey directing her to express the song's turmoil and pain physically as well as with her voice. It was a crash course in acting. When Mozhdah tried out for a movie role only a few months later, the lessons Audrey had drilled into her—take after take in freezing Vancouver rain—gave her the self-possession she needed to command the respect of directors—one in particular.

That director was Marie Clements, a renowned Canadian playwright, director, producer, screenwriter, and librettist. Marie is Métis, and her work often addresses issues of oppression, violence, and racism towards Canada's Indigenous peoples. Her latest project was *Red Snow*, and it had taken Marie eight years to raise the funds and organize the best production team she could muster to fulfill her vision for the film.

Marie had been deeply affected by images she had seen of Canadian troops in Afghanistan. The main objective of the Canadian Armed Forces was to overthrow the Taliban; however, contributing to the reconstruction of civil society and the restoration of civilian infrastructure, while engaging in active diplomacy, were also part of the mandate. In 2005, Canadian troops were deployed to Kandahar, with Canada directing the main military force in the region, the Multi-National Brigade for Command South. What NATO and U.S. intelligence missed, however, was the size and intensity of the resurgence of the Taliban in Kandahar, which was the religious group's capital during its rule of Afghanistan from 1996 to 2001. By the time Canada withdrew from Afghanistan in 2014, 158 Canadian soldiers had died and another 1,800 had been wounded.

Like other Canadians, Marie watched the news transfixed, wondering whether military involvement would truly help Afghans. She was struck by the facial similarities between some Afghans and Indigenous peoples. A creative thread wove in her mind: What would happen if two people from completely different cultures and countries were brought together, face-to-face, and placed in a situation where they are forced to understand each other—in order to survive?

This was rich earth for *Red Snow*. Marie wrote a script that was part romance, part action, part adventure, and part thriller. The film tells the story of a young Dene man named Dylan Nadazeau from the Gwich'in First Nation in Canada's Northwest Territories. Played by Vancouver's Asivak Koostachin, who is of Cree and Inuk descent, Dylan falls in love with his cousin, Asana. Being first cousins, their love is taboo, and they run away into the northern wilderness to be together. They are found by their families and forcibly separated. Asana cannot live with the heartbreak and commits suicide. Overcome by rage and anguish, Dylan joins the Canadian forces fighting in Afghanistan. It is a death wish.

Dylan is stationed in Kandahar. One day, while out on foot patrol, he and his fellow soldiers are ambushed by the Taliban. Dylan, the lone survivor, is taken captive and imprisoned in the home of his Pashtun translator, Aman, who had betrayed the soldiers to the Taliban. Dylan is tortured in a small interrogation cell in the back of Aman's home, which the Taliban has commandeered. It unfolds that Aman had led the Canadian soldiers into the ambush in order to protect his daughter, Khatira, whom the Taliban was threatening to kill if he didn't cooperate with their plan to slaughter Canadian soldiers. In the end, Khatira and Dylan escape together, fleeing in a ferocious winter snowstorm, their lives intertwined from that day forward.

I love it, Mozhdah thought, flipping the *Red Snow* script pages.

Mozhdah had known Marie for several years, after Marie had gone online to look for local Afghan actors when she started writing the script nearly a decade previously. They ended up meeting several times, casually, over the ensuing years, while Marie followed Mozhdah's activism on Facebook and in the media. As Khatira's character took shape, Marie envisioned Mozhdah, who seemed to naturally embody Khatira's grace and strength.

Two years previously, Mozhdah's former acting agent hadn't sent her on any auditions. "This acting thing is impossible," Mozhdah had complained to Nasrin. "How can I get any parts if I'm not even sent to audition?"

Because of the hundreds of American movies and TV series that are shot every year in Vancouver, amounting to a multi-billion-dollar-a-year industry, that city is often referred to as "Hollywood North." But it is a highly competitive business, especially for young female actors, and even more so for those who are ethnic minorities. Mozhdah, who also barely had any acting training or experience, languished on the periphery.

However, an enthusiastic new agent began sending Mozhdah to audition for lead roles, thanks in part to the confidence and poise that *"Dernière Danse"* had given her. And when Marie asked Mozhdah to audition for Khatira's part, and then offered her the role, it felt fated—as if Mozhdah had been training for this her whole life.

The winter scenes began shooting in March 2018 in minus-thirty-six-degree weather in Yellowknife, in the Northwest Territories. The summer scenes were shot in April and May in hot, arid Kamloops, B.C. Similar to Afghanistan, Kamloops is surrounded by rolling mountain ranges of varying elevations. The weather can be sweltering—also mimicking Afghanistan's climate. Marie's production team carefully made the scenes look authentic, constructing a low-slung, beige mud home with a surrounding wall deeply pockmarked with bullet holes from gun battles. This building was where the character of Dylan would undergo torture.

One thing was vital to the role of Khatira—a burka. Marie's wardrobe crew had spent considerable time, to no avail, looking for one in the Vancouver area. Finally, Marie asked Mozhdah if she or a family member had one.

"Maybe," Mozhdah said. "I'll check."

Unexpectedly, Nasrin had kept her burka from when she, Bashir, baby Safee, Mozhdah, and Masee had fled over the Paktia mountains into Pakistan three decades ago.

Marie was in the production office when Mozhdah brought in Nasrin's burka, carefully unwrapping its tissue-paper packaging.

"Where did you get it from?" Marie asked, holding the silken blue cloth, letting the cool material run through her hands like water. "The material—it's beautiful."

"It's my mom's," Mozhdah replied.

"May I try it on?" Marie asked.

"Please, go ahead," said Mozhdah.

Mozhdah watched Marie pull the burka awkwardly over her head, could hear how it impeded her breathing. While Marie was wrapped in its blue confines, Mozhdah began to tell her the story of the burka: how Bashir was forced to flee from Kabul with his family to avoid being arrested, how they traversed the war-torn countryside to Logar province, then ascended the rugged Paktia mountains in the back of an old truck to escape into Pakistan. Everyone pretended to be poor Afghan farmers, and the burka was Nasrin's disguise during the perilous journey.

"We stayed at this house, which was actually headquarters for a mujahideen group in Logar," Mozhdah told Marie. "It was bombed shortly after we left in a truck we had rented to take us to Pakistan. I remember being so cold, and hungry, and how much it hurt going over the rough roads. I thought the journey would never end," she said in a small voice.

When Marie pulled the burka off, there were tears glittering in her eyes, and she excused herself and left the room—needing, Mozhdah realized, to regain her composure.

Later, as the filming of *Red Snow* continued in Kamloops, Asivak Koostachin, as Dylan, was playing a scene with Mozhdah, garbed in the burka. During a break, Mozhdah lifted the garment up over her head, her face red and sweaty.

"It's hard to breathe in here it's so hot," Mozhdah complained, turning away to get a drink.

The props woman, working nearby, said quietly to Asivak, "The burka belonged to Mozhdah's mom, Nasrin. She used it to pretend to be an Afghan peasant during the family's escape from Afghanistan during the war."

Overhearing the comment, Mozhdah smiled sadly, thinking, *Yes, this burka isn't a costume; it is real—a real piece of Afghanistan.* Waiting in the shade, sipping from her bottle of water, Mozhdah mused on how time in Afghanistan seemed to follow a circular pattern, history repeating itself, over and over. *Red Snow* was not only capturing a time in history; it also showed how life was today for so many Afghans, especially those in the rural areas, which were still rife with forced marriages, domestic violence, and high maternal mortality rates.

"We're ready to go. Back to first marks," Mozhdah heard a voice call. Setting her water aside, she took a big breath of air, pulled the burka back down over her head, and walked slowly back to her place in the scene.

Mozhdah stood patiently, her thoughts drifting back to 2001, when she first watched the coordinated attacks by American and coalition forces to destroy Al-Qaeda and the Taliban. Since then, more than 38,000 Afghan civilians had died. Another 58,000 Afghan police and soldiers had perished, many in Taliban suicide attacks. United States military analysts estimated that the Taliban controlled, or were contesting, 60 percent of the country. The situation was made worse,

Mozhdah thought darkly, by misgovernance by Afghanistan's national leaders, who acted in their own interests, or as puppets of the West, rather than in the interests of Afghans. Any peace talks with the Taliban, whether they were brokered by the United States or any other country from the West, were a sham, she thought. The Taliban didn't want peace. They wanted power. The Taliban's brutal reign wasn't close to ending, she thought; rather, it was gaining momentum.

"Final checks, please," the voice called again.

Mozhdah shook the burka slightly, making sure it fell straight.

"Picture is up! Quiet please."

The thoughts kept tumbling in Mozhdah's mind. If Western and United States military forces were to withdraw, the unthinkable could happen—Afghanistan would, once again, come under Taliban rule. All of her friends and family who had dedicated their lives to rebuilding the country would be consumed by Taliban malice.

Where would these Afghans flee? The borders across Europe and North America had slammed shut to the millions harmed by violence in war-torn places like Afghanistan and Syria. In today's uncharitable world, would Canada have allowed Mozhdah's family in? She wasn't so sure. Like so many others around the world, she might have languished in a refugee camp, or even drowned in the Mediterranean Sea like the desperate people in overcrowded boats seeking sanctuary.

"Roll sound! Roll camera!" Then the clapper loader yelled out, "Scene fourteen. Take three!"

Suddenly, it was Khatira, not Mozhdah, standing there, and when the director yelled, "Cut!" Mozhdah gratefully pulled the suffocating fabric off and gulped fresh air. How had Nasrin endured this burka day after endless day during the family's escape to Pakistan? Yet her mother, a tiny woman who had recently given birth, bearing two hundred coins sewn into a vest hidden under the burka, had endured. It was because of this burka that Mozhdah was even here. And she marveled at the irony—that this symbol of female oppression had provided the means of escape to a new life in a new land.

In truth, it wasn't the burka that had brought them to Canada but the courage of her parents. Even though they had faced possible arrest at military checkpoints, as well as starvation and death along hazardous Paktia mountain roads, they never gave up hope that a better life awaited.

But what created courage? Men had their weapons. For women, it was their voices, expressed in song, poetry, books, or film. Mozhdah envisioned these voices—alongside her own—rising like the winds heralding an impending hurricane, joining others all over the world in a never-ending crescendo that would shake governments, religions, and cultures. Mozhdah's parents, especially Nasrin, had shown this to be true: that the greatest courage of all could be found hiding under a burka—enough courage to change the world.

Acknowledgments

THIS BOOK HAS its genesis in Afghanistan, traveling a dusty highway into Panjshir province to visit teacher-training projects and schools eleven years after the United States launched Operation Enduring Freedom to root out Al-Qaeda and the Taliban. While in Afghanistan, I became enamored with the country's arid, mountainous beauty and courteous people. Most of all, I was awestruck by the Afghan girls and women, who aspired to achieve gender equality in the face of enormous cultural, educational, and religious impediments. In 2015, I returned to film a documentary about gender rights, which led to me meeting, for the first time, singer and human rights activist Mozhdah Jamalzadah, one of three main women featured in my film. After finding out about the documentary, Greystone Books' editorial director Jennifer Croll saw the potential for a biography about Mozhdah. Since then, Jennifer, who has edited *Voice of Rebellion* with skill, kindness, and patience, has been crucial in bringing this book to fruition. Thanks also goes to Shirarose Wilensky, for her meticulous, conscientious copy editing.

Mozhdah herself, as well as her parents, Nasrin and Bashir Jamalzadah, have courageously revisited some of the most traumatic experiences of their lives for the book, and for that I am in their debt. It is a remarkable odyssey documenting someone's life, and it couldn't have been done without Mozhdah's trust, guidance, wisdom, and patience. I am also grateful to Nasrin for the huge containers of delicious home-cooked Afghan food she sent me home with, fearing for my nutritional needs as I toiled on the book weekends and evenings. Where would the world be without the grace and love of people—of mothers—like Nasrin?

I give huge thanks to my early readers: Rob McLauchlin, Lauryn Oates, Jane Armstrong, Terry Glavin, and Lucas Aykroyd, who gave of their time so generously. The book would not be the same without their knowledge, guidance, and insights.

Friends and family, of course, are indispensable, and Tallulah, Ingrid, David, Dawne, and Brishkay, as well as my son, Alexander, cheered me on when finishing seemed a precipice too steep to climb.

Finally, these acknowledgments would not be complete without thanking my Simon Fraser University thesis supervisors Drs. Stephen Duguid and Gary McCarron, who supported me in the creation of the documentary as part of my requirement to graduate. Without their early encouragement, this book may not have happened at all.

References

Aside from the sources cited here, all information in this book comes from interviews conducted with Mozhdah Jamalzadah, Bashir Jamalzadah, Nasrin Jamalzadah, David Reid, Siobhan Berry, Steven D. Comrie, Brishkay Ahmed, Melanie Adams, Ovidiu Bistriceanu, Audrey Baunez, Omid Nezami, Asivak Koostachin, and Marie Clements between October 2017 and September 2018.

BOOKS

Bakhtiar, Laleh. *The Sublime Quran*. Chicago: Kazi Publications, 2007.

Barfield, Thomas. *Afghanistan: A Cultural and Political History*. Princeton, NJ: Princeton University Press, 2010.

Bonner, Arthur, *Among the Afghans*. Durham, NC: Duke University Press, 1987.

Braithwaite, Rodric. *Afgantsy: The Russians in Afghanistan, 1979–89*. London: Oxford University Press, 2011.

Byrne, Rhonda. *The Power*. New York: Atria Books, 2010.

Coll, Steve. *Ghost Wars: The Secret History of the CIA, Afghanistan, and bin Laden, from the Soviet Invasion to September 10, 2001*. New York: Penguin Books, 2004.

Courtois, Stéphane, Nicolas Werth, Jean-Louis Panné, Andrzej Paczkowski, Karel Bartošek, and Jean-Louis Margolin. *The Black Book of Communism: Crimes, Terror, Repression*. Cambridge, MA: Harvard University Press, 1999.

Emadi, Hafizullah. *Culture and Customs of Afghanistan*. Santa Barbara, CA: Greenwood Publishing Group, 2005.

Giradet, Edward. *Afghanistan: The Soviet War*. Abingdon, UK: Routledge, 2011.

Giradet, Edward. *Killing the Cranes: A Reporter's Journey through Three Decades of War in Afghanistan*. Hartford, VT: Chelsea Green Publishing, 2012.

Harry, Naeem. *Understanding Pakistani Culture*. Bloomington, IN: Author-House, 2012.

Jalali, Ali Ahmad, and Lester W. Grau. *The Other Side of the Mountain: Mujahideen Tactics in the Soviet-Afghan War*. Tales End Press, 2012.

Kakar, Hassan M. *Afghanistan: The Soviet Invasion and the Afghan Response, 1979–1982*. Berkeley, CA: University of California Press, 1995.

Laber, Jeri, and Barnett R. Rubin. *A Nation Is Dying: Afghanistan under the Soviets, 1979–1987*. Evanston, IL: Northwestern University Press, 1988.

Lohbeck, Kurt. *Holy War, Unholy Victory: Eyewitness to the CIA's Secret War in Afghanistan*. Washington, D.C.: Regnery Publishing, 1993.

MacArthur, Kathleen. *Annisa: Daughter of Afghanistan*. Morgan Hill, CA: Bookstand Publishing, 2004.

Yousaf, Mohammad, and Mark Adkin. *Afghanistan: The Bear Trap—the Defeat of a Superpower*. Havertown, PA: Casemate, 2001.

PERIODICALS AND WIRE SERVICES

Abawi, Atia. "Afghanistan's 'Oprah' Helps Heal Country's Wounds." *Afghanistan Crossroads*, July 15, 2010. http://afghanistan.blogs.cnn.com/2010/07/15/afghanistans-oprah-helps-heal-countrys-wounds/.

"Afghan Woman: The Victim of Ultra-Conservatism and Ultra-Liberalism." Center for Strategic & Regional Studies, March 17, 2018. http://csrskabul.com/en/blog/afghan-woman-the-victim-of-ultra-conservatism-and-ultra-liberalism/.

"Afghanistan: Mozhdah to Perform 'Ghoroore Tu, Shikaste Ma.'" Eurovoix World, September 23, 2015. https://eurovoix-world.com/afghanistan-mozhdah-to-perform-ghoroore-tu-shikaste-ma/.

Auletta, Ken. "The Networker: Afghanistan's First Media Mogul." *New Yorker*, July 5, 2010.

Aykroyd, Lucas. "Meet the Vancouver-Raised Woman Who Is the 'Oprah of Afghanistan.'" *Vancouver Magazine*, April 24, 2017. http://vanmag. com/city/mozhdah-jamalzadah-oprah-afghanistan/.

Baker, Aryn. "Introducing the Oprah of Afghanistan: Mozhdah!" *Time*, July 28, 2010. http://content.time.com/time/world/article/0,8599, 2005504,00.html.

Balde, Lisa, BJ Lutz, Alex Perez, and LeeAnn Trotter. "Oprah Fills United Center for Final Shows." Chicago 5, May 17, 2011. https://www. nbcchicago.com/news/local/Celebrity-Rumors-For-Surprise-Oprah-Show-122032629.html.

Burr, Ty. "From Life in the Spotlight to Hiding for Her Life." *Boston Globe*, January 26, 2011. http://archive.boston.com/ae/tv/articles/2011/01/ 26/silencing_the_song_looks_at_the_fallout_of_female_celebrity_ in_afghanistan/.

Coll, Steve. "Canada Had It Right When It Comes to Afghanistan." *Globe and Mail*, February 9, 2018. https://www.theglobeandmail.com/ opinion/canada-had-it-right-when-it-comes-to-afghanistan/ article37917216/.

Colville, Rupert. "Famous Pakistan Camp Closes as Last Convoy Heads Home." UN Refugee Agency, May 21, 2002. https://www.unhcr.org/ news/latest/2002/5/3cea5f544/famous-pakistan-camp-closes-convoy-heads-home.html.

Empey, Erin. "Afghan Pop Singer Stands Up for Women." *Thunderbird*, April 14, 2009. https://thethunderbird.ca/2009/04/14/afghan-popstar-stands-up-for-women/.

Ghafour, Hamida. "Kabul's Sweet-Smelling Bakeries Conjure Memories of a Life Lost." *Star*, August 12, 2013. https://www.thestar.com/news/ world/2013/08/12/kabuls_sweetsmelling_bakeries_conjure_ memories_of_a_life_lost.html.

Guest, Iain. "UN Report Accuses Soviets of Massive Rights Abuses in Afghanistan." *Christian Science Monitor*, March 1, 1985. https://www. csmonitor.com/1985/0301/oghan.html.

Haidari, M. Ashraf. "Afghanistan's Silk Road Dream." *Pioneer*, October 17, 2017. https://www.dailypioneer.com/2017/columnists/afghanistans-silk-road-dream.html.

Haidari, M. Ashraf. "Securing the Future of Afghanistan: The Diaspora's Debt of Service." *The Diplomat*, February 13, 2018. https://thediplomat.com/2018/02/securing-the-future-of-afghanistan-the-diasporas-debt-of-service/.

Harris, Paul. "Oprah Winfrey Begins Farewell with Star-Studded Final Shows." *Guardian*, May 18, 2011. https://www.theguardian.com/tv-and-radio/2011/may/18/oprah-winfrey-final-shows-star-guests.

Hendren, John. "Magazine Aims to Introduce Positive Image of Afghan Women." *Al Jazeera*, June 10, 2017. https://www.aljazeera.com/video/news/2017/06/afghan-womens-magazine-gellera-challenges-local-traditions-170610142052576.html.

"Icons of Afghan and Global Music, Arts and Culture to Headline Ariana Television's 10th Annual ATN Awards in Istanbul on 5 April 2016." *Cision PR Newswire*, April 1, 2016. https://www.prnewswire.co.uk/news-releases/icons-of-afghan-and-global-music-arts-and-culture-to-headline-ariana-televisions-10th-annual-atn-music-awards-in-istanbul-on-5-april-2016-574262721.html.

Joscelyn, Thomas. "Taliban and Islamic State Target Religious Opponents in Afghanistan." Foundation for Defense of Democracies, May 31, 2018.

Kargar, Zarghuna. "Farkhunda: The Making of a Martyr." BBC World News, August 11, 2015. https://www.bbc.com/news/magazine-33810338.

Kelso, Paul. "Taliban Secret Weapon: Ancient Irrigation Trenches." *Guardian*, November 5, 2001.

Khan, Adnan R. "From Peshawar to Kabul: The Afghan Part of the Journey Used to Be Dangerous. Now That Side Is Thriving—While Pakistan Is Not." *Maclean's*, April 5, 2012. https://www.macleans.ca/news/world/from-peshawar-to-kabul/.

Kumar, Ruchi. "In Reproduced Miniatures, Afghans Regain a Lost Cultural Heritage: A Collection of Exquisitely Enlarged Reproductions of Rare Miniature Afghan Paintings Brings the Images Back to Their Now Troubled Place of Origin." *Friends of the American University of*

Afghanistan, July 27, 2018. https://friendsofauaf.org/in-reproduced-miniatures-afghans-regain-a-lost-cultural-heritage-a-collection-of-exquisitely-enlarged-reproductions-of-rare-miniature-afghan-paintings-brings-the-images-back-to-their-now-troubled-pla/.

Kuperman, Alan J. "The Stinger Missile and U.S. Intervention in Afghanistan." *Political Science Quarterly,* Vol. 114, No. 2 (Summer 1999): 219–63.

Macdonald, Nancy. "Mozhdah: The Oprah of Afghanistan." *Maclean's,* December 17, 2010. https://www.macleans.ca/culture/the-oprah-of-afghanistan/.

Mahdi, Sami. "Sami Mahdi: Revolutionizing TV News in Afghanistan." *International Center for Journalists,* 2013. https://www.icfj.org/sami-mahdi-revolutionizing-tv-news-afghanistan.

Nawa, Fariba. "I'll Make a Difference—If I Can Stay Alive." *Times* (London), June 19, 2011. https://www.thetimes.co.uk/article/ill-make-a-difference-if-i-can-stay-alive-dvmq9vnhxmj.

Nordland, Rod, and Fahim Abed. "Most Afghans Can't Read, but Their Book Trade Is Booming." *New York Times,* February 3, 2018. https://www.nytimes.com/2018/02/03/world/asia/afghanistan-kabul-books-publishing.html.

"The Oprah of Afghanistan." *The Week,* June 23, 2011. https://theweek.com/articles/483680/oprah-afghanistan.

"Profile: Ex-King Zahir Shah." BBC News, October 1, 2001. http://news.bbc.co.uk/2/hi/south_asia/1573181.stm.

Rubin, Alissa J. "The Killing of Farkhunda." *New York Times,* December 26, 2015.

Saberi, Helen. "Tea and Hospitality in Afghanistan Part I." *Afghan Culture Unveiled,* October 10, 2013. http://www.afghancultureunveiled.com/humaira-ghilzai/afghancooking/2013/10/tea-and-hospitality-in-afghanistan.html.

Sands, Chris, and Fazelminallah Qazizai. "Mullah Mansour: The Story behind the Former Leader of the Afghan Taliban." *The National—World,* May 28, 2016. https://www.thenational.ae/world/mullah-mansour-the-story-behind-the-former-leader-of-the-afghan-taliban-1.191947.

Silverstein, Ken. "Stingers, Stingers, Who's Got the Stingers?" *Slate*, October 3, 2001. https://slate.com/news-and-politics/2001/10/stingers-stingers-who-s-got-the-stingers.html.

Snow, Lalage. "Kabul's Hidden Gardens Offer Afghans Haven from War." *Financial Times*, September 13, 2013. https://www.ft.com/content/f1b9f768-1635-11e3-a57d-00144feabdc0.

Staley, Roberta. "The Kabul Markets: Afghanistan." *Montecristo Magazine*, June 30, 2017.

Steele, Jonathan. "10 Myths about Afghanistan." *Guardian*, September 27, 2011. https://www.theguardian.com/world/2011/sep/27/10-myths-about-afghanistan.

Taylor, Alan. "Afghanistan in the 1950s and '60s." *Atlantic*, July 2, 2013. https://www.theatlantic.com/photo/2013/07/afghanistan-in-the-1950s-and-60s/100544/.

Taylor, Alan. "The Soviet War in Afghanistan, 1979–1989." *Atlantic*, August 4, 2014. https://www.theatlantic.com/photo/2014/08/the-soviet-war-in-afghanistan-1979-1989/100786/.

Tyler, Patrick E. "The Horrors and Rewards of the Soviet Occupation of Afghanistan." *Washington Post*, February 13, 1983. https://www.washingtonpost.com/archive/opinions/1983/02/13/the-horrors-and-rewards-of-the-soviet-occupation-of-afghanistan/8d155d41-10d6-4aef-b3c7-b45a57046bdd/.

Weinberg, Samantha. "Afghanistan, in All Its Colorful, Tragic Beauty." *Economist 1843*, August 9, 2017. https://www.1843magazine.com/culture/look-closer/afghanistan-in-all-its-colourful-tragic-beauty.

Williams, Holly. "How Did the AK-47 Become the Most Abundant Weapon on Earth?" *Independent*, November 6, 2010. https://www.independent.co.uk/news/world/how-did-the-ak-47-become-the-most-abundant-weapon-on-earth-2124407.html.

World Peace Foundation. "Afghanistan: Soviet Invasion and Civil War." Mass Atrocity Endings. https://sites.tufts.edu/atrocityendings/2015/08/07/afghanistan-soviet-invasion-civil-war/.

Yahr, Emily. "'Surprise Oprah! A Farewell Spectacular,' Part One." *Washington Post*, May 23, 2011. https://www.washingtonpost.com/blogs/tv-column/post/live-blog-surprise-oprah-a-farewell-spectacular-part-one/2011/05/23/AFLGPy9G_blog.html.

VIDEOS

"Afghanistan's Oprah Stands Up to Taliban." ABC News, December 6, 2010. https://abcnews.go.com/GMA/video/afghanistans-oprah-mozhdah-jamalzadah-stands-up-to-taliban-12322311.

Ali, Samina. "What Does the Quran Really Say about a Muslim Woman's Hijab?" TEDxUniversity of Nevada. TEDx Talks. February 10, 2017. https://www.youtube.com/watch?v=_J5bDhMP9lQ.

"Ghoroore Tu, Shikaste Man | Mozhdah Jamalzadah." DilNawaz Music. YouTube, October 15, 2015. https://www.youtube.com/watch?v=BHGAO_JeGO8.

"Mozhda—DARDAMANI SARA." TOLOTV. YouTube, May 18, 2011. https://www.youtube.com/watch?v=qxbnQ4GNQHS.

"Mozhdah—Boro (Official Video)." Ethnobeast. YouTube, October 22, 2016. https://www.youtube.com/watch?v=hONCPhiwDYU.

"Mozhdah—CBC News Part 1." YouTube, March 30, 2012. https://www.youtube.com/watch?v=SNiofAW5MZk.

"Mozhdah—CBC News Part 2 2012." YouTube, March 30, 2012. https://www.youtube.com/watch?v=SKIPVJWZ6TY.

"Mozhdah—Dernière Danse (Cover) | #Ethnosessions." Ethnobeast. YouTube, December 17, 2016. https://www.youtube.com/watch?v=030tRBO5zbk.

"Mozhdah—Feathers feat Kresnt (Official Video)." Ethnobeast. YouTube, January 6, 2018. https://www.youtube.com/watch?v=gn5zCj7M8QQ.

"Mozhdah Jamalzadah—daf BAMA MUSIC AWARDS 2016." Daf Entertainment. YouTube, December 3, 2016. https://www.youtube.com/watch?v=JdvutxavN90.

"Mozhdah Jamalzadah on Breakfast Television." CitytvEdmonton. YouTube, April 15, 2011. https://www.youtube.com/watch?v=zeqsKRZWF9w.

"Mozhdah Jamalzadah—Your Pride—My Poison—New Afghan Song 2015." NiKZAD PRODUCTIQN. YouTube, October 16, 2015. https://www.youtube.com/watch?v=xg4RUZ5M6cg.

"Muzhda Jamalzadah. Better with You New Song in Afghan Star Tolo TV." Soroosh Ahmadi. YouTube, February 25, 2011. https://www.youtube.com/watch?v=804GXq9-FV4.

"The Winner of Best Female Artist in 9th Ariana Award Show." Ariana Television. YouTube, June 6, 2015. https://www.youtube.com/watch?v=E3By7Ua6uvk.